What Daniel Boorstin in *The Discoverers*, Colin Wells now does for history in *A Brief History of History*. An accessible and lively biography of history as a living idea, this book brings together evocative sketches of the great historians with concise summaries of their most important works. Moving forward through the ages, Wells shows us how such brilliant minds have changed our understanding of history, how history itself moved forward over time as a way of approaching the past, and why "history" is a startlingly fluid concept, with an evolutionary course—a story—all its own.

History is the turf on which we fight our culture wars. Given its humble origins as a minor literary genre in ancient Greece, the study of history stands today as perhaps the most successful monument to the global spread of Western civilization, rivaling even science in its ubiquity. Yet it did not have to turn out that way. While tracing the evolution of history, Wells shows how this branch of knowledge has at times been rejected and scorned by those who questioned its very legitimacy.

Wells begins by arguing that history has two "parents" in the ancient Greek world, epic poetry and science, and that its first two practitioners, Herodotus and Thucydides, each took after one of those parents respectively. This dichotomy serves as a backdrop for the larger narrative that follows, in which "the scientist" dominates the writing of history until very recent times, when "the storyteller" makes a comeback.

A riveting blend of vibrant prose and penetrating insight, *A Brief History of History* is a must for anyone interested in how we look at the past.

A BRIEF HISTORY of HISTORY

A BRIEF HISTORY of HISTORY

*Great Historians and the Epic Quest
to Explain the Past*

COLIN WELLS

The Lyons Press

Guilford, Connecticut

An imprint of The Globe Pequot Press

For Theodore Quin Bickford Wells

May all your stories have happy beginnings and happier endings.

Contents

Prologue   The Traveler's Tale   ix

One   "A Possession for Always"   1
Two   "From the Foundation of the City"   19
Three   Barbarians (and Believers) at the Gate   40
Four   Clio Nods   62
Five   The Wall of Faith   84
Six   History Reborn   107
Seven   Point, Counterpoint   129
Eight   New Worlds   141
Nine   The Challenge of Reason   163
Ten   Reason and Imagination Pass Each Other
                     in the Night   182
Eleven   Making It (Sort of) in the Enlightenment 200
Twelve   History Goes to School and Gets a Job   221
Thirteen   The Last Amateur   237
Fourteen   History Discovers Art and Culture   247
Fifteen   Deep Time   264
Sixteen   Vast Impersonal Forces   279
Seventeen   The Return of the Storyteller   294
Epilogue   History Comes of Age   311

Suggested
Reading   315
Acknowledgments   319
Notes   321
Index   331

The Traveler's Tale

*T*he traveler had many questions. He had come to the city seeking answers, for it was here, he had been told, that the most
knowledgeable men were to be found. In this city, a religious center,
those men were priests, and accosting them with his interpreter—the
traveler was an outsider and did not speak the language—he dog-
gedly took up and pursued one line of inquiry after another. Here,
as elsewhere, religious practices seemed especially to pique his lively
interest, but he had long conversations with the learned priests on
matters ranging from astronomy and the yearly calendar to local
customs, landmarks, and wildlife. He was a patient and attentive
listener, if at times appearing perhaps to curb some mild and possibly skeptical outburst.

He asked repeatedly about the strange behavior of the famous
river, which flooded in the summer when other rivers ran dry, and
whose origins nobody knew for certain. In the land from which the
traveler had journeyed, many outrageous theories about the river
jostled for credibility, and the traveler was especially determined to
lay them to rest.

A curious man from a people noted for their curiosity, he never
seemed completely satisfied. At length, however, he relented, thanking his informants profusely for their help. Then he moved on to
another town, another round of questions.

As he had many times already, the traveler repeated this same
basic procedure again and again over the years to come. His quest

ultimately took him to the far corners of the known world—to places near and far, familiar and exotic, lush and barren, civilized and barbarian, friendly and suspicious. If in one land he sought out priests, in others he tracked down old soldiers to hear them tell again the battles of their youth, those bright blood- and fear-soaked days that had colored every succeeding moment of their long lives. He paid special attention to the old soldiers.

He was a gregarious man, the traveler, and everywhere he went his warmth and enthusiasm softened the blows of that probing, implacable curiosity. He had a knack of enlisting the aid of others in his project, the precise nature of which remained somewhat obscure even to those who assisted him. But for all his inquisitiveness concerning anything at all out of the ordinary, more than one observer remarked that he grew most intent when tracing the events of the past. These he seemed to collect, much as a worker might gather up olives to be pressed into clear golden oil.

And always he wrote, carrying with him an apparently endless supply of reed pens that he would sharpen down before discarding, little clay jars stoppered with cork and filled with ink that stained his fingers a rather alarming shade of black, and dry, rustling papyrus rolls on which he scribbled his notes and queries. These were his tools.

In some half-glimpsed way, like a ship emerging from fog, it became known that the main object of his interest was the great war that had shaken the world nearly a lifetime ago, when the old soldiers had fought their famous battles. For this reason, many who encountered the traveler assumed he was a poet. Though normally reserving their words for the legendary or mythic past, the poets among his own people had begun singing this war when its triumphs and catastrophes were still fresh in living memory. No one had questioned its fitness as a subject for poetry. Yet the traveler was not a poet.

Finally there came a time when the notes and queries were finished, when the last witness had spoken, when the journeys—for the moment, anyway—had ended. The traveler sat down to compose the work itself, the work that had lived in his head for so long, and in whose aid his restless odyssey had been undertaken.

The traveler whose portrait we have just plausibly, if somewhat fancifully, drawn was Herodotus, an Ionian Greek from the city of Halicarnassus, now Bodrum, Turkey. Born in the early fifth century BC, Herodotus lived in a time and place that must be counted among the most exciting in history. It was in fifth-century Greece that the very idea of history first took shape, and Herodotus was its inventor. The brief sketch offered above, based on his own writings (along with some informed speculation), imagines that process. Our sketch attempts as well to capture how novel and strange the idea of "history" must have seemed to a world that lacked it.

We first saw Herodotus in the holy city of Heliopolis, Egypt, and the alert reader may have guessed that the "famous river" in question was the Nile, the source of which was a mystery that intrigued the ancient Greeks almost as much as it did the eminent Victorian explorers who finally solved it more than two thousand years later. From Egypt we followed him to some of the other lands that, like Egypt, had formed part of the mighty Persian empire in the years just before Herodotus's birth, which is traditionally dated to 484 BC.

The "great war" of our sketch is the series of conflicts between Greece and Persia that began about a decade and a half before that date, and continued into the years of Herodotus's boyhood. That struggle resulted in a series of momentous victories for the Greeks, in battles whose names—Marathon, Thermopylae, Salamis—still resonate with heroism, self-sacrifice, and daring. The old soldiers Herodotus sought out had fought in these battles and many others, as the Greek city-states drove back two separate Persian invasions, preserving against all odds their cherished independence. Poets who had broken with tradition by treating the Persian Wars included the Athenian dramatist Aeschylus, whose remarkable tragedy, *Persians,* showed the battle of Salamis from the enemy's point of view, and even portrayed the defeated Persian king Xerxes as a tragic hero.

Inspired by these same epoch-making events, Herodotus's idea represents a profound revolution in human thought. Yet we don't usually think of "history" as something that might fit into such a category. We've always had a past, after all. Doesn't it follow that we've always had history?

Well, no.

History, the discipline, goes beyond the "simple past." It goes beyond the official record-keeping and palace chronicles, even quite sophisticated ones, which existed in older civilizations such as Persia, Egypt, Babylon, and China, or the lists of kings and the prophetic narratives found in Jewish scripture. All of these are admirable in their own right, and they are sometimes put forward as early versions of history. But Chinese or Jewish, Hindu or Muslim, when we write history today, we write in the tradition of Herodotus, not the tradition of Confucius or Moses, estimable as such figures might be.*

As an intellectual discipline, a particular way of thinking about the past (not better or worse, but peculiar to itself), the tradition of history that began with Herodotus has an essential ingredient that separates it from other traditional approaches to the past. History's defining characteristic is not record-keeping or list-making, though it shares its interest in the past with these pursuits (not to mention using them as source material). What distinguishes history's attitude to the past is the overarching goal of rational explanation. History is about *explaining* the past, not just recording it.

And there was a time when it simply didn't occur to anyone, anywhere, to sit down and attempt, in writing, a disinterested explanation of past events, deliberately and self-consciously ascribing the hows and whys to particular

---

* In hopes of forestalling inquisitorial accusations that this book is a Eurocentric, triumphalist account of a Western cultural tradition, I should say at the outset that this book is a Eurocentric, triumphalist account of a Western cultural tradition. I would, however, qualify that potentially heretical statement by pleading that most history so far has been written in a Eurocentric cultural context, and that the book's triumphalism will be limited to the global spread of European-style historical writing, which has only relatively recently been taken up by other cultures (often, to be sure, in combination with their own preexisting traditions). I'd also venture, more piously, that such an account can be accomplished without privileging Western civilization itself. Whatever that is.

human interactions rather than solely to the gods, or God, or fate, or the tao, or karma, or any of the other supernatural explanatory shortcuts to which the rest of humanity had previously ascribed the hows and whys, when it thought of them at all. As far as we know, Herodotus was the first to do this, though it is significant that he keeps a place for divine agency—and especially for *nemesis*, the Greek version of bad karma—in his view of the past.

Yet it's also significant that Herodotus was an independent observer, a *writer*, and not someone's royal advisor, government bureaucrat, high priest, or prophet. We might go even further and say that intellectual independence is more than significant; it's necessary. Not only was Herodotus beholden to no one, but he also belonged to an individualistic culture in which political power was contested and relatively diffuse. Though history has survived great empires and priest-ridden bureaucracies, it seems unlikely that it would have been born in one.

Since Herodotus first applied it to his investigation of the past, the word *history* has taken on many meanings, and we'll make free use of them in tracing our own story. As our main subject, however, we'll limit ourselves to the tradition of historical writing that began with Herodotus, with a short digression or two chosen for the light they throw on that tradition.

Considered, even momentarily, the import of the invention goes against our image of the inventor: a kindly, bearded, somewhat fuzzy figure, spinning thrilling, exotic tales to a reader perched on his avuncular knee. But this approachable, unintimidating man possessed a startlingly original and creative mind. Like other revolutionary figures (Darwin especially comes to mind), Herodotus took ideas that were floating around out in the contemporary cultural ether and reassembled them in a compelling new way. In doing so, he forever altered our cultural landscape. The past would never be the same.

ONE

"A Possession for Always"

*Herodotus of Halicarnassus here produces his history, so that
the vestiges of humankind might withstand the erosion of time,
and the great and wonderful exploits of both Greeks and barbarians be saved from ignoble obscurity, and especially the reason
why they went to war against each other.*

—Herodotus I: 1

When Herodotus sat down to compose his *Histories*, these portentous and rather ambiguous words were the first to tumble out onto the papyrus. With them, history begins . . . sort of. A large part of what makes history's first sentence ambiguous is precisely its incomplete, anticlimactic feel. Look at the way Herodotus tacks on that last bit, which appears, in the original Greek as in our translation, to lack a verb of its own. Is "the reason why they went to war" part of what he hopes to save "from ignoble obscurity"? That doesn't really seem to fit. Then is it part of another idea, one that Herodotus doesn't quite manage to articulate?

Modern translators of Herodotus seem to think so. To make the end of the sentence sound like good English, they routinely fabricate a verb from nothing and slip it in, as in "to put on record" (Rawlinson) or "to show" (de Selincourt) the reason for the fighting. By modern standards that also makes it sound like good history, but unfortunately, it's simply not there in the Greek. This opening sentence acted like a title page, an advertisement for the whole work—yet after such a grandiose start, what a dull, confusing thud at the end! The way that last part just hangs there . . .

Almost like an afterthought.

Which, in a way, it might have been. History arose from two cultural traditions which don't necessarily sit so well together, either in Herodotus's own work or in that of his successors. With its dangling afterthought, history's first sentence clearly reflects this ancestral tension, and so it offers us a convenient key to history's origins.

One of those origins sprang from the relatively straightforward urge to preserve and celebrate the past, to commemorate significant achievements and the people who took part in them. (For the mostly male historians of the past, that almost always meant men—though Herodotus is more inclusive of women than his immediate, and not-so-immediate, successors.) This celebratory impulse gets all of the sentence's glamour and high-sounding polish—in short, all the glory, which is what it's really about: "so that the vestiges of humankind might withstand the erosion of time, and the great and wonderful exploits of both Greeks and barbarians be saved from ignoble obscurity. . . ." Herodotus here uses the Greek word *aklea*, literally, "ingloriousness."

Like many other cultures, the ancient Greeks expressed this sort of yearning first in epic poetry, originally an oral tradition. They did so especially in *The Iliad* and *The Odyssey*, which celebrate the heroes of Greece's legendary war against Troy. As written down by Homer, probably in the eighth century BC, these two epic poems represent the beginnings of Greek, and thus, Western, literature. To be an educated Greek, in Herodotus's time as forever afterward, was to know them intimately.

So it's not surprising that the high-sounding part of history's first sentence has a distinctly Homeric feel, like much of the rest of the book (which also shares Homer's twin preoccupations of war and travel). *Aklea* is a Homeric concept. The word itself appears prominently in both *The Iliad* and *The Odyssey*, as do its more common positive versions *klea*, "glory" (it is an insult to his *klea* that incurs Achilles' wrath) and *kleos*, "glorious."

Later generations of Greeks would designate the muse Kleio as history's patron goddess. Her name, rendered in English as Clio, comes from the same root. As a verb in epic poetry, the word *kleio* means "I celebrate."

If people everywhere share an urge to celebrate the past and glorify its heroes, the other urge that gave rise to history was specifically and at first uniquely Greek: the impulse to explain things in secular, rational terms. And if epic poetry reached back to the very foundations of Greek civilization, rational explanation was a relative newcomer, a radical innovation that first appeared around the beginning of the sixth century BC, about a century or so before Herodotus's birth.

It did so, moreover, at a place almost within shouting distance of Herodotus's hometown of Halicarnassus: the Greek city of Miletus, a day or two's easy sail up the Aegean coast of what is now Turkey.

Centuries earlier, the Greeks had colonized this coast, which was known as Ionia. Settling amid local peoples like the Caryans and Phrygians, the Greeks had established a number of prosperous cities on the Ionian coast, of which Miletus was the acknowledged leader.

Ionia lay closer than the rest of Greece to fascinating older cultures like those of Egypt, and especially Persia, which incorporated the ancient mathematical, astronomical, and wisdom traditions of the Babylonians and others. Modern scholars believe this proximity may have helped spark the birth of scientific thinking in Ionia around the year 600 BC, when the earliest philosopher, Thales of Miletus, made the first attempt to explain the natural world in secular, rational terms (by theorizing that all matter is ultimately composed of water).* His reputation as a sage made Thales one of the most famous men of his time, and Herodotus mentions him several times in the *Histories*.

Herodotus's special contribution was to take the Ionian tradition of rational explanation and apply it not to the natural world but to the human past, the subject matter previously covered by epic poetry. And it is this innovation that is rather inchoately reflected in the last part of history's first sentence, with Herodotus's groping stab at including in his purview "the reason why they went to war against each other."

---

* The reader may wonder why mathematical and astronomical knowledge wasn't sufficient reason for these older civilizations to be considered scientific. As with history, however, the accumulation of information is less important than the mental approach. Numerous ancient civilizations built up quite detailed information about both the natural world and their pasts, in other words, but (as far as anyone can tell) when they used that information to explain anything, it was within the context of religion or mythology. This oversimplifies a complex situation, however. A fuller account may be found in G. E. R. Lloyd, *Magic, Reason and Experience: Studies in the Origins and Development of Greek Science*, especially pages 229 ff.

The birth of reason in the ancient Greek world doesn't mean that no one had ever thought in secular, rational terms before. Nor does it mean that these early scientists were as consistently and methodically secular in their thinking as their intellectual descendants are supposed to be today. Thales, for example, wove strongly religious strands into his thinking, as did many of his successors.

But it does mean that these ancient Greeks were the first to seek naturalistic explanations of the world in a deliberate and culturally coherent way—in a way that was progressive, that built on work of earlier thinkers to create a self-consciously rational body of thought, a recognizable movement.

Thales was followed by a growing crowd of students and imitators, who critiqued everyone else's explanations and offered their own. From Ionia the movement rapidly spread throughout the rest of Greece, but for some time it remained especially strong in Ionia, and this vitality extended into the fifth century BC, when Herodotus was exposed to it as a young man.

History's parents, then, are epic poetry and science. Yet the intellectual values that these two fertile traditions represent have never fit seamlessly together. It's striking that history's first sentence embodies all this so perfectly—not only the parents, that is, but also the prickly relationship between them.

We know next to nothing for certain about Herodotus's life outside of what he himself tells us in the *Histories*, which is little (and mostly about his travels). The sketchy details we do possess—including the traditional date of 484 BC for his birth—may simply have been made up by later writers eager to concoct a suitable biography for "the Father of History." On the other hand, as the Oxford classicists W. W. How and J. Wells observe in their wonderfully dry Edwardian-era commentary on Herodotus, the *Histories* enjoyed immediate success, and there's no reason to think that the basic details of its author's life should have remained hidden from posterity.

Herodotus, we may safely say, was born to a socially prominent family in Halicarnassus sometime in the early fifth century. From here the ground gets progressively both shakier and more scenic. We're told that his father was named Lyxas and his mother Dryo, a Caryan name, which suggests that Herodotus may have been of mixed parentage. He is also given a brother, Theodorus, and another relative, an uncle or cousin named Panyasis. We hear next to nothing about Theodorus, but Panyasis cuts an interesting figure. Described as an epic poet and seer, Panyasis is reported to have been put to death by Lygdamis, the tyrant of Halicarnassus. Evidently Panyasis's political activism, if that's what it was, rubbed off on his younger relative. Herodotus himself is said to have been expelled as a young man from Halicarnassus by Lygdamis, returning later to help in the tyrant's own expulsion. During his exile from Halicarnassus, tradition has it, Herodotus sojourned on the large island of Samos, which lies off the Ionian coast just to the north of Miletus.

This has a ring of truth, since Samos and its sights figure more prominently in the *Histories* than we might otherwise expect. Always one for stupendous tourist destinations, Herodotus gushes about the long tunnel cut through a Samian mountain, the giant pier in the Samian harbor, the huge Samian temple of Artemis. The tunnel is lost, but the ruins of the others may still be seen.

Herodotus also dwells on Samos's tyrant, the rich and powerful Polycrates, who provides the occasion for one of the *Histories'* best-known tales. Polycrates's wise friend Amasis, pharaoh of Egypt, warns him that he risks incurring the jealousy of the gods for his unbroken success, and should throw away something he treasures. Polycrates duly throws his favorite golden ring into the sea. When the ring turns up in the stomach of a fish served to him at dinner, Amasis (along with the reader) knows that Polycrates's doom is sealed. Shortly afterward Polycrates is overthrown and murdered, and his corpse crucified.

It's a quintessentially Greek story. Familiar from Athenian tragedy, the message that inordinate prosperity or pride (*hubris*) leads inevitably to divine retribution (*nemesis*) lies at the heart of Herodotus's understanding of history. Over and over, Herodotus suggests that Greece's victory represents divine retribution for inordinate Persian pride.

As an Ionian Greek born under Persian rule, Herodotus would have had ample exposure to the Persian empire, and an extended description of its lands and peoples in fact takes up the first half of the *Histories* (the work as whole runs to some 600-plus pages in English translations). In his geographical bent, Herodotus was clearly influenced by a previous writer of prose nonfiction—perhaps the very first in the West, though Herodotus is the first whose work survives—called Hecataeus of Miletus. Hecataeus's books have been lost, but we do know the titles given two of them by Hellenistic commentators: one was *Journey Around the World*, and the other was a work of mythology called the *Genealogies*. Herodotus, who mentions Hecataeus several times, was especially indebted to the first, which described the lands and peoples to be encountered on a sailing voyage around the Mediterranean coastline, as well as some more-remote places like India and Scythia.

A few quotations from Hecataeus by later writers survive, and they show that Hecataeus took a rationalistic if somewhat crusty view of his subject matter. "I write what I believe to be the truth," one of *his* opening sentences declares, "for the stories of the Greeks are many and foolish." He may have included among his aims elements of what we would consider historical explanation. One of the alternate titles Hellenistic commentators gave the *Genealogies* was the by-that-time generic *Histories*.

Unfortunately, we will never know the full extent of Herodotus's debt to Hecataeus, but wanderlust was certainly part of it. Herodotus spent years in travel, ranging from Libya and Egypt in the south, to beyond the Danube in the north, and east as far as Scythia, in today's southern Ukraine. It's been suggested that he began his project as a book of Hecataean travel writing, and that this original conception, embodied in the first half of his book, became the Persian background for the more "historical" subject matter in the second half (the Persian Wars themselves). Both authors clearly emerged from the encounter between epic poetry and science, and both seem to have taken after the epic parent more than the scientific one.

Above all, we feel on reading him, Herodotus loved a good yarn. Like the travel material, most of the tale-spinning happens in the first half of the *Histories*, though not exclusively. (This, too, may show a Persian influence, since many of these tales clearly come from Persian sources.) After a brief introduction, Book I opens immediately into a magic garden of exotic and enchanting tales from the past, each leading straight to the next with hardly a break, like a fast-paced Hollywood action movie. Digression piles upon digression in a dizzying parade of Greeks and others: foolish kings and tyrants (the Greek word, meaning a sort of popular dictator, lacked the negative connotation it later took on), crafty royal advisors, bold pretenders, a strong-willed queen or two, heroic young men.

A central figure in Book I is Croesus, the extravagantly wealthy and powerful king of Lydia, Ionia's neighbor in Asia Minor, whose downfall will later be echoed by that of Polycrates. Croesus, who considers himself the most fortunate of men, receives a visit from Solon, the Athenian sage and lawgiver. Solon warns him that no man can be called truly fortunate until he's safely in the grave. Croesus's contempt for this very Greek advice foreshadows what happens next. The powerful Croesus is brought low by the even more powerful Cyrus the Great, founder of the mighty Persian empire, who conquers Lydia in the late sixth century BC and adds it to his growing dominions. All too late, Croesus realizes the wisdom of Solon's words.

Along with tourist marvels, diverting tales ostensibly from real life, and divine retribution for immoderate success, Herodotus is always impressed by oracles and omens, neither of which was ever in short supply in the ancient world. Here he shows the Persian king Xerxes, marching to invade Greece and hubristically dismissing not one but two perfectly obvious signs of impending doom: first, a mare gave birth to a hare, and then "a mule dropped a foal with a double set of sexual organs—male and female—the former uppermost. Xerxes, however, ignored both omens and continued his march at the head of his army." Oh rash, oh vain! Clearly we're a ways yet from the crystalline realms of hardcore modern-style rationalism.

Yet just a few pages later we get a detailed, closely reasoned argument in support of Herodotus's main thesis that Athens, with its formidable navy, deserved the credit for defeating Persia. The key was mastery of the sea. If the Athenians had not been able and willing to face the main Persian force at sea, Sparta, the Greeks' major land power, would not have been able to resist the Persians by land. "It was the Athenians who held the balance," Herodotus declares definitively, and so it was "the Athenians who—after God—drove back the Persian king." This is as logically persuasive as anyone would wish—and that final devout protestation undercuts the analytical rigor not one iota.

For today's readers, it may be hard to see how both passages could have been written by the same person. We must remember that Herodotus was not a modern historian, and he had no way of knowing what history would become once it left his hands. We feel he must have known he was doing something new, but we can't be certain about precisely how he conceived of his project.

We can only recognize that Herodotus shows none of the discomfort that modern historians (even if themselves religious) would feel at putting religious factors in a parallel historical track with rational ones. Divine agency is a constant in epic poetry. The gods continually intervene in human affairs. Their bickering lay behind the Trojan War, and one of them is always strengthening Achilles's arm here or marring Agamemnon's judgment there. While he sharply reduces their role to low-level background material, Herodotus does retain a place for them in his thinking. Like "the Father of History," most of Herodotus's contemporaries are likely to have taken the gods' role in past events for granted.

There was, however, one glaring exception.

Thucydides the Athenian belonged very much to the next generation. As a young man Thucydides was said to have heard Herodotus reading from his work in Athens, where Herodotus almost certainly lived for some time before moving to his final home, the Athenian colony of Thurii in Sicily. Herodotus would have been in Athens at the height of its Periclean glory, as it enjoyed wealth, empire, and unparalleled cultural vitality in the wake of the Persian Wars. His extensive treatment of Athens' history shows that he had important and well-placed sources there, including in the family of Pericles himself, the great Athenian statesman who has lent his name to the age. It was a natural place for Herodotus to spend time, considering the prominent and flattering role he assigns to the city in the struggle against Persia.* The readings Herodotus is thought to have given in Athens may have constituted the *Histories'* original "publication." Inspired by them, the story goes, Thucydides decided right then and there to become a historian.

His work, *The Peloponnesian War*, chronicles the long and destructive war that broke out between Athens and Sparta a half-century after the Persian Wars. At first glance, it's as different from Herodotus's book as one could possibly imagine. Herodotus seems to wander at will; Thucydides stays tightly focused. Herodotus covers a huge area both geographically and chronologically; Thucydides restricts himself to Greece and the years leading up to and during the war. Herodotus has an eye for any interesting detail; Thucydides has eyes only for war and politics. A reluctant revolutionary, Herodotus remains essentially conservative and traditional; Thucydides stands on the cutting edge.

By Thucydides' time, Greece's foaming rationalism had spilled over from philosophy into areas as diverse as medicine and rhetoric, the latter being of central importance in the culture of democratic Athens. Influenced by the appearance of new types like the physician and the professional sophist, the tenor of the times was rapidly moving in a distinctly secular direction, at least for the intellectual

---

* As Herodotus acknowledges, his favorable portrait of Athens wouldn't have won him friends anywhere else. Imperial Athens was also unpopular Athens, and for good reason, despite our rather rosy picture of it.

vanguard.* Nowhere in Thucydides are the gods allowed any influence over human events. Thucydides' mask is that of the cold, clinical observer, a chilly but effective counterweight to Herodotus's warm, reassuringly conventional congeniality.

Thucydides was born around 460 BC, just as Pericles was coming to the period of his long political ascendancy. It's likely, though he doesn't say, that he was related to another Thucydides, the leader of the aristocratic party opposed to Pericles and the Athenian democrats. If so, then Thucydides the historian turned his back on this connection, praising Pericles and his policies without reservation in *The Peloponnesian War*.

Our image of Pericles will always be the one Thucydides draws, just as our Richard III or Prince Hal will always be Shakespeare's. And the Funeral Oration Thucydides has Pericles deliver draws our eternal image of democratic Athens: versatile, proud, self-reliant, an object of admiration for succeeding generations. Only a close look at this often-quoted speech shows the muscle under the fine suit of clothes, for Pericles also celebrates Athens' naked imperialism. He would not be around to guide his city much longer, dying soon after leading Athens into a war whose devastating outcome not even he could foresee.

---

* Everyone else, then as now, most likely professed conventional beliefs. Just after the end of the Peloponnesian War, for example, in a reaction against military and political disaster as well as against skeptical inquiry, Athenians voted to execute Socrates for impiety (399 BC). Yet right around the same time, medical studies in the Hippocratic tradition contain the earliest surviving blanket rejections of magic and the supernatural. For that, see Lloyd, *Magic, Reason and Experience*, pages 15–29 (though you may wish to keep reading for the enlightening discussion of Herodotus that starts on page 29); for the conservative reaction, see E. R. Dodds's classic, *The Greeks and the Irrational*, pages 179–195.

We're told and then shown how Pericles' successors lacked his stature, substituting violent demagoguery for hard-headed leadership. Power, in a word, is Thucydides' real subject—power and its corrosive effects. From the heights of Pericles' Funeral Oration we rapidly descend into the bleakest depths of cruel, self-interested calculation, watching Pericles' noble Athens commit genocide, enslavement, and other atrocities. At its worst, Athens turns out to be no better than any other city-state. Thucydides, it is often remarked, invented *realpolitik*.

Thucydides' writing has a knotted intensity that makes it a great work of art as well as of history, but one that puts up a wall between author and reader in a way that Herodotus never does. There are numerous unresolved tensions in *The Peloponnesian War*. Thucydides' ambivalent attitude toward Herodotus is a large part of this picture.

Unlike his predecessor, who wrote from more than a generation's remove, Thucydides tells us that he began his book early in the war, which lasted from 431 to 404 BC, and wrote as the events unfolded. In that sense, Thucydides' work is closer to what we think of as "current events" than it is to "history."

It was probably to distance himself from Herodotus that Thucydides never once uses the word "history," *historia*. Even though he focuses on contemporary events, there was no reason not to apply the word to his efforts. At the time *historia* simply meant "research," "inquiry," "investigation," and it carried no implication that the subject of the investigation had to be the distant past, or even the past at all. A few years after Herodotus wrote, it would even be briefly claimed by the medical writers, such as Hippocrates, who represented another growing offshoot of secular ratio-nalism. But Herodotus had used the word in that famous opening sentence, as well as in various forms throughout his work (most commonly as a verb, "to inquire"). It was Herodotus who eventually made the word stick.

In contrast, the word Thucydides uses for what he's doing is *syngraphein*—literally "to write together"—which lies somewhere between "to write up" and "to compose in writing." Simon Hornblower speculates that an immediate model for Thucydides' famously terse style was the reports that Greek generals in the field sent back to their politi-cal superiors at home. This makes sense, since Thucydides himself was an Athenian commander during the war. In other words, he was a participant in the events he recorded. He may even have used such reports, his own and others', in writing his book on the war. Another modern scholar has called him "Colonel Thucydides," which fits him perfectly.

Only once or twice does he really tell us anything about himself, but in a way that captures all this with surprising poignance. The Spartan general Brasidas, whose energy and initiative Thucydides praises, had moved to threaten the strategic city of Amphipolis, an ally of Athens. "Thucydides, the son of Olorus, the author of this history," Thucydides reports, "was then at the island of Thasos... about a half a day's sail from Amphipolis" and was asked to come to the relief of the city. But before he could do so, Brasidas won the city over by negotiating generous terms of surrender. Thucydides moves on with his narrative, and only later does he reveal, in a matter-of-fact way, that the Athenians exiled him for twenty years for his failure to defend Amphipolis. Rather than dwelling on it, though, he mentions it only to observe that his exile gave him a unique opportunity as a historian. "I saw what was being done on both sides, particularly on the Peloponnesian side, because of my exile, and this leisure gave me rather exceptional facilities for looking into things."

Thucydides never names Herodotus, but his criticism of Herodotus is implicit from the opening lines of his work:

> *Thucydides the Athenian covered the war between the Peloponnesians [i.e., the Spartans] and the Athenians, how they went to war against each other, beginning as soon as the war broke out in the expectation that it would be great and more worth telling about than any that had come before . . . For this was the greatest turmoil ever among the Greeks and in the barbarian world as well—even, so to speak, for the whole of humanity.*
>
> —Thucydides I: 1

From the start, Thucydides asserts his primacy (my war is bigger than yours) even while paying Herodotus the supreme compliment of imitation. Note the familiar "how they went to war against each other," an obvious echo of Herodotus's first sentence. Here is the common kernel of intent: to explain how the war happened.

Thucydides minimizes his great general debt to Herodotus by painstakingly distinguishing himself from Herodotus in method, and, above all, in style. He tells us that he either witnessed the events he describes himself, or at least subjected the accounts of others to the closest scrutiny (implying that Herodotus did not). In short, he presents himself in a role that we would think of as closer to a war correspondent than a historian, and his work as one of objective, unemotional reportage, which is why the journalistic verb "covered" seems an appropriate translation of *syngraphein* in the passage above.

This, he makes clear a bit later, is what other writers ought to confine themselves to, even at the expense of reaching a broad audience. Having conspicuously corrected several "popular misunderstandings" about the state of Greek affairs—mistakes that just happen to have been made by Herodotus—Thucydides goes on to deliver the *coup de grâce* against his rival:

> *My work's lack of sensational stories may make it seem less engaging in the telling. Yet it will suffice for me if the work is judged useful by those wishing to plan for the future by clearly comprehending the past, since—human nature being what it is—the one is always bound to resemble the other. It is composed to be a possession for always, rather than a puff-piece for easy listening.*
>
> —Thucydides I: 23

In its impact on future historians, this is the most influential passage any historian ever wrote, and a nearly mortal blow to the Herodotean vision. It strikes us, too, as a bit hard on Herodotus, however much glee "the Father of History" took in retailing stories about giant ants, winged snakes, and men with their faces in their bellies.

But it was certainly effective as a way of staking out one's turf. Herodotus may have taken after the poets, but

Thucydides would model himself on history's other parent. If one was going to present himself as "the storyteller," the other would be "the scientist."

So powerful was Thucydides' analysis of the war, and so compelling his self-presentation, that none who came after him dared depart too conspicuously from the model he offered. Few came close to measuring up. Few even really tried, though most dutifully aped the rationalistic pose.

History soon established itself as a minor literary genre dealing, by and large, more comfortably with great contemporary events than with past ones. Thucydides had indicted the past as unknowable, privileging the verifiability of the present. This was one side of his legacy. The other was the narrowing of subject matter, which he successfully intertwined with the pose of rationalism, as if war and politics were the only topics suitable for rational inquiry. Yet the ultimate adoption of Herodotus's word, *history*, suggests the tacit appeal of the Herodotean approach, even if few historians openly modeled their style on his, and even if none were as broadly inclusive of other sorts of subject matter than war and politics.

History was duly passed along, with other literary genres, from the Greeks to the Romans, and from the Romans to the rest of the world. But for almost 2,500 years, the majority of those who followed history's path stayed to the narrow channel laid down by Thucydides, steering clear of the meandering trails that Herodotus had blazed in searching out the wider human past.

TWO

"From the Foundation of the City"

*I*n 1923, a German historian named Felix Jacoby began what would turn out to be one of the great heroic efforts of modern scholarship: the attempt to collect and catalog the quotations by other writers of Greek historians whose work has since been lost. Taken up by his colleagues on Jacoby's death in 1959, *The Fragments of the Greek Historians* now fills eighteen volumes and includes some 12,000 snippets from the lost writings of 856 historians. Its massive ranks, solid and forbidding in austere blue with gold print, have become a familiar and indispensable resource for classicists and ancient historians. Brill, the academic publisher of this monumental work, have begun putting an expanded "New Jacoby" online, no doubt to sighs of resignation from the old school and gasps of excitement from the technophiles.

While some of the 856 authors come from later times (the collection includes Greek historians from the Byzantine period), the vast majority lived and wrote in the ancient world. In other words, their lives took place during the roughly 800-year span between Herodotus and Constantine the Great, the Roman emperor who converted to Christianity in the early fourth century, hastening the transition from a pagan empire to a Christian one.

One way of putting it is to say that, on average, there was a vanished Greek historian for approximately each year of this immensely long span of time. This is an astonishing and rather disheartening thought, all the more so when we remember that Jacoby's eighteen fat volumes may represent just the tip of the iceberg. How many more were there who were never quoted in a surviving work? Whose names and writings are *completely* lost, so that nothing whatsoever survives to mark their efforts?

Of course, all this leaves aside the substantial Greek historical works that *do* survive from this period, as well as the much smaller body of surviving works by Roman historians. But, as students of ancient history commonly complain, the relative paucity of extant sources makes studying ancient history feel like trying to live for a year on an acorn, compared with the well-fertilized, industrially grown, packaged and processed abundance churned out onto the supermarket shelves of modern history today.

As we turn to the Greek and Roman historians who came after Herodotus and Thucydides, we'll do well to keep Jacoby and his eighteen volumes in mind—not to mention the poor unknowns who never made it even that far.

Thucydides' history of the Peloponnesian War breaks off abruptly in the year 411 BC, nearly a decade before the war ended with Athens' catastrophic defeat. From clues in the text we know that Thucydides lived past the end of the war, but apparently not long enough to finish his book. One measure of his immediate prestige is that the next generation of historians resumed where he left off, near the end of the war. Xenophon, the best known of those who tried to take up Thucydides' baton, begins his history precisely where Thucydides ends, with the words, "And after all that . . ."

An Athenian aristocrat with a flair for adventure, horsemanship, and self-promotion, Xenophon also thrilled readers for centuries with the *Anabasis* ("The March Up-Country"), a gripping account of a daring Greek military expedition deep into Persian territory. He was held in high regard by historians until very recently. Alas, modern scholarship has revealed that this hero to numerous Victorian schoolboys was, as far as reliability goes, a total dud. Xenophon may have been a wonderful writer and a fine soldier, but despite a slick pretense, that's all he had in common with Thucydides—and besides, he was wonderful and fine in a different sort of way altogether. One clue might have lain in his versatility, for his works (which also include popular biographies of the philosopher Socrates and the Persian king, Cyrus the Great) are each strikingly different in tone and content. In contrast, it's hard to imagine Thucydides writing any differently than he did.

Xenophon died around the middle of the fourth century BC. By that time, the northern half-Greek kingdom of Macedon had begun to assert itself over the Greek world. After consolidating mastery of Greece, the young Macedonian king Alexander the Great undertook the explosive conquests that would push a tidal surge of Greek ways as far east as India before it slowly ebbed back toward the Mediterranean. In this new Hellenistic world, an official veneer of Greek language and culture was overlaid on the ethnically variegated cosmopolitanism of the old Persian empire, which Alexander had vanquished and absorbed.

We might expect history to do well in the lush, riotous growth that resulted when Greek forms were cross-fertilized by still-vital local traditions. And it did at first. But it soon becomes clear that something was missing. Historians had thrown their lot in with contemporary politics, and Alexander the glamorous boy-king put paid to the fractious but free political life of the independent Greek city-states. Instead, the Hellenistic world dealt in kingdoms, with local elites held firmly under the thumbs of ambitious kings who often claimed divine prerogatives. The atmosphere discouraged Thucydides' sort of skeptical, even pessimistic, analysis of power politics.

That left—what? Blunted by the walls thrown up to protect divine kings, historians' spear thrusts went in several oblique directions. Some paralleled the several already-established literary genres closely associated with, but still separate from, history itself. Biography was one such genre, and it received a huge boost from the inspiring figure of Alexander. Another took up the ethnographic vein so richly worked by Herodotus, so that Greeks were soon writing ethnographies of the exotic peoples they now ruled in places such as Egypt, Persia, and India. In the same spirit, Hellenistic scholars also began methodically raking over the past, but with an eye toward accumulating detail more than explaining events. Like the ethnographers, these antiquarians compiled facts rather than told stories, arranging their material in thematic sections, not in the chronological narratives that distinguished history.

The master accumulator, of course, was Aristotle, Alexander's tutor and the man who codified the systematic approach to knowledge for the ages. Aristotle's awesome breadth spanned cultural, political, literary, philosophical, and scientific studies. When it came to history, however, he turned Thucydides' implied rejection of the distant past into a deadly weapon. Because by its very nature history is empirically unverifiable, Aristotle said, it has no proper place among the branches of knowledge. That charge makes Aristotle history's first enemy. In one form or another, we shall hear the same accusation echoed over and over, right down to the trendy postmodern academicians who level it against history today.

Still, even if relegated to the margins of learning by Aristotle's indictment, history didn't go away, as Jacoby's eighteen volumes and the Penguin Classics together remind us. In the rise of Rome the Greek historians once again found a sympathetic subject, and an encore of the Herodotus-Thucydides matchup was played out as the Hellenistic world first took notice of the new power.

In the Herodotus mask is Timaeus of Taormina, born in that Sicilian city around the time of Xenophon's death, as the Greek world was falling under Macedonian hegemony. Timaeus (number 566 in Jacoby) survives only in fragments that belie a long lifetime of work and an extensive posthumous influence. Like Herodotus, whom he may have openly styled himself after, Timaeus was exiled from his city as a young man by a hostile tyrant and went to Athens, where he is reported to have lived for fifty years. His literary approach included Herodotean elements—geographic and ethnographic excursuses, omens and portents, tales and marvels—but Timaeus appears to have lacked his model's most endearing quality: human warmth. Punning on his name, later writers called him Epitimaeus, meaning "fault-finder," and he comes off a pedantic and mean-spirited wretch indeed, at least in those later portraits.

But for centuries (until his work was lost during the Byzantine period), Timaeus was the standard source for the early history of Sicily and the western Greek world, though he is best known today as the first Greek historian to cover Rome in any detail. He died sometime around the middle of the third century, reportedly in his nineties, having chronicled the rise of Roman power, first over Italy itself, and then over his native Sicily, Rome's first overseas colony. The stage was now set for Rome's epic clash with Carthage, the other major power in the western Mediterranean. What we don't know is the significance Timaeus gave to these events— whether he saw the rise of Rome as relevant only to his history of the western Greeks, or whether he perceived instead the first hints of an emerging new world order.

Perhaps because of his own nastiness, Timaeus's successors felt free to carp at him (while using him freely in their own histories, of course). None buried him so thoroughly as the mighty Polybius, who played Thucydides to Timaeus's Herodotus. Polybius devoted an entire book to Timaeus's many faults.[*] Chief among them was Timaeus's

---

[*] When used to mean a part of a larger literary work from Greco-Roman antiquity (as here), the word *book* refers to a conventional division in the text, in length somewhere between a "chapter" and a "part" in modern terms. It originally meant the amount that fit onto a single scroll of papyrus.

reliance on written sources alone, rather than the use of travel and personal investigation to supplement them. If true, this suggests that Timaeus was missing Herodotus's sense of adventure as well as his humanity, though that hardly sets him apart from most modern historians, at least. But Polybius makes Timaeus's bookish ways sound cowardly, painting himself, by contrast, as a worldly man of action. Experience in politics and war, not book learning, makes the real historian, he says.

Born in mainland Greece around 200 BC, Polybius lived the life he extols as essential to his craft. A confederation of mainland Greek cities, the Achaean League, had managed to break free of Macedonian rule, and the young Polybius followed his father into political life as a leader of the league. By this time, Rome had beaten Carthage in the first two Punic Wars and was unchallenged in the West. When the Macedonian king Perseus moved against the league, the Greeks formed an uneasy alliance with Rome, which made short work of Perseus. Several earlier Roman interventions in the East had been followed by withdrawal, but this time the Romans stayed. Greek misgivings were well founded. Rome's presence in the East took on a harsher edge, soon verging into the naked expansion of that permanent power the Romans came to call *imperium*, "empire."

Polybius was one of a thousand prominent Greeks arrested by the Romans and whisked off to Rome as hostages to Greek obedience. He spent nearly twenty years there, numbering among his Roman friends some of the most powerful men of the day, including Scipio Aemilianus, whom he tutored. When Rome found a pretext to declare yet another war on now-docile Carthage, it was Polybius's student Scipio who commanded the Roman legions and oversaw the old enemy's final destruction, famously razing the city, plowing up the land, and sowing salt in the furrows to symbolize its permanent abandonment. Polybius was there and witnessed it all. He tells how Scipio, envisioning the possibility of a similar fate for Rome one day, turned to him in tears and quoted Homer on the sack of Troy.

The story reflects one of Polybius's pet concepts—the idea that history moves in cycles, which he inherited from the Hellenistic theorists. One aspect of this cyclical view of history explained the rise and fall of empires, while another involved an elaborate theory that political constitutions progress from monarchy to aristocracy to democracy, each with a corrupt version that comes before it is overthrown. Thus monarchy decays to tyranny, aristocracy to oligarchy, democracy to mob rule. The finest and most stable constitution was one that mixed all three in proportion. Though the idea ultimately goes back to Plato, Polybius provided the classic articulation of it, and through him it would influence subsequent political theory. A century later, using Polybius as a source, Cicero put it in the mouth of Scipio Aemilianus, the central character Cicero's dialogue, *De Republica*.

Polybius wrote his *Histories* in forty books, covering what he saw as the biggest story of all time: the rise of the Roman empire. He began with the First Punic War in 264 BC, and ended with the Third, which brought the destruction of Carthage in 146 BC and soon afterward, that of Corinth, the last remaining Greek power, as well. But Polybius's main focus was the pivotal, hard-fought Second Punic War

(218–202 BC). It is largely owing to him, for example, that we have the story of Hannibal bringing the elephants over the Alps.

Speaking of elephants, the first thing we notice about his work is its sheer size. History had grown, in the most basic way, since its beginnings; both Timaeus and Polybius wrote works that were much longer than those of Herodotus and Thucydides. To get an idea of the difference, consider that the Loeb Library publishes Herodotus's entire work in four volumes, while the surviving part of Polybius takes up six. And that surviving part amounts to perhaps a third of the original, which makes Polybius's *Histories* something on the order of four to five times longer than Herodotus's—some eighteen volumes, if it survived to be published whole by the Loeb Library! Small wonder that, a few centuries later, another historian numbered Polybius's work among those that "nobody endures to read through to the end." Small wonder, too, that only a (relatively) small part survived the age when all books had to be laboriously copied out by hand.

Length wasn't all that stood between an intact Polybius and posterity. His style is graceless and repetitive, conveying a woodenness that Polybius clearly felt to be consonant with his ideal of "pragmatic history." Timaeus's more ornate style, by contrast, was praised by later writers, including Cicero, who appreciated its "Asiatic" sophistication. Like Thucydides, Polybius explicitly rejects such ornamentation, along with the entertaining and marvelous tales associated with it, but he goes further than Thucydides in adopting an openly didactic tone. Thucydides had hoped his work might be useful to future generations, but left it up to them to figure out how. Polybius always comes right out and tells his readers the message he wants them to take away. To the point of numbness, we might add.

Numbing didacticism aside, all those lessons stand squarely in the Thucydidean tradition. From its earliest beginnings, Polybius tells us, history had two purposes: training political leaders (who will benefit from learning the mistakes of others), and helping its students withstand the vicissitudes of fate (by showing how others have stood up to similar disasters in the past). Next to Thucydides himself, Polybius would be the most highly regarded of the Greek historians, regardless of whether anyone actually made it through his entire work. His elaboration of the Thucydidean model did much to reinforce the link between reason (in Polybius's case, flavored with pragmatism) on the one hand, and the subject matter of war and politics on the other.

Despite the loss of so much of his work, Polybius has stood up quite well. When Renaissance humanists rediscovered the Greek historians, it was Polybius who enjoyed the first real vogue. Historians today still give him high marks for reliability, if not for insight on a par with the awe-inspiring Thucydides. The flyleaf of the Penguin paperback selection from his surviving work describes him as a "scientific" historian. If that's faint praise in the ears of postmodern critics, when it was originally offered a generation or two ago, it was the highest seal of respectability (but that's a story for a later chapter).

Already by Polybius's time, history had jumped the tracks and was no longer being written exclusively by Greeks. What's interesting about this development, however, is that even when non-Greeks took it up, they still wrote it in Greek. Early in the third century BC, one Manetho, an Egyptian, wrote a history of Egypt in Greek, while a certain Berossus wrote one of Babylon in Greek. Later that same century—around the time Hannibal was bringing the elephants over the Alps, along with several Greek historians to chronicle his exploits—a Menander of Ephesus wrote a history of the Phoenicians in Greek. Despite his Greek name, this Menander may have been Phoenician himself, which would make him near-kin to the Carthaginians.* About the time of Polybius's birth, a Hellenized Jew named Demetrius wrote a Jewish history in Greek that was based on the Hebrew Bible, which someone had translated into Greek earlier in the century. So close was the identification of history with the Greek language that the two seemed inseparable.

So it isn't surprising that when the first Roman tried his hand at history, he did it in Greek, too, just like everyone else. Quintus Fabius Pictor, an aristocratic Roman born into a well-known branch of a well-known family, lived in the generation before Polybius. A member of the Roman senate, he fought in the Second Punic War. After

---

* Carthage was founded by Phoenician traders, hence *Punic* (the Latin word for "Phoenician"). The Phoenicians, an ancient trading people who roamed the Mediterranean, had originally come from the Lebanon.

the great Roman victory, he decided that his country's new status as a world power meant it was high time someone wrote a history of Rome.

Like Polybius, Fabius Pictor relied heavily on Timaeus and other Greek historians in writing his history. Even for a history of Rome, a Roman had to go to Greek sources. Only a few scraps of his work survive, but they show a Herodotean interest in customs, religious practices, and good stories that probably came from Timaeus. But Fabius Pictor also brought some new and peculiarly Roman elements to the mix.

If the Greeks were interested in the past, the Romans were obsessed by it. To a Roman aristocrat, tradition was all. These were people who literally worshipped their illustrious ancestors, and what made one's ancestors illustrious (or otherwise) was what they had accomplished as Romans. It was natural, then, for a Roman to write history as a Roman, and to focus on Rome itself as a historical and political entity.

Fabius Pictor took Rome from its mythical founders, Romulus and Remus (a rival tradition had the city being founded by the Trojan warrior Aeneas), to its expansion in Italy, its battles against Gauls and Carthaginians, and the beginnings of its overseas empire. His approach became the standard one among Roman historians, and later passed to the rest of Europe. We know it as national history, but the Romans summed it up in the phrase *ab urbe condita*—"from the foundation of the city"—a generic title for Roman historical works, which were usually presented in annalistic form, year by year. Fabius Pictor was followed by a number of imitators, who like him hoped to fold Roman history smoothly into the Hellenistic cultural mix.

If Fabius Pictor was the first Roman historian, in the next generation another Roman senator became the first Latin historian: Cato the Elder, who took the unprecedented step of writing history in a language other than Greek. He's best known, of course, as a statesman. A zealous patriot and archconservative, it was he who pushed so relentlessly for Carthage's final annihilation, famously ending all of his speeches in the senate, on whatever topic, with the words, "Furthermore, Carthage must be destroyed." He followed Fabius Pictor's *ab urbe condita* storyline, but the fact that he embraced Latin, the language of Rome, as a medium for historical writing had momentous consequences. A few poets had dared to write in Latin before Cato, but Cato's prominence and prestige emboldened the other Latin writers who, self-consciously and deliberately, would soon begin inventing a national literature to stand against that of the Greeks. History would be an important part of this patriotic literary impulse.

Like other archconservatives we know of, Cato emphasized "traditional values." One reason for his choice of Latin was no doubt his often-expressed alarm at the growing influence of Greek culture (seen as soft and effeminate) among the Romans (seen as virtuous and manly). Succeeding Roman historians picked up on Cato's values-based history, eventually turning it into a rolling condemnation of the supposedly degraded present, which always comes off in Roman history as a corrupt and pathetic shadow of the good old days when men were men and Greeks were nervous. The idea of a lost "golden age" of national purity and strength became Roman history's main theme.

This was the paradox of empire. Even as Rome vanquished all her old enemies and came to rule the known world, her new position brought unforeseen disasters. To many, these fresh problems seemed worse than the old ones. Hannibal and other external threats could be countered by fielding armies, at which the Romans excelled. The new threats were internal, and they struck deeply at Roman social and political institutions—the very traditions that Romans prized so highly. A century of civil war accompanied them.

Rome's internal problems approached their climax in the figure of Julius Caesar, who also happened to be one of the best Roman historians. We think of Caesar as a man of action, not letters, but we wouldn't know about his actions if he himself hadn't written about them. His best known line—"I came, I saw, I conquered"—says it all. Concise, elegant, active. And, despite a huge element of self-promotion, insightful and surprisingly accurate. His most famous line notwithstanding, Caesar generally wrote about himself in the third person, abandoning the annalistic approach for swiftly flowing narrative. Caesar did this, Caesar did that. Like most other Roman historians, Caesar was a military and political leader. He was known for the stunning speed with which he could move an army from one place to another, and his prose has the same purposeful rapidity. He wrote to justify first his campaigns in Gaul and then his relentless prosecution of civil war against his rival, Pompey. He put history in the service of his political career, and thus also of the Roman state and Roman tradition. The idea was to present these things as one and the same.

After Caesar's murder in 44 BC, his lieutenant Sallust, forced out of public life, carried on historical writing in the monograph format that Caesar had used. Two short works survive in full. One describes the notorious conspiracy of the Roman senator Cataline some two decades earlier, and the other narrates the war that Rome fought against the Numidian king Jugurtha in the previous century. From a literary standpoint, these works are polished and absorbing, if less than authoritative in the eyes of modern scholars. Sallust then turned to annalistic history, covering the decade before Caesar's rise to power in five books that have since been lost. Enough fragments remain to show that in this longer work, as in the shorter ones, Sallust was concerned above all to hammer home the now-familiar theme of Rome's moral decline. Though modeling himself on Thucydides (right down to the gnarly syntax), Sallust has charm but lacks depth, an Ian Fleming trying to pass as a Graham Greene.

In the next generation, Roman historical writing reaches its peak in the magisterial figure of Livy, who wrote, appropriately enough, just at the climax of Rome's transformation from republic to empire. Livy composed the definitive history of Rome that no one before him had quite been able to bring off. His massive work, fittingly entitled *Libri ab Urbe Condita*, "Books from the Foundation of the City," represents the culmination of the annalistic tradition.

Unfortunately, we know very little about Livy's life. A few lonely details stand out. He was born not in Rome but in the northern city of Padua, around 60 BC; he was not active in politics, which was otherwise unheard of for a Roman historian; and he was on friendly terms with Julius Caesar's nephew and adopted son, Octavius Caesar, who became the first Roman emperor Augustus around the time that Livy began writing. We don't know when he came to Rome, but it was probably not long after the battle of Actium in 31 BC, in which Augustus defeated his last rival, Mark Antony. Later, Livy tutored the young Claudius, who would eventually be the last emperor in the family line (though hardly the last emperor). While sympathetic to Augustus and the new regime, Livy was not a toady. He viewed one-man rule as a necessary evil, a temporary measure. He died in AD 17, perhaps never really seeing that imperial rule was firmly established and the republic well and truly buried.

Livy's history of Rome originally filled a whopping 142 books, of which only the first third or so survive in sustained stretches, and that with significant gaps. This brings the story down to the clash with the Macedonian king Perseus in 168 BC, which had resulted in the captivity of Polybius. That critical investigator would no doubt have dismissed Livy as an armchair historian, for like the despised Timaeus, Livy relied solely on written sources. At least Timaeus had used documents as well as earlier histories. Livy spun his history entirely out of the work of other historians, which, to be sure, was considered by most to be entirely acceptable practice. His strengths lie not in his investigative powers, which were nil, or even his judgment, which was fair, but in his extraordinary gifts as a writer, which were prodigious.

Livy's celebrated preface is a short masterpiece of delicious authorial conspiracy with the reader. In just a few tactically deployed paragraphs, Livy draws you in by careful stages, letting you know that he intends to be both story-teller and scientist in a way that promises the best, and leaves out the worst, of both worlds. He leads off with the mythic element, but instead of rejecting it like a Thucydides or a Polybius, he allows that it lends a certain "dignity" to the past—adding piously that such legendary stories mean little compared to a hard analysis of war, politics, power, and (naturally) the decline in traditional moral values. Then he artfully tips his hand:

> *But bitter comments of this sort are not likely to find favour, even when they have to be made. Let us have no more of them, at least at the beginning of our great story. On the contrary, I should prefer to borrow from the poets and begin with good omens and with prayers to all the host of heaven to grant a successful issue to the work which lies before me.*
>
> —Livy, *Praefatio*, 13 (de Selincourt trans.)

In other words, we'll save the serious stuff for later, if we get to it at all. Meanwhile, let me show my true intentions by invoking the muses to help me, just like the epic poets at the beginning of their works. Sweeping pageantry and gripping action are what really lie in store, not any of that nasty intellectual stuff, though I'll put just enough of that in the mix to let you feel like a smart reader—no more than that, though, I promise!

As far as we can tell, Livy keeps that implicit promise. Romulus and Remus, Hercules and Evander, the Rape of the Sabine Women, Horatius at the Bridge—in his opening pages Livy rolls out one majestic set piece after another, before proceeding to a stirring, action-filled narrative. Livy is not so much a Shakespeare as he is a David Lean or Richard Attenborough. The loss of any ancient literary work is sad, but the loss of Livy's later books comes especially hard. It would be fascinating to see how he handles events of his own time—the civil wars, the accession to power of Augustus, the events of Augustus's rule. Livy withheld publication of those books until after Augustus's death in 14 BC, which suggests his analysis may have had some teeth. There's a story that Augustus objected mildly to Livy's account of the war between Pompey and Julius Caesar, reproaching the historian for "Pompeian" sympathies.

Livy was not in with the Roman literary crowd, though even as he worked on his history the poet Virgil was composing his own equivalent to it in epic verse, *The Aeneid*. But Livy's work was an immediate hit. Pliny the Younger tells us that one reader was so taken with it that he journeyed all the way from Cadiz to Rome, just to lay eyes on its author.

Livy combined a Herodotean zest for narrative drama and epic scope with a Thucydidean focus on war and politics, tying it all together with the overarching emphasis on morality and individual character that always marked (and limited) the Roman approach to such matters. Jettison the Herodotean elements, exaggerate the others to the point of obsession, then drop the whole thing in an acid bath of biting sarcasm, and you'll begin to get an idea of the historian sometimes called Rome's greatest: the incomparable Tacitus.

Tacitus was born around AD 55, somewhere (it's believed) in the northern provinces, perhaps Gaul. We don't know anything about his family, but it must have enjoyed some means and social standing, because Tacitus received the classical education of the Roman gentleman. He came to Rome as a young man and worked as a lawyer and orator, marrying the daughter of a prominent Roman politician and embarking on a modestly successful political career himself. He began writing in his mid-forties, turning out three short works in succession. The first, *Agricola*, amounts to a eulogy of his father-in-law, who had been a governor of Britain. His second work, *Germania*, provides a detailed ethnographic and political description of the German tribes north of the empire's borders. The third, *Dialogus de Oratoribus*, is a dialogue in the Ciceronian style on the nature and practice of oratory. In these early works, Tacitus developed the distinctive themes and literary style that he would enlarge upon with such effectiveness in his longer historical works, the *Histories* and the *Annals*.*

---

* The titles are modern ones. The *Histories* covers events from the years 69 to 96, though only the parts dealing with the first two years of that period survive. The *Annals*, Tacitus's last work, fills in the background, as it were, covering the period from Augustus's death in AD 14 to Nero's in 68. It survives more fully, though still far from complete (we possess only a single, badly damaged manuscript).

Writers like Livy and Virgil had lived through civil war and the rounds of mass political assassination that accompanied it. For them as for Rome, a sense of genuine relief constituted the bedrock beneath the contrived, slightly nervous serenity of the Augustan settlement that they celebrated. By Tacitus's day a century or so later, relief was long gone and had taken serenity with it. Nervousness threatened to demolish the imperial project, or so it seemed. Not for nothing does Tacitus begin his first overtly historical work, the *Histories*, in AD 69, infamous as "the year of the four emperors."

He opens with a complaint that would have sounded familiar, we feel, to the Greek historians who struggled to write history under the Hellenistic kings. In the open atmosphere of the republic, he tells us, historians "wrote with eloquence and freedom." But Rome's political transformation undermined the writing of history:

After the conflict at Actium, when it became essential to peace that all power should be centered in one man, these great intellects passed away. Then too the truthfulness of history was impaired in many ways—at first, through men's ignorance of public affairs, which were now wholly strange to them, then through their passion for flattery or their hatred of their masters.

—Tacitus, *Histories*, I: 1 (Church and Brodribb trans.,
slightly altered)

In Tacitus the sense of a lost golden age that had always haunted Roman history finds its fullest and most bitter expression. Envy, sloth, corruption, flattery, stupidity, malevolence—these are the qualities Tacitus reveals in the sharply etched characters who fill his pages. Inadequate emperors fail to cope with their scheming, murderous wives; obsequious senators fawn and wheedle; the blood-crazed mob that is the imperial army makes and disposes of new emperors with seeming impunity.

Alone among ancient historians, Tacitus possesses intellectual integrity and powers of insight and artistry that approach those of Thucydides. But it's as if Thucydides had lived several centuries later than he did, at a time when history was gasping for air rather than stretching its limbs. Tacitus is twisted by his times. The worst part is, he knows it full well, but the self-awareness can't quite correct the deformation. Historians today prize Tacitus for his accuracy, if not always for his interpretations. Without him, we'd know very little about the early decades of Roman imperial rule. Yet from our perspective, the most moving and fascinating story in Tacitus's writing is the titanic struggle of the historian with himself.

THREE

Barbarians (and Believers) at the Gate

A few decades before Tacitus began writing, a defeated rebel commander was captured and brought to Rome in much the same way that Polybius had been taken two centuries earlier. Joseph ben Matthias had already been to Rome once, only a few years previously, as a self-appointed Jewish representative, petitioning for the release of several imprisoned priests. At that time, Joseph was only twenty-six, but already he was widely respected for his wisdom and learning. Or so he tells us—and fortune has left no one to gainsay him.

On his first visit Joseph had been impressed by the city's imperial splendor. Now he found himself back in Rome as a captive. However, like Polybius, Joseph had taken steps to secure his future by insinuating himself into the good graces of a powerful Roman, in this case the very general to whom he had surrendered. As he was brought before the general, first he boldly demanded a private audience, and then he appealed to the general's vanity by predicting that the general would one day rule as emperor.

The long shot paid off. Within a few years of Joseph's arrival in Rome, his prophecy came true. The general, whose name was Vespasian, became emperor, the last to seize the throne in AD 69, the notorious "year of the four emperors" with which Tacitus opened his *Histories*. Joseph was promptly rewarded for his flattering clairvoyance with a public stipend and a comfortable home. Latinizing his name to Josephus, and taking also the family name, Flavius, of his imperial patron Vespasian, he began writing a history of the failed revolt he had helped lead in Judaea.

To call Josephus one of history's great survivors is to flirt with catastrophic understatement. More fitting instead, perhaps, to call him Lucky Joe. Like the hapless yet ultimately triumphant antihero of Kingsley Amis's comic novel *Lucky Jim*, Josephus blends shameless opportunism with a breathtaking and at times hugely entertaining genius for improvisation. If these qualities are merely suggested in the story of his prophecy for Vespasian, they're revealed more starkly in the events surrounding his capture by that Roman emperor-to-be. Again, Josephus himself tells the story, though hardly in a way that compels trust; if his work were fiction, literary critics would put him firmly in the category of "unreliable narrator."

Born into a priestly family that traced its lineage to the Hasmoneans, Josephus in his early career was a cautious moderate bedeviled by extreme circumstances. Reluctantly drawn into the revolt that swept Judaea starting in AD 66, when the Jews drove the Romans out of Jerusalem, Josephus accepted command of the northern region of Galilee. He knew the Romans were bound to win in the end, but smarted under accusations that he was a collaborator. Soon afterward, a large Roman force invaded Galilee, and Josephus and his troops withdrew to the fortress at Jotapata. The ensuing siege lasted two months. It ended with Josephus and a small group of soldiers holed up in an old cistern as the Romans overran the fortress. Over Josephus's objections they decided on a suicide pact, agreeing to kill each other rather than face capture. They drew lots to see who would be the last two to go. Supervising the procedure, Josephus cheated his fellows by contriving to emerge at the right end of things. When the others had dispatched one another, Josephus persuaded his sole remaining comrade that captivity might not be so bad after all. Shortly afterward, Josephus was captured and brought before Vespasian, where he sustained the display of virtuoso improvisation long enough to secure a place in Rome, and history.

We don't have to piece this story together entirely by reading between the lines of Josephus's flagrantly self-aggrandizing *Jewish Wars*, the account of the rebellion he wrote later in Rome. Uniquely, a manuscript survives that appears to be a copy of the rough draft, in which the historian admits that "he counted the numbers cunningly and so managed to deceive all the others." In later versions he literally rewrote history, making his survival look like sheer luck.

Josephus is fond of portraying himself in dramatic situations and explaining at great length how behavior that might appear cowardly in fact reflected steely-eyed courage. At one point, finding himself "alone in the midst of a howling mob" of hostile fellow Jews, "he showed no trace of fear" but coolly assumed the clever disguise of a quivering wreck. He assures us that "the real purpose of this self-abasement was to prepare the way for a stratagem by which he would induce his enraged critics to quarrel among themselves." We can easily imagine Peter Sellers in the role.

And yet, like the bumbling Inspector Clouseau, somehow Josephus comes out on top in the end, paradoxically preserving the dignity that so often crosses into self-importance and self-parody. Josephus brings us face-to-face with our own human shortcomings. Who wouldn't choose to survive, if given the chance? And who wouldn't rather look like a hero? To the charitably inclined modern reader at least, his ineptness itself, the very transparency of his efforts to carry off the pose, evokes a certain sympathy and invites us to identify with him, as we do with Clouseau, even while laughing.

Authorial antics aside, Josephus stands as virtually our only major historical source not only for this crucial period in Jewish history, but also for the development of Judaism itself, and for the lives of Jews, within the larger Greco-Roman world. So we won't begrudge him the great popularity enjoyed through the ages by his two major works, *The Jewish Wars* and *Jewish Antiquities* (which might more appropriately be called *A History of the Jews*), though we may wonder how readers in earlier times perceived the historian himself. It's because of Josephus that we know in any detail about the revolts in which he took part, including the siege of Jerusalem, the destruction of the Second Temple, and the siege of Masada. It's also because of him that we have a relatively full picture of Jewish life under Roman occupation: the Maccabees, who had led an earlier revolt against Rome; the Zealots and their extremist fringe, the *sicarii* or "dagger men," who lurked in public places to assassinate those who worked with the Roman occupiers; and other sects such as the Pharisees (to which Josephus belonged), the Sadducees, and the Essenes. As the interpreter of Judaism to the Hellenistic world, he gives us a coherent account of Jewish secular history down to his own time, including the reign of Herod the Great, providing insight into the psychology of occupation and, incidentally, filling out our understanding of Roman military operations.

Reviled as a turncoat by the Jews, Josephus would have been long lost to posterity had it not been for his enduring interest to Christian readers. Thanks to him, we have a better understanding of events in Palestine during the first century AD than in any other part of the empire at any other time. Josephus himself doesn't take much notice of Jesus or of early Christians, aside from one or two fleeting, indirect, and indeed rather dubious references. (These were clearly not enough to satisfy medieval Christian scribes, who took it upon themselves to insert passages into the text that conveniently supplied some of the details they felt to be missing.) But he does provide an invaluable backdrop to the events portrayed in the New Testament, which accounts for his wide popularity during the Middle Ages and beyond.

For we're now entering the Christian era.* As the new faith gathered adherents in the empire, it was perhaps only a

---

* Or as the more politically correct but intellectually shabby recent locution would have it, the "Common Era," as if calling the very same numerals "common" should somehow lessen their inappropriateness for Jews, Muslims, and others. In fact, this no doubt well-intentioned procedure does the reverse, by implying that *Christian* should equal "common." A truly "common era" would find some other starting point than the supposed year of Christ's birth—perhaps a mathematical average of the years in which Moses, Zoroaster, Confucius, Buddha, Socrates, Christ, Muhammad, Joseph Smith, L. Ron Hubbard, and Sam Harris were born. The reader of this book may already have noted the traditional BC and AD designations, which may be "Christocentric," but at least are honestly so. More on how these Christian designations arose later in this chapter.

matter of time before history did take notice of it—and vice versa. Indeed, the emergence of Christian history seems inevitable, especially when we consider Christianity's historical roots and its quasi-historical nature. Being a Christian meant accepting that certain events actually took place in the past, a historical element inherited from Christianity's parent faith, Judaism. Just as Jews looked to their "historical" covenant with God, so did Christians look to their "historical" incarnation of God. But Christianity went further, because it also invested itself in ensuring the proper interpretation of those events. This was new, and it means that Christianity trespassed into history's turf in a way that Judaism did not.

Where Jews had focused on practice, Christians focused on belief. That entailed a strict and jealous defense of the institution charged with enforcing belief, the Christian church. Unlike Jewish history, Christian history is *church* history—a history, in other words, of thought control, which appears (shall we say) somewhat antithetical to the notion of free inquiry, *historia*, upon which the ancient historians had based their work.

Church history was invented by a man whose impact on posterity rivals that of Herodotus himself: Eusebius, bishop of Caesarea during the crucial reign of Constantine the Great, Rome's first Christian emperor. Born into a Christian family around AD 260, Eusebius came of age at a time when Christianity was expanding rapidly within the empire. A wave of persecutions had just ended, and for the first four decades of Eusebius's life, as a Christian he was free to practice and study his faith relatively unhindered. Eusebius is thought to have been born and raised in Caesarea, a good-sized provincial city on the coast of Palestine, and the place where he would live throughout his adulthood. Founded by Herod the Great and endowed by him with spectacular buildings and public spaces, Caesarea (which Herod had sycophantically named after Augustus Caesar) was the capital of Roman Judaea.

By the third century, it was also an important center of Jewish and Christian studies. The pioneering Christian teacher and theologian Origen lived and taught there during the persecutions of the mid-third century, and Eusebius later wrote a biography of the great man. As Eusebius tells it, Origen was famous for having castrated himself as a sign of his dedication to Christian chastity. It's a striking image, to say the least, though scholars are divided on whether Eusebius made it up. Eusebius himself studied with Origen's follower Pamphilus, whose name Eusebius added to his own as a sign of respect, so that he became Eusebius Pamphili, or "Eusebius of Pamphilus."

The relative security and calm of Eusebius's formative years ended in 303, when the emperor Diocletian kicked off another round of persecutions. It lasted a decade, though Diocletian himself abdicated and retired within a few years. Eusebius survived the persecutions unscathed, but pagan hostility—imperial and, more commonly, popular—created numerous Christian martyrs. It was during this period that Constantine, whose father had been co-emperor with Diocletian, rose to power, beating out various rivals. The turning point came in 312, when Constantine vanquished the strongest of those rivals, Maxentius, at the battle of the Milvian Bridge near Rome.

Eusebius later wrote up the classic version of the battle in his *Life of Constantine*, turning it into one of History's Great Moments. He assures us that he got the story from Constantine himself. As they marched toward Rome, the emperor and the entire army all saw a blazing cross in the sky with the words WITH THIS SIGN, YOU WILL CONQUER wreathed around it. Jesus also appeared to Constantine in a dream, showing him the *labarum*—which combines the first two letters of the word *Christ* in Greek, X (Chi) and P (Rho)—and telling him to put it on his standard. Constantine promptly converted to Christianity, fighting under the Christian symbol and winning the battle with divine aid.

Constantine's conversion was undoubtedly sincere, whatever the truth about the circumstances. He ended the persecutions and gave the church his full support, with the result that almost overnight the church went from a suppressed renegade operation to an imperially favored public institution. This is the story that Eusebius tells in his *History of the Church*, starting (after an Old Testament preamble) with Jesus and ending with a Technicolor version of Constantine's victory. "From that time on a day bright and radiant, with no cloud overshadowing it, shone down with shafts of heavenly light on the churches of Christ throughout the world . . ."

It was just as well he stopped there. The years after Constantine's accession saw the Christians bitterly divided by numerous disputes over what it was exactly that they were supposed to believe. This was the price of triumph. Within a century Christianity was the state religion and the old paganism was outlawed. But if Christianity transformed the empire, no less did the empire transform Christianity. When Christians had been united by oppression, it mattered less if they disagreed on a little detail like whether the Father was coeternal with the Son. When they ran the cosmos—i.e., the empire—the cosmos itself hinged on it. Suddenly the consequences of wrong belief were literally cosmic.

Eusebius defined the task of Christian history for all time: not to explain anything, but to rectify belief. "My book will start with a conception too sublime and over-whelming for man to grasp—the dispensation and divinity of our Saviour Christ." And if something is beyond human understanding, explanation is pointless. Eusebius replaced it with theology: "The nature of Christ is twofold; it is like the head of the body in that He is recognized as God, and comparable to the feet in that for our salvation He put on manhood as frail as our own. My account will therefore be complete if I begin my exposition of His entire story with the basic and essential points of the doctrine." With Euse-bius history takes a huge step backward, away from expla-nation and into dogma.

Though Eusebius ransacks earlier histories (relying, for example, on Josephus for most of the first century), his own work lacks a narrative feel. In that sense it's more of a chronicle than a history, a collection of paraphrases and often lengthy quotations patched together year by year without any interpretative glue.

Immensely learned as he was, Eusebius had no capac-ity for insight. Nor did he strive for one. When God is the reason for everything, secular explanation is worse than unnecessary; it's dangerously close to blasphemy. In Western Europe, Eusebius's basic approach held the field for the millennium that we call the Dark Ages—our no-doubt smug, generalizing, and judgmental label for an era that by and large turned its face resolutely away from explanation.

If history withered when grafted onto the vine of faith, its cousin, biography, fared better. Biographers weren't encumbered by the expectation that they would explain anything. Like the historian, the biographer was supposed to offer moral instruction in his narrative. Otherwise, accuracy was optional and juiciness mandatory, which was the reverse of the situation with history.

The most popular and influential of all ancient biographers was Plutarch, a contemporary of Tacitus in the first century. An aristocratic Greek from the island of Boeotia, Plutarch studied philosophy at Athens, traveled widely, and enjoyed powerful connections at Rome. Like so many other Greek and Roman writers, he hoped through his writing to bring the two worlds closer together. His originality lay in the appealing formula he devised of pairing biographical sketches of Great Men, one Greek and one Roman, based on similarities between them. (We can imagine that he thought of his project as requiring the capital letters.) Thus, for example, he paired Demosthenes with Cicero, Alexander the Great with Julius Caesar, and Aristides the Just with Cato the Elder. Of these *Parallel Lives*, twenty-three such pairs survive, all of them meant to exemplify particular virtues or vices. His other major work was a collection of philosophical essays known as *The Moralia*. Despite his constant moralizing, Plutarch's presence is almost always an easy one, cosmopolitan and comfortable.

Plutarch was one of the first ancient authors "rediscovered" by Western humanists during the Renaissance, and his surviving work was rapidly translated into the European languages, deeply influencing later writers. Michel de Montaigne, who invented the genre of the personal essay in the sixteenth century, used *The Moralia* as his model. The English version of the *Lives* by Sir Thomas North, which appeared in 1579, gave William Shakespeare most of the material for those of his plays set in the ancient world, including *Antony and Cleopatra*. The extended description of Cleopatra's barge ("Purple the sails, and so perfumed that / The winds were lovesick with them") is taken almost word for word from it, though the lovesick winds are Shakespeare's.

As Plutarch makes clear, he's not really interested in history, and modern historians return the favor by not putting much stock in him. Fittingly, perhaps, one of the rare occasions on which his characteristic magnanimity deserts him is his vituperative attack on Herodotus, "On the Malignity of Herodotus," in which the malignity, sad to say, is all on the author's part.

Plutarch's younger Roman contemporary, Suetonius, whose *Lives of the Caesars* offers racy, gossipy sketches of emperors, gets a slightly higher grade from modern historians, who use him to round out Tacitus. But Suetonius, too, has morals in mind more than historical accuracy. Here we get the Rome familiar to television audiences—decadent, sensual, dangerous. Suetonius was the major source for Robert Graves's excellent novel and television series *I, Claudius*, as well as the more recent HBO series, *Rome*—though don't look to either if you're looking for history. (*Caveat visor*—viewer beware. *Lector*, too, for that matter.)

Because it restricted itself to character, morals, and edifying entertainment, biography made the transition to the Christian era more smoothly than history, which was hobbled by its pesky insistence on secular explanation. Nothing about biography was inherently secular. And so as Christians went "establishment" over the course of the fourth century, biography was one of the literary genres they took over intact, as it were—except that now it celebrated Christian heroes rather than pagan ones. Since the Christians' biggest heroes were saints, Christian biography in the form of saints' lives became known as *hagiography* (from the Greek *hagios*, "holy").

Eusebius offers an early example with his *Life of Constantine*, who is considered a saint by Eastern Orthodox Christians. Later in the fourth century, another bishop, Athanasius of Alexandria, wrote the classic saint's life, that of St. Antony, the Egyptian ascetic regarded as the founder of Christian monasticism. And in the fifth century, Augustine, bishop of the North African city of Hippo, gave the genre an invigorating if self-absorbed new twist by inventing the autobiography. *The Confessions* of St. Augustine (he was later canonized), a masterpiece of world literature by any standard, shows how profoundly the energy of Christian belief was transforming creative endeavor in the Greco-Roman world.

Secular history limped along for a while, but its role as a hobby of aristocrats, statesmen, and soldiers grew even more pronounced. Increasingly, too, its scope was restricted to the eastern or Greek part of the empire. A flash in the pan, secular history written in Latin soon disappeared entirely.

It's revealing that the last major historian to write in Latin was in fact a Greek soldier from the eastern city of Antioch, who wrote in Latin because he wanted to pick up where Tacitus had left off. Ammianus Marcellinus was born around 330, toward the end of Constantine's reign, probably a few years after Eusebius put the finishing touches on his *History of the Christian Church*. Of noble birth, as he came of age in Antioch Ammianus faced a problem common to upper-class young men in those days: what to do about the ruinous financial burdens of local service that the empire now imposed on its wealthy citizens. Most chose a career in the imperial bureaucracy, which exempted them, but Ammianus instead took the less popular way to avoid the local obligations, which was to join the army. He rose rapidly to the high rank of a staff officer, serving on imperial campaigns first in Gaul and then in Persia. Like Polybius, Ammianus sees history through a soldier's experienced eyes.

Just as important in this age of Christian triumph, Ammianus also sees history through the eyes of a committed pagan. He is very much of the old school, fighting a rearguard action to uphold "traditional" Roman values against the tide of Christian novelty. And both in Gaul and later in Persia, Ammianus was close to the quixotic figure who represents paganism's last gasp, or at least its last opportunity to retain political status in the Roman world: Constantine's young nephew Julian, known as Julian the Apostate, whose brief reign marks the final time a pagan emperor held the throne. "It seems that the life of this young man was guided by some principle which raised him above the ordinary and accompanied him from his illustrious cradle to his last breath." Our romantic picture of Julian, as relayed in popular books such as Robert Browning's *The Emperor Julian*, comes largely from Ammianus.

Although Ammianus begins his history in AD 96, the year Tacitus breaks off, he moves relatively quickly through the first 250 years, then devotes the second half of his work to the quarter-century from 354 to 378, the period he knew firsthand. This is the part of his history that survives—the first half has been lost—and modern historians give it high marks in all areas: reliability, insight, narrative power, and, above all, that great bugbear, objectivity. For despite his pagan outlook, which he doesn't try to hide, Ammianus is remarkably fair in his treatment of Christianity and Christians. Julian's three years in power aside, the shoe of persecution was now firmly on the other foot. Christians' intolerance toward pagans was exceeded only by their intolerance, in bloody riots that raged throughout the empire, toward other Christians who professed the wrong beliefs. Yet Ammianus shows no animus toward the Christians, and unlike other pagan writers of the time, he never blames them for the empire's many troubles.*

"Scrupulous honesty," this admirable fellow tells us earnestly, "is the duty of every writer of history." What historian would disagree? But the proof of the pudding is in the eating, and Ammianus does better than most in making this commonplace a real goal, not just a rhetorical pose. Despite his approval of Julian, his portrait of the emperor is evenhanded, balancing praise with criticism. Ammianus's basic fairness shines through, for example, in his reproach of Julian for banning Christians from teaching rhetoric.

If Ammianus spends less time than modern scholars would like on the social and religious tensions hinted at in such passages, he does give us lots of information on war and politics. And he tells a ripping good story to boot. In addition to an exciting narrative of the ill-fated expedition against Persia during which Julian died after being wounded in battle, we also get a vivid picture of the barbarian tribes, such as the Goths and Huns who pressed on the empire's northern borders in this turbulent century. It is with the devastating Gothic victory at Adrianople—where, alarmingly close to Constantinople, the emperor Valens fell in battle—that Ammianus ends his history in the year 378. He closes with the following words: "The rest I leave to be written by better men whose abilities are in their prime. But

---

* It was for this impartiality that Edward Gibbon, for example, writing in the eighteenth century, would praise Ammianus strongly, even while disagreeing with him about Christianity's role in the empire's "decline." In this regard, ironically, Ammianus's objectivity is probably greater than Gibbon's. For Gibbon and his masterpiece, *The Decline and Fall of the Roman Empire,* see chapter 11.

if they choose to undertake the task I advise them to cast what they have to say in the grand style."

There were no takers. As the western empire fell to the barbarians, it was Christian Latin culture, not secular, that beckoned Europe's new masters. To Franks, Burgundians, Lombards, and Visigoths, each of whom had their religious chroniclers, *Rome* meant the papacy—an impression that the growing church monopoly on literacy did nothing to dispel. Inspired by Eusebius, not Tacitus, packed with miracles, and oozing sanctity and gore in almost equal measure, these accounts of the past—like other writing in the Latin West—were composed now mostly by bishops, priests, and monks for other bishops, priests, and monks.

That said, however, if the austere Tacitus was remote from their minds, a more engaging writer like Livy was not necessarily so. The past never disappeared completely, only parts of it. Others survived, though often conveying little more than a vague sense of pageantry and spectacle to pious scribblers.

One of the liveliest was Gregory of Tours, an influential, curious, and deeply superstitious sixth-century churchman who lived in what would become central France, and wrote the history of his local church along with the bloody intrigues and internecine strife of the Frankish royal family. Gregory belonged to an aristocratic Gallo-Roman family with a long tradition of service to the church. As he tells us proudly, all except five of his predecessors as bishop of Tours were blood relatives. A prolific writer, he produced numerous works, including lives of saints, books of miracles, and commentaries on scripture, in addition to his *History of the Franks.** He was close to power, and when he gets to his own times, he himself steps onto the stage as a major player in the events of the day.

Gregory is one of those writers whom the reader strongly suspects of playful humor without ever being able to clinch the case. His style is easy and conversational, and he writes in the simple spoken Latin of his time rather than tying himself in knots trying to resurrect the complex literary language of the classical authors. He opens the preface to his *History* with this wonderfully deadpan first line: "A great many things keep happening, some of them good, some of them bad." Throughout the work, omens and portents abound, saints work wonders, kings grimly wage war for Jesus, and bad men suffer horribly painful deaths.

Gregory's personal enemy Leudast comes in for some particularly grisly treatment. The king has him tortured and then healed so that he can be tortured some more. Finally, "his wounds began to fester and it was clear he would not last much longer. At the personal command of the queen he was placed flat on his back on the ground, a block of wood was wedged behind his neck and then they beat him on the throat with another piece of wood until he died. His life," Gregory adds cheerfully, "had been one long tale of perfidious talk: so that he met a fitting end."

Despite Gregory's considerable charms, the most impressive church historian of the Middle Ages was the

---

* The title is not Gregory's. He referred to his work as an "ecclesiastical history."

English monk Baeda, born in the latter half of the seventh century and better known to posterity as the Venerable Bede. But like Gregory and the others, Bede wrote theology first and history second. Judging by the number of surviving manuscripts, his commentaries on scripture were more widely read than his *History of the English Church and People*, even if it's on the latter that his reputation rests today.

Much of what we know about Bede's life comes from the short autobiographical note with which he concludes his *History*. He was born in 673 near Sunderland on the North Sea coast, and when he turned seven his parents gave him over to the abbot of the nearby monastery of Wearmouth so that he could become a monk. When the abbot founded the sister monastery of Jarrow nearby a couple of years later, the not yet so Venerable Bede was sent there with some twenty other monks. "I have spent all the remainder of my life at this monastery and devoted myself entirely to the study of the Scriptures," he writes. "And while I have observed the regular discipline and sung the choir offices daily in church, my chief delight has always been in study, teaching, and writing." Fortunately, the monastery's library was an unusually good one. Bede is thought to have left only twice, once to visit the Holy Island of Lindisfarne some forty miles up the coast, and once to visit York, about fifty miles to the south. He died in 735, and eventually his remains were brought to Durham Cathedral, where his tomb may still be seen.

Like Gregory, Bede salts his narrative liberally with omens, portents, and above all, miracles, miracles, miracles.

So frequent are God's spectacular interventions in human affairs that some modern scholars suggest Bede was merely pandering to his audience. Forgetting history's Herodotean origins, perhaps, they refuse to accept that Bede himself could really have believed in such unhistorical stuff. They might be right, of course. On the other hand, we could turn the suggestion around and suspect the moderns of pandering to their own audience of mostly secular history professors, and of projecting their values back onto Bede, who never gives the slightest hint anywhere that he viewed these alleged goings-on with anything other than wholehearted pious endorsement.

There's St. Alban, the first British martyr, who had been a Roman soldier until he was converted by a priest on the run during the persecutions of Diocletian. Alban traded places with the priest to save him, and after having Alban tortured at length (naturally, Alban refused to renounce Jesus), the authorities ordered that he be executed down by a river. But when he came down before a vast crowd assembled by God, "the river ran dry in its bed and left him a place to cross." The executioner himself was so impressed that he refused to do the dirty deed and laid down his sword, converted at once to the faith. Alban climbed a nearby hill and asked God for water, whereupon "a perennial spring bubbled up at his feet." There he was finally executed. "But the man whose impious hands struck off that pious head was not permitted to boast of the deed, for as the martyr's head fell, the executioner's eyes dropped out on the ground." We are not told why having his eyes drop out would prevent the impious executioner from boasting, but this unseemly observation is not likely to have interrupted many readers in the grip of such a thrilling narrative.

Or the noble Fursey, an Irish holy man who founded several monasteries in East Anglia, and whose extraordinary visions of the fires that will consume the earth were vouchsafed to him by angels carrying him up to what today would be considered cruising altitude. Or the time a plague was ended by the intercession of good King Oswald—which might merely indicate prescient medical skills on that devout ruler's part had it not happened on the anniversary of his death in battle at the hands of the heathen. Or even the relatively pedestrian St. John of Beverley, performing the traditional laying on of hands to heal the sick . . . and so it goes.

But behind all the song and dance, Bede gives us a wonderfully full picture of early British history: the Celts who were Britain's first inhabitants; Britain's incorporation into the Roman empire, beginning with Julius Caesar ("the first Roman to reach Britain"); the Anglo-Saxons who occupied the island as Roman power ebbed back toward the Mediterranean. He also gives a biographical sketch of the first poet known to us by name who wrote "in his own English tongue"—Caedmon, a monk at Whitby, whose beautiful verses "have stirred the hearts of many folk to despise the world and aspire to heavenly things." Though Bede wrote his *History* in Latin, he promoted the use of vernacular Old English in religious education.

A steady torrent of miracles notwithstanding, the overarching narrative that takes shape around them is as helpfully explanatory as any modern professor could wish.

That story revolves around the tension between the idio-syncratic, loosely organized Celtic missionaries from Ireland, who had lost touch with Rome, and Roman Catholic missionaries who arrived (starting with St. Augustine of Canterbury) around the year 600. Both hoped to convert the Anglo-Saxons. Though Bede endorses the Roman side, his treatment of the Celtic missionaries is always generous (Fursey was one, for example). A period of Celtic ascendancy ended when the two sides met at the synod of Whitby about a decade before Bede was born. Bede describes it at length in the *History*. The Roman success at that convocation reshaped the British church in his lifetime, tying it more closely to papal authority and bringing Britain once again within Rome's cultural orbit.

One of the issues addressed at Whitby was the calendar, since the Celtic and Roman churches used different systems for figuring out when Christians should observe important holy days like Easter. Time in general was a major preoccupation of the medieval church, and it's here we owe Bede our biggest debt. Before Bede, there was no standard way of identifying years. Anglo-Saxons used regnal years, but there were many kingdoms, and so regnal years rapidly got confusing. Similar problems had plagued historians all the way back to Herodotus and Thucydides. Regnal years; lists of annual municipal magistrates; tax cycles called indictions, each of a set number of years that could change from one emperor to another—it was a hodgepodge. Everyone reinvented the wheel. "In the third year of the first indiction of Constantine, when Ephorus was magistrate in Athens, and Cethylwist had ruled in Northumbria for twelve years . . ."

That's a made-up example, but it gives the idea. There was no universal time, just a patchwork of local times.

In his *History*, Bede counts years from the birth of Christ. Though he did not invent this system (it had been suggested by a sixth-century Roman monk named Dionysius Exiguus), the popularity of his *History* did much to spread it. Bede also wrote several other works about the measurement of time in which he laid out arguments in favor of the system. The eventual effect was to synchronize the West. Obviously, this had huge implications in all sorts of areas, from trade and politics to literature and art. It's hard to imagine life without universal, easily reckoned years. Not to mention history.

FOUR

Clio Nods

*H*ere's a question: What if Thucydides had written smut?

In the Latin West, writers like Gregory and Bede may have abandoned secular history, but on its home turf in the Greek East, the tradition of Herodotus and Thucydides proved more, shall we say, robust. This part of the old Roman empire morphed into the Byzantine empire of the Middle Ages—ethnically diverse but held together by the glue of Greek culture, centered on Constantine's new capital of Constantinople, and proudly celebrating Orthodox Christianity as its state religion. In its Byzantine form the Roman empire can be said to have survived until 1453, when the Ottoman Turks finally ended it by capturing Constantinople.*

If history survived in Byzantium, it still faced some hard times, especially during the difficult transformation from a "Roman" empire to a "Byzantine" one. No one illustrates the challenges of this transition better than the strange and puzzling figure of Procopius, whom modern scholars once celebrated as the Thucydides of his time, but who has more recently been revealed as a very different kind of writer indeed. Thucydides, for a start, never wrote about sex performers and their orifices.

---

* I tell the story of the Byzantine empire and its cultural legacy in my book, *Sailing from Byzantium: How a Lost Empire Shaped the World.*

Procopius was born around AD 500 in Caesarea, the prosperous city in Palestine that had also been the home of Eusebius. Judging from his writing—both what he says, and how he says it—he likely came from Caesarea's provincial gentry and received a fairly standard education (for his class) as a lawyer. But we don't really know anything about his early life, except that by 527 he was serving on the staff of Belisarius, the general who was leading the emperor Justinian's military campaign against Persia. Procopius's ambivalent attitudes to these two men would color everything he wrote, and in turn, his writings would forever influence how history has seen them.

Procopius was with Belisarius when the general returned to Constantinople in 531, after decisively beating a much-larger Persian army at the border town of Dara. It was Byzantium's (or Rome's) first clear victory in years against this old enemy, but the rosy glow which now bathed Belisarius in Procopius's eyes didn't last. Persia was just the opener. Justinian had other wars to fight, in Africa and Italy. He hoped to reclaim these former imperial lands from their barbarian occupiers in an ambitious plan of grand reconquest, and Belisarius was the man he had chosen to get the job done. But by the time these wars had been fought to their hard and bitter end, Justinian had soured on Belisarius, and Procopius had long since soured on them both.

Procopius tells the story of Justinian's imperial reconquest in *The Wars*, his major work of history, which is divided into three parts that cover Persia, Africa, and Italy in turn. Procopius witnessed many of the events he recounts, and to all appearances, *The Wars* is good, old-fashioned military history in the scientific Thucydidean mold. (It was also the major source for Robert Graves's *Count Belisarius*, a good read if not quite up to the standard of *I, Claudius*.) If this was all that we had of Procopius, things for today's historians would be a lot simpler. It's his other two works that mess up what would otherwise be a relatively tidy—if totally misleading—picture.

These other works, *The Buildings*, and, especially, *The Secret History*, have led some modern commentators to doubt Procopius's sanity. And taken together, they do give a schizophrenic impression. *The Buildings* is a protracted and fawning description of Justinian's ruinously expensive building program. Big yawn. But *The Secret History*—this scandalously titillating attack on Belisarius and Justinian (and, most salaciously, their wives) reads like something from the darker corners of the Internet. That didn't stop Penguin from publishing it while ignoring the rest of Procopius's writings, though the reader is primly warned on the back cover of my old edition that the author's "candour" is "often revolting." As it turns out, though, we can forget about "candour" with Procopius, and as for "revolting"—well, some warnings sound more like advertisements.

The Secret History really was a secret, and it remained a well-kept one until discovered in the Vatican Library in 1623. Its title in Greek, *Anekdota* (from which we get "anecdote"), literally means "unpublished," and as Procopius says, to publish it during Justinian's lifetime would have meant certain death. It's easy to see why. Procopius portrays Belisarius as a corrupt and spineless coward, and his wife Antonina as a scheming, domineering slut who's continually yanking the puffed-up general around by the short hairs. And he literally demonizes Justinian, asserting that the emperor he praised so lavishly in his other works was in fact a demon in human form, whose greatest aspiration was to slaughter as many of his subjects as possible.

Then, of course, there's Theodora. The way Procopius tells it, Justinian's beautiful and celebrated empress makes Paris Hilton seem like Mother Teresa. Claiming that Theodora had been a sex performer in her earlier life, he shows her servicing ten fellow guests at a dinner party, leaving them spent, and moving on to their slaves, thirty at a time. Then he gets truly inventive:

And though she brought three openings into service, she often found fault with Nature, grumbling because Nature had not made the openings in her nipples wider than is normal, so that she could devise another variety of intercourse in that region.

Yikes! But the real dirty secret is that historians love this kind of thing, just like everyone else. Witness the great Gibbon, who certainly had his fun with it, observing of the empress that "she murmured most ungratefully against the parsimony of nature . . . but her murmurs, her pleasures, and her arts, must be veiled in the obscurity of a learned language." Accordingly, he gives the passage in a footnote in Greek, without translation, remarking only that "she wished for a *fourth* altar on which she might pour libations to the god of love." Just imagine what generations of English schoolboys did with that.*

Set this Procopius against the stiff, "official" Procopius of *The Buildings* and *The Wars*, and you begin to see why for centuries many historians—Gibbon being a prominent exception—refused to accept that Procopius had written *The Secret History*. But by the twentieth century, a close study of all three texts established conclusively that they had indeed been written by the same author, forcing the magisterial J. B. Bury, the authoritative editor of Gibbon and a strong Procopius "denier," to admit that he'd been wrong.

Yet that only made things worse. The problem was that our whole idea of this crucial period in history—a big focal point of the "decline of the Roman empire" storyline that Gibbon had developed—was based on the old Procopius, who is the only major historical source for it. Everything rested on the rationalistic historian of *The Wars* (most modern scholars also quietly ignored *The Buildings*). Bury and his ilk had exalted him as the only truly great Byzantine historian: a paragon of Thucydidean objectivity, a scientific defender of the old classical ideal as everything around him was about to descend into darkness. Justinian, too, was seen as upholding this classical ideal, the greatest of the late Roman or Byzantine emperors—reconqueror of lost lands, lawgiver to Europe (through the famous Justinianic code), and builder of magnificent monuments such as Hagia Sophia.

---

* In addition to adolescent fantasies, Procopius's portrayal of Theodora in *The Secret History* has also inspired several would-be Galahads to come to her defense, most notably, perhaps, Antony Bridge, whose romantic biography *Theodora* (1978) stands Procopius on his head.

"It was one of the glories of Justinian's age," Bury declaimed, "to have produced a writer who must be accounted the most excellent Greek historian since Polybius." How to reconcile that Procopius with the smutty and venomous *Secret History*, or for that matter, the nauseatingly obsequious *Buildings*?

In the end, modern historians had to let go of their Procopius and replace him with the sixth century's Procopius.* That meant reassessing other elements of the old picture, especially the view of Justinian embraced by Bury and the others. Recent approaches don't see so many "glories" in Justinian's reign. Instead, they emphasize the extraordinary stresses that wracked this emerging Christian society.

From this perspective, Procopius's contradictions can be seen as mirroring the larger contradictions of a society that was shedding its classical skin but had not quite wriggled free of it. Each of Procopius's three works can also be seen as a modestly talented writer's strained effort at fulfilling the requirements of a classical genre in an atmosphere of extreme political risk—*The Wars* as "scientific history," *The Buildings* as panegyric (fulsome praise of a ruler that we've lost a taste for but that autocracy demands), and *The Secret History* as invective. Procopius was trying to jump through literary hoops that were just a bit high off the ground, and getting higher all the time.

Closer examination reveals Procopius the historian to be far less objective, insightful, or reliable than his earlier

---

* Averil Cameron established this in her brilliant book, *Procopius and the Sixth Century* (1984), to which I'm indebted for my handling of Procopius (and the sixth century) here.

champions would have liked. Even his supposedly Thucy-didean style evaporates under inspection—lip service in the shape of clichéd remarks about the value of history, self-conscious verbal echoes, the dutiful trotting out of set pieces, with none of the searching intelligence or clarity of thought. Under the secular veneer, so admired by Gibbon and Bury, lie all sorts of religiosity, excluded by the rules of the genre but shaping the narrative in hidden and some-times not-so-hidden ways.

Rather than a rock of classicism standing nobly against the stream of unreason, Procopius was in reality a twig being swept before it. All of his voices were the "real" Proco-pius; at the same time, none of them was.

Procopius, it seems likely, died sometime around 550, well before Justinian. And just as that emperor's overam-bitious reconquest crumbled away with his passing, so too did secular history crumble away after Procopius. He had a handful of successors in the century after his death, but they survive only in fragments. Procopius is the last (osten-sibly) secular historian from the ancient world whose work we can actually sit down and read cover to cover. Small wonder that Bury and his fellow gentlemen scholars pinned such high hopes on him.

Secular history now fell into slumber in Byzantium, as it had already in the West. Exhausted by barbarian incursions, devastating outbreaks of plague, and constant warfare with Persia, the Byzantines turned their backs on the entire cul-tural legacy of ancient Greece. In effect, they abandoned the knife-edge complexities of secular reason for the blunt cer-tainties of faith. The rise of Islam and the conquests that established a vast new Arab empire in the East reinforced their choice.

By the end of the seventh century, these pressures had cracked the old Mediterranean world into three pieces—Western, Byzantine, and Arab—each of which would develop its own distinctive version of monotheism. (The Arabs were by far the richest and most powerful, and Byzantium was the weakest, having lost its wealthiest areas to the Arab conquest.) But these three monotheistic civilizations were also the three heirs of the classical world, and as such, each would try in its own way to awaken the sleeping Clio, with varying degrees of success.

In the West, the main development was the rise of the Franks, whom we encountered briefly in the person of Gregory of Tours. Since Gregory's time, the Franks had acquired a large empire in Europe and a valuable alliance with the papacy. Both were solemnized together on Christmas Day in the year 800, when Pope Leo III crowned the Frankish king Charlemagne, "Charles the Great," emperor of a restored "Holy Roman" empire. Charlemagne had just spent three decades conquering various peoples in northern Europe and forcibly converting them to Christianity, and his empire took in what are now France, Germany, Belgium, the Netherlands, Switzerland, and parts of Italy and Spain.

As befit a restored empire, Charlemagne aspired also to restore learning and culture, not least in order to bring the administration of civil and church affairs up to scratch. Illiterate scribes and priests don't get much done in the way of efficient bureaucracy. The focus of this so-called Carolingian Renaissance* remained on such practical matters (religion being very much a practical issue in the medieval world), but because education rested on proficiency in Latin, it inevitably brought the attention of some of Charlemagne's elites to the pagan works that still remained the highest standard in Latin literature.

While it might seem natural for these two sets of interests—empire and education—to converge on the revival of classical history, that never really happened for the Carolingians. Perhaps the time span was too short, since Charlemagne's empire dissolved after his death in bitter fighting among his heirs. But two outstanding writers, Einhard and Nithard, show how close history was to coming back to life. They'll serve as guides on our brief tour of the fascinating Carolingian court before we return to Byzantium, where classical history did indeed enjoy the revival that we look for in vain among Charlemagne's learned (but not excessively so) courtiers.

Einhard was born around 775, in the early years of Charlemagne's long reign, and like Bede—another promising lad a century earlier—he was given over as a young boy to be raised in a local monastery. When Einhard was still a teenager, at the abbot's urging Charlemagne accepted the boy at court. At that time the Palace School was run by the celebrated English scholar Alcuin of York, and Einhard must have impressed Alcuin deeply. A few years later, when Charlemagne asked Alcuin a question pertaining to the

---

* *Carolus* is the Latin for Charles. "Carolingian" refers to the Frankish royal house to which Charlemagne belonged.

classics, Alcuin referred the emperor to the young Einhard, still less than twenty years of age. From that point until Charlemagne's death in 814, Einhard remained within the emperor's closest circle, carrying out numerous missions of state on his behalf.

Einhard then became personal secretary for the new emperor, Louis the Pious, Charlemagne's only surviving legitimate son. In this position Einhard had access to state documents and archives. He wrote several works, but he's best known for the remarkable *Life of Charlemagne* that he began composing a few years after the old emperor died.

This short, simple, and deceptively unassuming work was in fact a bold departure: the first biography of a secular figure written in the West for centuries, since hagiography had become the norm. Accordingly, Einhard went back to classical times for inspiration, modeling his account of Charlemagne's life and achievements on Suetonius's biography of Augustus in *The Lives of the Caesars*. But he also relied on his close friendship with Charlemagne, and we in turn come to know the emperor through Einhard's vivid portrayal. Einhard shows him in action—conquering, conversing, welcoming foreigners to court, enthusiastically hunting, struggling without much success to master Latin and Greek (charmingly, he kept his notebooks under his pillow hoping to absorb their learning that way).

Einhard's physical description of Charlemagne as being unusually tall was borne out in the nineteenth century, when the emperor's tomb was opened and his body measured at over six feet, three inches. Other details ring true as well: "the upper part of his head was round, his eyes very large and animated, nose a little long, hair fair, and face laughing and merry." Though openly written to honor the memory of a friend as well as a ruler and patron, *The Life of Charlemagne* gives a clear-eyed portrait of the man who would go down in memory as the founder of Europe, including a number of his quirks and eccentricities.

One of them was that Charlemagne, though possessed of three attractive daughters, could never stand to let them marry, saying that he relied on their company too much to let them leave the palace for good. Yet this lusty ruler's offspring—Charlemagne himself had had several wives as well as numerous concubines—weren't about to let paternal vigilance be the price of liberty. Apparently father and daughters reached an understanding. As Einhard says delicately, the emperor "concealed his knowledge of the rumors current in regard to them, and of the suspicions entertained as to their honor." Dalliances between the emperor's courtiers and his daughters were an ill-kept secret at court.

It was from one such dalliance, between the emperor's daughter Bertha and the poet Angilbert, that our second guide, Nithard, was born around the year 790. As a grandson of the emperor, even if illegitimate, Nithard was brought up at court, where his father belonged to a group of writers whose humanistic interest in ancient literature went beyond the chilly ecclesiastical purposes of an Alcuin. These enthusiasts called each other by classical nicknames, and Angilbert's was "Homer," which suggests the esteem in which his verses were held by his peers. Nithard's writing gives the impression of a relatively broad, if not terribly deep, education in the classics. We may speculate that his father played a role in it, though probably not in sparking his interest in history.

Like so many of his ancient predecessors, Nithard was first and foremost a soldier. But where Einhard chose an ancient biographer as his model, what surprises us about Nithard is that he doesn't seem to have read any of the classical historians. As he tells us, he came to history by accident, at the request of his king (and cousin), Charles the Bald, youngest son of Louis the Pious. Nithard's assignment was to justify Charles's behavior in the disreputable bickering among Louis's sons, which forever shattered the unity of Charlemagne's empire.

The basic problem was that Frankish tradition, which required a king to divide his realm equally among his sons, went against the notion of "empire" that the Franks were now trying to embrace. Louis's halfhearted and unconvincing attempt to leave everything to his oldest son, Lothair, was easily challenged. Louis went back on it, but it was too late. His credibility was shattered and he was unable to reassert control. Fighting between Louis's sons ultimately resulted in the Treaty of Verdun (843), which divided the empire into three parts. These three parts became France, Germany, and the lands between them that they have fought over ever since.

A simple man of action, Nithard remains true in his *Histories* to his own highest value, which as he makes clear is loyalty to his king, Charles. And of the brothers involved, Charles does appear the most sympathetic. As we might expect, then, Nithard's highly readable history of these internecine civil wars is heavily biased toward Charles. But it is biased in a disarmingly candid way, one that makes it hard not to feel that Nithard's got a valid point. Part of that point was the upholding of tradition, even at the cost of empire.

Nithard himself died fighting for his king in 844, the year after Verdun. Despite the intelligence and style he commanded in nearly reinventing history on his own, his work was not widely read in the years that followed. And secular history did not reappear in the West for over five hundred years.

In Byzantium during all this time, what historians there were had more in common with writers like Bede than with their classical predecessors. And none possesses Bede's artistry or insight. Theophylact Simocatta, an advisor to the emperor Heraclius in the early seventh century, wrote a history that reads like an awkward hybrid between the classical approach and the ecclesiastical one. No one wrote much history at all in Byzantium for the century and a half after that. Around the time of Charlemagne, Byzantine writers once more began taking an interest in the past, but again, they're a rather stiff and charmless lot. And now they lack any remnant of the classical tradition.

But by the time Nithard was chronicling the breakup of Charlemagne's empire, the Byzantines were recovering from the earlier threats to their own. As their confidence grew, they no longer felt that a Christian identity required turning their backs on ancient Greek learning. The most erudite Byzantine of the age was Photius, born two decades after Nithard, who possessed a breadth of classical learning that put anyone at the Carolingian court to shame, even an Alcuin.

The brilliant Photius stimulated a lasting revival of the classics in Byzantium. To say that he single-handedly saved ancient Greek literature might be an overstatement, but only just. He and his students dug out the dusty old unread manuscripts from their hiding places in aristocratic homes and monastery libraries, and began the slow process of bringing them back to life. They also copied many of them out themselves, which is a blessing for us, since virtually all of the oldest surviving manuscripts of Greek literature that we have come from this period.

This Byzantine renaissance took a while to bear real literary fruit of its own. Ironically, by the time it did, the Byzantines were just falling into another period of rapid decline. But there to record it was one of the most polished and urbane writers ever to take up the pen in Byzantium, the refined Michael Psellus—courtier, philosopher, theologian, monk, tutor to royalty, and secular historian in the grand old style.

Michael Psellus was born to a noble Constantinopolitan family of modest means in the year 1018, as the long and prosperous reign of the Byzantine emperor Basil II was drawing to a close. As a boy Michael was taught by the capital's most famous scholar, and then as a promising young man he joined Byzantium's sophisticated civil service. When he was about thirty, he was appointed president of Constantinople's school of philosophy, receiving the prestigious-sounding title "consul of the philosophers." Michael was a voracious reader and a prolific writer, a cultivated polymath whose enormous body of work embraces the law and rhetoric as well as philosophy, theology, and history.

As he himself reveals in his history, he was also insufferably vain (vanity being the besetting sin of learned Byzantines). And somewhere along the line, he put a foot wrong in Byzantium's slippery corridors of power. In 1078—at which point his history abruptly breaks off—Michael was banished from the capital by the emperor Michael VII, an ungrateful former student, no less. After that his fate is unknown. Modern scholars surmise that he died in poverty and obscurity, perhaps sometime in the 1080s.

Michael begins his history, the *Chronographia*, with an absorbing account of the fifty-year reign of Basil II, the grim and implacable warrior-emperor who brought Byzantium to the height of its medieval power, and who died unmarried and childless when Michael was a boy. "All his natural desires were kept under stern control," Michael writes. "The man was as hard as steel." It's largely owing to Michael's portrait that some Byzantinists credit Basil with being the greatest of all Byzantine emperors, especially since Justinian has been downgraded. To this day, Greeks know Basil II as *Bulgaroctonos*, "Slayer of the Bulgars," for his utterly ruthless subjugation of Bulgaria, which had rebelled from Byzantine rule.

As Michael makes clear, Basil's successors lacked his steel and his ferocity, and his once-mighty Macedonian dynasty petered out in a succession of elderly relatives. Two of them,

Basil's nieces Zoe and Theodora, ruled as co-empresses for a number of years, with three of Zoe's husbands in succession as emperor. (Theodora remained unmarried.) If Michael's political analysis strikes us as shallow, his portraits of these sometimes hapless rulers are usually shrewd, often catty, and always entertaining.

Today, perhaps, we'd find him dissecting the private lives of political celebrities among the scented ads of *Vanity Fair*. Here he is on the affair that Constantine IX, Zoe's last husband, carried on after marrying Zoe:

> *The lady in question was the niece of his late wife, a beautiful and normally discreet woman. . . . With his physical eyes he beheld Zoe, but in his mind's eye was the image of his mistress; while he folded the empress in his arms, it was the other woman whom he clasped in the imagination of his heart.*

Constantine easily persuaded Zoe to recall his lover from exile and let her live in the palace with them. "The fact is, Zoe was no longer jealous. She had her own fill of trouble, and in any case she was too old to harbor resentment." Michael's gifts were well suited to his times. He inspired a number of imitators, though none so frothy, and the rest of Byzantine history is relatively well lit by gracefully written narratives in the classical mode.

Just over a decade after Michael's history breaks off, Byzantium's sharp decline was arrested by a young noble named Alexius Comnenus, who came to power at a time of truly desperate circumstances. Luckily for Byzantium, Alexius I turned out to be fully the equal of Basil II. And luckily for Alexius, he had a historian to chronicle his exploits who was fully the equal of Michael Psellus. That was his own formidable daughter, Anna Comnena, whose history of her father's reign she pointedly titled *The Alexiad*, just in case anyone missed the comparison she was making between Alexius and Achilles.

And who would demur? In just a few short years, Byzantium had suddenly found itself invaded on three fronts by fierce new enemies—Turks in the east, who had spent the last decade flooding into the Byzantine heartland of Asia Minor; nomadic Petchenegs in the north, loyal allies for a century, who were now pressed by more-savage nomads behind them, and had crossed the Danube to plunder and settle imperial lands in the Balkans; and Normans in the west, the warlike descendants of Vikings who had settled in southern Italy, and were now looking to cross the Adriatic and conquer new territory from a weakened Byzantium. And to face these enemies, Alexius Comnenus, age twenty-four, but already a seasoned commander, had . . . next to nothing.

Even as Alexius came to the throne, the Norman conqueror Robert Guiscard was known to be readying an invasion of northwestern Greece, an invasion which in fact materialized within weeks. With no time to catch his breath, Alexius had to act right away. He decided that the Turks and Petchenegs could wait. The worst threat came from Robert Guiscard and the Normans, who had taken the island of Corfu and besieged the Byzantine garrison at the coastal city of Durrazzo. Alexius assembled what was left of the army, bolstering it with anyone he could find—Turkish mercenaries, Paulician heretics, even asking for help from Venice and Germany. Venice came through with a fleet that trounced Robert's navy, but when Alexius attacked the besieging force at Durrazzo, the Paulicians deserted and his army was virtually annihilated. Alexius himself, one of a handful of Byzantine officers left standing, barely escaped. The Normans began to occupy northern Greece. There was no one to stop them. The army was gone.

This is where Alexius's genius comes into play. Somehow, he managed to engage the Normans a truly astounding three more times over the next several years, losing badly each time, always on the run, and yet cobbling together a new ragtag force—mercenaries, displaced retinues of Byzantine aristocrats, Norman deserters, young sons of soldiers killed in service, peasant boys pressed into service, sundry other misfits—to try again. With such troops, Alexius held the disciplined and war-hardened Normans to northern Greece, before Robert's timely (from the Byzantine point of view) death plunged Norman Sicily into civil war and Bohemund, Robert's son, had to pull the Norman forces back and try to secure his patrimony.

Next, Alexius turned his attention to the Petchenegs and the rest of the Balkans, and in a few years of further military improvisation backed by virtuoso diplomacy he restored the empire's borders along the Danube. In theory, anyway, and theory counted for a lot in the Byzantine world. Only in the 1090s was Alexius able to come to grips with the daunting task of recovering at least some of the huge territorial losses in Asia Minor. Meanwhile, things there had worsened, with Antioch lost in 1085 and Nicaea, uncomfortably close to

Constantinople, captured in 1092. Clearly, something had to be done about the Turks.

That brings us to the Crusades. The Normans, Alexius knew, were still hungry, and in an attempt to ward them off and get some help against the Turks at the same time, Alexius decided to forge an alliance with the papacy, whose influence, he also knew, was threatened by the Norman ascendancy. In 1095, responding to Alexius's appeals for help against the Turks, Pope Urban II addressed an appeal of his own to a crowd of French knights at the Council of Clermont, who took him perhaps a little more seriously than he had intended. The rest of Alexius's reign, along with those of his son and grandson, would be dominated by the results of that appeal, as indeed would the next several centuries. In the short term, though, Alexius's appeal succeeded in diverting the Normans from Constantinople and clearing much of Asia Minor of the Turks. While dealing with the Crusaders required its own tightrope act, it was one at which Alexius excelled. He was still performing it at about seventy years old, when he fell ill and died in August 1118.

This is the story Anna tells in *The Alexiad*, which is one of the few Byzantine literary works to receive the high honor of Penguinification (the *Chronographia* of Michael Psellus is another, under the title *Fourteen Byzantine Rulers*). If her style lacks the insouciant charm of a Michael Psellus, her historical judgment often cuts deeper. She also gives us a few details about her own life, which is almost as exciting as her father's—and in the end, perhaps, even more interesting.

Anna was born in 1083, a couple of years after her father came to power, which made her a "born in the purple" princess. She was also the oldest of Alexius's seven children. When she was about eight, she was betrothed to Constantine, the young son of a previous emperor, who at the time was considered the rightful heir to the throne (Alexius having originally been chosen as a sort of caretaker emperor). For several years—formative ones, as later events would demonstrate—Anna believed that she was destined to become empress of Byzantium.

But then Alexius decided to make his own oldest son, Anna's younger brother John, heir instead. At that point John was still a boy—*Kalo Joannes*, as he was called by an adoring public. Handsome John.

Anna's disappointment turned to hatred of her brother, and that hatred shaped the rest of her life. Constantine died shortly afterward, and Anna married Nicephorus Bryennius, the son of an old rival of her father's. A cultivated aristocrat as well as a political and military leader, Nicephorus was himself a historian whose work still survives. (Anna tells us that she undertook her own history of her father's reign because her husband's broke off just as Alexius came to power.) Though originally a political alliance, the marriage was a happy one. As far as it went, that is.

Which, for the ambitious Anna, wasn't far enough. After their father's death, Anna tried to overthrow her brother and put her husband Nicephorus on the throne instead. But Nicephorus himself refused to go along. He proved loyal to John, whom he died serving faithfully some two decades later. Anna, who might easily have been executed, got off lightly. She was sent to live in a convent, where, starting in 1148, she wrote *The Alexiad*.

By that time, John himself had died in a hunting accident, and Anna's nephew Manuel I Comnenus was emperor. Both John and Manuel proved worthy successors to Alexius, and the empire was by then doing quite well. But Anna can hardly stand to mention them—on the few occasions when they do come up, you can almost hear her teeth grinding. Anna died in her convent, probably sometime in the 1150s, a bitter and disappointed woman.

This certainly comes through in her narrative, which she interrupts frequently with "floods of tears" or "seas of misfortune" that sweep her into a self-pitying digression before she drifts back into the story. "Now that I have returned to my senses, I will swim against the tide, as it were, and go back to the original subject," she says after one particularly turgid eddy. It would be nice to know how much of this swooning is genuine, but whatever the answer to that question, she is hardly the feminist heroine we might hope to find in our first woman historian. Born in the purple she may have been, and always longing for the purple slippers worn by emperors, but it would define the word "anachronism" to look at her royal feet and see purple Birkenstocks.

As an unapologetically ambitious woman in a heavily patriarchal culture, Anna may have felt that her emotional literary displays would forestall accusations of unwomanliness. Her memorable portrait of her celebrated paternal grandmother, Anna Dalassena, may also be shaped by such considerations. Alexius relied on his mother's counsel in conducting affairs of state, but Anna Comnena portrays her namesake as assisting the emperor only reluctantly. She would much rather have done the proper thing and gone into a convent, we're told with a straight face, but she was too valuable. "The truth is that Anna Dalassena was in any case endowed with a fine intellect and possessed besides a really first-class aptitude for governing."

There speaks a writer who saw these same capacities in herself and raged at the unfairness that kept her from exercising them. We have benefited from that unfairness, since it gave us Anna's memorable voice. Small consolation, perhaps, when we consider how many other voices it silenced.

FIVE

The Wall of Faith

We call them Crusaders, and distinguish Norman from French, English from German. But to Byzantines and Muslims alike they were all simply "Franks"—*Frangoi* in Greek, *Franj* in Arabic. Around noon on July 15, 1099, amid dense smoke and flames from a tower burning close by, and to the mingled sounds of trumpets behind and terrified screams ahead, they entered the ancient city of Jerusalem. Thousands of Muslims fled to the Temple of Solomon, where they were slaughtered, like every other Muslim in the city, along with many of its Jews and Christians. "If you had been there," writes the chronicler Fulcher of Chartres (who wasn't either), "your feet would have been stained to the ankles in the blood of the slain. What shall I say? None of them were left alive."

Despite professing speechlessness—and despite being elsewhere at the time—Fulcher does in fact find quite a lot to say in celebrating this glorious event. In words that bring to mind similar bloodlettings closer to our own time, he describes the Franks as paragons of piety. "They desired that this place, so long contaminated by the superstition of the pagan inhabitants, should be cleansed from their contagion. It was a time," Fulcher continues blandly, "truly memorable and justly so because in this place everything that the Lord God our Jesus Christ did or taught on earth, as a man living amongst men, was recalled and renewed in the memory of true believers." Hmmm . . . Can't say we noticed that.

Still, it was indeed "a time truly memorable," if perhaps not quite for the reason Fulcher suggests. In circular fashion, one of the things that made it memorable was the diversity of voices doing exactly that—making it memorable, in chronicles like Fulcher's. History suddenly explodes during the Crusades. And not just among Crusader chroniclers, but also among the Muslims, who had their own chroniclers, as well as among the Byzantines, the Crusaders' fellow Christians, their allies, and often their victims as much as the Muslims.

Yet, as we've seen, there is history and there is history. Throughout this fascinating and much studied period,* the Byzantines retained their somewhat spotty monopoly on secular history, however personally devout they may have been outside their classically inspired narratives. Among the Franks and Arabs we find only true believers.

If Byzantine historians during the Crusades possessed a secular outlook that their Western and Islamic counterparts lacked, it may have been reinforced by the fact that Byzantine interests in the whole Crusading enterprise were largely political—and historical. Byzantine rulers hoped to

---

* Some exciting new interpretations of the Crusades have been offered for general readers in the past few years. In particular, Christopher Tyerman's *God's War: A New History of the Crusades* (2006) supercedes Steven Runciman's three-volume *A History of the Crusades*—masterfully written but over half a century old—as the standard work.

recover places, like Antioch and Jerusalem, which had once been under Byzantine rule but had been lost to the Muslims. Of course, a place like Jerusalem always had strong religious pull. But Byzantines saw other reasons than religion for being there, while for Catholics and Muslims, it was all about the faith.

Like Fulcher, Latin and Arabic sources writing about the Crusades tended to obsess over ideas like cleansing and purity.* And not just religious purity, but sexual as well, as the two are so frequently connected in all religious traditions. "How many Muslim women's inviolability has been plundered? How many a mosque has been made into a church!" laments an anonymous Arab poet around the time of the First Crusade. "The cross has been set up in the *mihrab* [the niche in a mosque's wall that shows the direction of Mecca]. The blood of the pig is unsuitable for it. Qur'ans have been burned under the guise of incense."

When the Muslims recaptured cities like Jerusalem—which they did under Saladin in 1187—they celebrated with the same language of purification and cleansing that the Catholics had used upon taking those cities in the first place. Saladin's biographer, Imad al-Din al-Isfahani, was there in 1187, and he recorded the painstaking ritual purification needed to make the holy places once again suitable for Muslim worship after nearly a century of pollution at the hands of the *Franj*. Most urgent was the magnificent Dome of the Rock, Islam's first public building, built on the

---

* Of course, these concepts are useful for murderous campaigns undertaken in a secular context as well, when applied (for example) to race or ethnicity instead of religion.

site where Muhammad ascended to heaven. The Franks had installed Christian furnishings which had to be removed, whereupon the walls and floors were carefully rinsed with rosewater and fumigated with incense. Only then could he report that "The Rock has been cleansed of the filth of the infidels by the tears of the pious," as he fancifully described the rosewater.

The retaking of Jerusalem was the turning point of the Crusades, and was notable for Saladin's remarkably humane treatment of the Christian captives, which contrasted sharply with the Frankish atrocities of 1099. Saladin impressed Latin chroniclers as much as he did Arabic ones, inspiring a substantial body of literature in both languages. He became an important figure in the Western tradition of chivalry, which he was seen as perfectly embodying.

The two chroniclers who most impress modern historians are William of Tyre, who died shortly before Saladin's reconquest of Jerusalem, and Ibn al-Athir, who was in his late twenties at the time. William was born around 1130 in the Latin Kingdom of Jerusalem, which gave him a native perspective on the East and a certain openness to its non-European cultures.* It's thought he would have learned Arabic and Byzantine Greek as a child, along with French. At about fifteen he was sent to France for his education, and he didn't return home for some two decades. When he did, he won the favor of the Latin king, Amalric, and rose at court, becoming archbishop of Tyre, an important coastal

---

* New arrivals from Europe, full of rigid zeal, were often shocked at the mutual tolerance Crusaders and Muslims came to show for each other's ways. When they weren't killing each other for God, that is.

city in the kingdom, around 1175. But Amalric died soon afterward, and William fell out of favor at court. Eventually he moved to Rome, where he died knowing that Saladin was almost certain to retake Jerusalem but spared the anguish of seeing it happen.

William wrote two works, of which only one survives: an account of the First and Second Crusades called *The History of the Deeds Done Overseas*. The lost book, a history of the Arab lands in which the Crusaders found themselves, was written at Amalric's request. Its loss is a shame, since we would very much like to know more about how this relatively open-minded and humane Westerner saw Islamic civilization.

An important player in many of the events he describes, William was also chosen by Amalric to tutor Amalric's young son, Prince Baldwin IV. He writes touchingly about Baldwin, whom he admired and loved, and who contracted leprosy and died at thirteen. His history was heavily used by later chroniclers, and it remains our most balanced and authoritative source for the period from Jerusalem's capture by the Crusaders to shortly before its recapture by Saladin.

Ibn al-Athir, who fought as a twenty-eight-year-old soldier in that campaign, originally came from Mosul, an important city in Mesopotamia (now Iraq). His major work is a universal history of the Islamic world called *The Complete History*, which, like its Christian equivalents, started with the Creation and went on from there. His writing is spirited and colorful, if less impartial than William's. He throws in frequent exclamations ("May God curse his name" comes up regularly in connection with Crusaders), and while he

praises Saladin, he reserves his strongest endorsement for
Saladin's predecessor, Nureddin.

In addition to being the best Arabic source for the first
three Crusades, Ibn al-Athir witnessed a second calami-
tous assault on the Islamic world, this time from the east,
in the form of the Mongols under Genghis Khan. Between
1218 and 1221, the Mongol conqueror swept in from Central Asia, destroying fabled cities such as Samarkand and
Bukhara, annihilating their Muslim inhabitants. "No,"
wrote Ibn al-Athir, "probably not until the end of time will
a catastrophe of such magnitude be seen again." He died a
few years later in Mosul. Sadly, the prediction proved shortsighted, not least when Genghis Khan's grandson Hulagu
Khan came back for more a couple of decades later. He
struck even deeper into Islamic territory, meting out the
same devastating treatment to the Arab capital of Baghdad
and ending the Abbasid caliphate.

By the time the Mongols were devastating the Islamic world,
the Byzantines had new problems of their own. These were
chronicled by one of the most engaging and accomplished
of Byzantine historians, Nicetas Choniates, who was Ibn al-
Athir's younger contemporary. The balancing act so skillfully executed by Alexius, John, and Manuel Comnenus
blew apart with the spectacular dissolution of their dynasty
at the end of the twelfth century. Taking up the story where
Anna Comnena left off, with the death of Alexius Comnenus and the accession of John, Nicetas follows it through
the chaotic years after the death of Manuel Comnenus. His

history culminates in the Latins' horrific sack of Constantinople during the Fourth Crusade in 1204, when thousands of Byzantines perished and untold cultural treasures were destroyed or looted. Nicetas himself lived through this national catastrophe, and though we have other sources for it, his account is the fullest and best informed.*

Nicetas Choniates was born around 1155 in Chonai, the Greek city in Asia Minor from which his family took its surname. The family (whose name is pronounced *kohn-YAH-dees*) belonged to the provincial gentry, privileged enough for access to an excellent education but lacking high connections in the capital. Nicetas had several brothers and sisters, the oldest of whom was his brother Michael, some eighteen years his senior. Soon after Nicetas was born, Michael went off to study in Constantinople. When Nicetas was nine, he joined his older brother, who took over responsibility for his upbringing and education. Mentor, guardian, career counselor, and second father, Michael would always be there for Nicetas. The relationship would be the most important one in Nicetas's life.

Michael's own mentor was Eustathius of Thessalonica, a brilliant and original writer and teacher who has been called "one of the most attractive Byzantine intellectuals of any age" by a modern authority. Eustathius was a leading figure in the church and the head of Constantinople's patriarchal school. Later he would be appointed metropolitan (archbishop) of Thessalonica, the empire's second city. Michael himself, as a promising oldest son, was funneled

---

* I describe these events briefly in my book *Sailing from Byzantium*, pp. 29 ff. See also Jonathan Phillips, *The Fourth Crusade and the Sack of Constantinople* (2004).

into the service of the church and would eventually also rise to the rank of metropolitan. But Eustathius was also an accomplished classical scholar with a deep love of ancient Greek literature and a decidedly secular bent in his thinking. He promoted secular values in his writings, and conceived of history as a record of progress from savagery to civilization. Both Michael and Nicetas owed much of their own sophisticated literary and intellectual *personae* to his influence.

Nicetas began a career in the imperial administration, and by 1189 he had been put in charge of Thrace, the crucial region west of the capital. Later that year, however, Thrace was overrun by the Germans of the Third Crusade under Frederick Barbarossa. These were turbulent years for Byzantium, years of coups and countercoups as different branches of the Comnenus dynasty battled over the throne. Nicetas kept his feet on the uneven political ground and eventually rose to become the head of the civil service, a position he held until shortly before the fall of Constantinople to the Fourth Crusade in 1204.

Bursting with florid quotations from scripture and classics alike, Nicetas's account of the rape of Constantinople reads like an ornate dirge:

> *There were lamentations and cries of woe and weeping in the narrow ways, wailing at the crossroads, moaning in the temples, outcries of men, screams of women, the taking of captives, and the dragging about, tearing in pieces, and raping of bodies heretofore sound and whole.*

It takes some effort to glimpse reality through pages and pages of wailing at the crossroads. But then a sharp passage will pierce the gauzy rhetoric, snapping the picture into grainy focus. Fleeing the city with his family on the fifth day, Nicetas sees a Latin soldier snatch a terrified young girl off the street. She is the daughter of a judge he knows.

> *The girl's father, afflicted by old age and sickness, stumbled, fell into a mud-hole, and lay on his side wailing and wallowing in the mire; turning to me in utter helplessness and calling me by name, he entreated that I do everything possible to free his daughter. I immediately turned back and set out after the abductor, following his tracks . . .*

Nicetas shames a group of loitering Latins into joining the pursuit, cornering the man and forcing him to give up the girl.* In Nicetas's version, this happens only after he mercilessly subjects the would-be rapist to a lengthy and rhetorically tricked-out speech on the finer points of lust versus civilization. Michael Choniates wrote about the episode, too, and he says that Nicetas persuaded the man to release the girl by swearing that she was his wife. Not as flowery, perhaps, but even more courageous, as he certainly put his own life at still greater risk by posing as her husband.

---

* Umberto Eco takes this episode as a starting point for his picaresque novel *Baudolino*, in which one of the Latins (the fictional character Baudolino) saves Nicetas's life. The two become friends and Baudolino narrates his life story to Nicetas, who "records" it for the reader. Baudolino is an inveterate liar, and Nicetas's skepticism about his grandiose tales turns the book into an entertaining and philosophically informed meditation on the nature of historical truth.

Most historians sit around reading at a safe distance, which is perfectly okay. We've seen some in action as soldiers, which is fine, too. Historians who would actually risk their lives for fair damsels (yes, she was "fair-tressed" on top of everything else) are rare. Those who would downplay their own courage in doing so are rarer still. In fact, I can't think of another one.

Of course, courage won't necessarily help you write good history. Yet Nicetas scores well here, too. To be sure, his narrative is packed with omens, portents, demons, and miracles, unlike those of, say, a Michael Psellus or an Anna Comnena, both of whom largely excluded religion beyond conventional expressions of piety. But, as with Bede, under the superstructure of superstition lies a foundation of explanation. (In this connection we might propose that secular history is less about excluding faith than it is about including reason.) This is what separates Nicetas and most lesser Byzantine historians of the period from the Latin and Arabic chroniclers. The shortsighted dismantling of Byzantium's navy, squalid infighting among the various branches of the Comnenus dynasty, growing hostility between Westerners and Byzantines, Western savagery and Byzantine cowardice—by weaving these and other contributory strands into his narrative, Nicetas gives it momentum and real analytical depth. In comparison, the pious chronicles of Westerners such as Geoffroy de Villehardouin or Robert of Clari, both of them French knights who participated in the Fourth Crusade, seem simplistic and naive.

Still, they're not bad fellows. It's informative and entertaining to read their overawed descriptions of

Constantinople's imposing majesty and glittering riches. At the time, the city was some ten or twenty times larger than Paris. Geoffroy describes the Crusaders' reactions as the fleet approached the great walls:

> *I can assure you that all those who had never seen Constantinople before gazed very intently at the city, having never imagined there could be so fine a place in all the world. They noted the high walls and lofty towers encircling it, and its rich palaces and tall churches, of which there were so many that no one would have believed it to be true if he had not seen it with his own eyes, and viewed the length and breadth of that city which reigns supreme over all others. There was indeed no man so brave and daring that his flesh did not shudder at the sight.*

No less were these bluff soldiers impressed by the spoils of conquest. "No one could estimate its amount or its value," Geoffroy tells us breathlessly. "Geoffroy of Villehardouin here declares that, to his knowledge, so much booty had never been gained in any city since the creation of the world." The even wider-eyed Robert of Clari goggles on for pages about it, at times seeming almost to stutter. "And it was so rich, and there were so many rich vessels of gold and silver and cloth of gold and so many rich jewels, that it was a fair marvel, the great wealth that was brought there." How delightful that in the midst of treasure what he needs most is a thesaurus, which of course literally means "treasure."

We don't know what became of Nicetas, whose history closes elegantly in 1206. He seems to have died about a decade later, at around sixty years old. We do know that Michael Choniates, now pushing eighty, survived him. Looking after his younger brother even in death, Michael composed an eloquent eulogy. As for the Byzantines, perhaps Nicetas would have taken comfort if he'd known that they would recover their capital in 1261, and that the remarkably resilient Byzantine empire would last a further two centuries after that.

Byzantium's reprieve can be chalked up to the terrible destruction wrought upon the Islamic world by the Mongols. But the Mongols weren't the only problem for Islamic civilization. In North Africa, Berbers and Arab nomads constantly besieged and harried the Arab elites who ruled from urban centers such as Tunis; in Spain, once home to the glories of Moorish civilization, Christian Spanish forces were in the process of expelling the Muslims altogether; and the eastern reaches of Iraq and Iran that suffered most from the Mongols had already been ravaged by the incoming Seljuk Turks. By the early decades of the fourteenth century, the once-prosperous lands of Islam had fallen into decay.

The great Arab historian Ibn Khaldun, who would make it his life's work to explain how such things happen, was born in Tunis on May 27, 1332.* The Ibn Khalduns were an illustrious family, he tells us in his autobiography. (The historian is known by his family name, his full name in

---

* Or 1 Ramadan, 732 by the Muslim calendar. Muslims count years from the *hijra*, the sojourn in Medina that followed Muhammad's expulsion from Mecca (AD 622). In Western languages this is often denoted by the initials AH, for *anno hijrae* ("in the year of the hijra").

majestic Arabic fashion being approximately two Muham-
mads longer than your arm.) Originally from southern Arabia, the family had helped conquer Spain for the Muslims
and had owned property in Seville before it fell to the Christian Reconquest. Welcomed by the powers-that-be in Tunis,
they assumed their place in that city's ruling elite. When
angry nomads came to the walls, the Ibn Khalduns would
have been very much on the inside.

Ibn Khaldun received a rigorous education not only in
Islamic scripture, theology, and law, but also in rationalistic philosophy, which was based on ancient Greek sources,
especially Aristotle and Plato. The Arabs had discovered
ancient Greek learning centuries earlier, and had taken it
up enthusiastically at first. But they had not embraced the
Greek classics wholesale. Focusing on science, medicine,
mathematics, and philosophy, which they considered to be
useful areas of knowledge, they had eschewed much of what
we consider integral to Greek literature, including poetry,
drama, and, most importantly for our purposes, history.
There is no evidence that Ibn Khaldun ever heard of Herodotus or Thucydides, much less read them, which makes
his ultimate achievement all the more remarkable.

When he was sixteen, Ibn Khaldun began studies with
a celebrated mathematician and philosopher whom Ibn
Khaldun's father, himself learned in these fields, invited to
live with the family. The next year, however, was 1348, and
the first of several personal misfortunes befell Ibn Khaldun when the Black Death, which ravaged the Old World
beginning in that year, took both of his parents. He continued his studies for three more years, until his teacher was

summoned to Fez by its ruler. Ibn Khaldun was able to secure a secretarial post at the same court. While he continued his studies, his position at court in Fez became a springboard into the Machiavellian political world of North Africa and Islamic Spain, which was rife with intrigue and danger as alliances shifted, patronage was doled out or withheld, and rebellions failed or succeeded. At one point, he spent nearly two years in jail for allegedly plotting against Fez's ruler.

Having repeatedly burnt his fingers in Fez in his twenties, as he turned thirty the still-ambitious Ibn Khaldun tried his luck in Granada, the last stronghold of Muslim Spain. But there, if anything, his experience was worse. Ibn Khaldun undertook a concerted effort to shape Granada's young ruler, Muhammad V, into a Platonic "philosopher-king," but in so doing he crossed an older and more seasoned teacher named Ibn al-Khatib, who was a good friend but had a different take on Muhammad V. Concluding that Ibn Khaldun was playing with fire, Ibn al-Khatib forced him to leave Granada. Ibn al-Khatib turned out to be entirely correct, as Muhammad V revealed himself to be a bloodthirsty tyrant. As for Ibn Khaldun, it was fingers burnt again, and off to new horizons. But some people just have to learn the hard way. Over the coming years, as he served petty rulers in various North African cities and even returned once to Granada, Ibn Khaldun increasingly sought, without any success whatsoever, to stay clear of political intrigue and pursue his studies in relative isolation.

At length, while on a diplomatic mission to the Algerian interior, he simply abandoned his current patron and took refuge in the remote castle of Qalat ibn Salama, sending for his wife and children to join him. At this point, Ibn Khaldun was in his early forties.

His first idea was to write a straightforward history of the Maghrib, as coastal North Africa is known in Arabic (the name means "the West"). But the more he got into it the less straightforward it seemed. His background in philosophy had taught him to look for the reasons behind things, which in Greek is expressed by the word *aitia*. It isn't entirely coincidental that this is precisely the word Herodotus uses in the first sentence of his history—but that example, of course, wasn't available to Ibn Khaldun. And the examples he did have weren't much help to him. Islamic history was just that—Islamic, in the same way that Christian history was Christian. The big difference was that Christian history grew out of a secular tradition that already existed, while Islamic history was born from Islam itself, in the Koran and the Hadith (non-Koranic sayings and deeds traditionally ascribed to Muhammad).

Yet like most Christian historians, and for that matter, like those in many other cultures who have written about the past in one manner or another, Islamic historians were interested mainly in recording and celebrating. Many were quite thorough, but like their Christian counterparts, they were chroniclers. As Ibn Khaldun complains, often they merely repeated the information in their sources without interpreting it. "They disregarded the changes in conditions and in the customs of nations and races that the passing of time had brought about," he writes. In short, they "neglected the importance of change over the generations . . . Their works, therefore, give no explanation for it."

It was this gaping explanatory hole that Ibn Khaldun, steeped in his isolated fortress of reason, felt so keenly when he began to think about the past. He decided in his methodical way that before he could write about history, he had to understand how history works, an approach that came directly from his scientific and philosophical training.*

At Qalat ibn Salama, Ibn Khaldun embarked on the massive project that would become the celebrated *Muqaddimah*, or "Introduction" to history. This imposing work (the final version fills three big volumes in the English translation) lays out an entirely "new science" of history. It amounts to a detailed road map for historians, one all the more necessary because history itself is so deceptively complex:

For on the surface history is no more than information about political events, dynasties, and occurrences of the remote past, elegantly presented and spiced with proverbs. . . . The inner meaning of history, on the other hand, involves speculation and an attempt to get at the truth, subtle explanations of the causes and origins of existing things, and deep knowledge of the how and why of events.

Ibn Khaldun's exploration of history's "inner meaning" is indeed subtle and systematic. Most notably, perhaps, he explores connections between physical environment and collective psychology, which he sums up with the term *asabiyah*, or "group feeling."

---

* The Iraqi-American scholar Muhsin Mahdi pointed this out in *Ibn Khaldun's Philosophy of History* (1957), which is half a century old but still sparkles. I'm heavily indebted to it here.

The *Muqaddimah* represents the first attempt anywhere to lay out a theory of historical practice. In short, it's the world's first work in the field that would later become known as the philosophy of history. Writing in the twentieth century, Arnold Toynbee called the *Muqaddimah* "undoubtedly the greatest work of its kind that has ever been created by any mind in any time or place."

Though it was widely read in Persia throughout the Middle Ages, the Arabs themselves largely ignored it. And not until a French translation appeared around 1850 was Ibn Khaldun "discovered" by the West. Ibn Khaldun's overall approach continues to resonate with recent thinking, even if many of his confident pronouncements are misguided in light of modern understanding, including explanations based on race, magic, and the supposed consequences of sedentary versus nomadic lifestyles. Still, he's been hailed as one of the fathers of sociology for his scientific treatment of human affairs, and his concept of *asabiyah* is still inspiring new sociological theories in the twenty-first century.

Ibn Khaldun wrote the early drafts of the *Muqaddimah* largely from memory. He knew that he needed to do a lot more research, especially since his idea for a history of the Maghrib was evolving into a far more ambitious "Universal History" of Islamic civilization. Formidable as it is, the *Muqaddimah* constitutes merely the first part of this larger work. Research for such an undertaking could be performed only in a good-sized city, and so after several decades' absence from his native Tunis, Ibn Khaldun returned home. He was welcomed by the Tunisian ruler, who soon became his patron, and the writer found himself slipping back into the courtier's life. He stayed in Tunis for four years, studying, thinking, writing, and teaching, as the old familiar brew of intrigues, suspicions, and jealousies bubbled up around him once more.

That, combined with Tunis's shortcomings as a place for research, pushed him to move on yet again. Giving out that he wished to make a pilgrimage to Mecca, in 1382 Ibn Khaldun left for Egypt, where he planned to settle in Cairo and, he hoped, find a permanent haven for teaching and writing. He was fifty years old.

Under its Mamluk dynasty, Egypt at this time was an island of comparative stability and prosperity in the sea of political chaos and cultural decay that was the rest of the Islamic world. Distance and Mamluk strength had so far fended off the Mongols to the east and the Berbers to the west. And Cairo itself was a great metropolis with, best of all, a large and famous university, al-Azhar, where Ibn Khaldun (whose reputation had preceded him) was immediately invited to teach. In Cairo Ibn Khaldun at last found the stable but stimulating cosmopolitan environment that he had been seeking for so long. There he made a permanent home, and there he brought his ideas about history, already partly formed, to their full maturity.

Ibn Khaldun's life in Egypt was not unburdened by loss. The worst came just over a year after his arrival. He had arranged for his family to join him, and they were sailing to Egypt when their ship was wrecked near the port of Alexandria. Everyone on board was killed, including Ibn Khaldun's wife and all his children. Nor did he disengage himself altogether from public life and its attendant irritations. After two years in Cairo, he was invited to become a grand judge, an important role he was widely accused of performing with undue strictness. He would be dismissed and reappointed numerous times in the coming years.

Yet the underlying stability of Ibn Khaldun's life in Egypt is revealed by the fact that this formerly restless traveler left his adopted country only three times in the quarter-century he lived there, and briefly at that. His first trip, in 1387, was the pilgrimage to Mecca that had been the pretext by which he had persuaded Tunis's ruler to let him come to Egypt in the first place. His second trip was a journey to Damascus thirteen years later, which he made in his capacity as grand judge, since Egypt's Mamluk dynasty also ruled Syria at the time.

Only a few months after returning from this journey, Ibn Khaldun again visited Damascus, in late fall of 1400, his third and last trip away from Cairo. This time he accompanied an expeditionary force led by Egypt's thirteen-year-old ruler, the Mamluk sultan Faraj, who had just taken over from his recently deceased father. Testing the new sultan, the Mongols were on the warpath once more, and their new leader, the ferocious conqueror Tamerlane, had marched on Damascus after sacking nearby Aleppo. Ibn Khaldun had been dismissed from his judgeship shortly beforehand, but the young sultan's advisors still valued his counsel.

The army made it to Damascus before Tamerlane, but a mere two weeks later Faraj's nerve broke and he fled back to Cairo, rumors of a coup against him there having reached him in Damascus. Taking part of his command staff with him, he left the rest, along with the entire army, high and dry in Damascus. Within days the army fragmented and began trickling back to Egypt. Ibn Khaldun was among those to whom the bewildered and demoralized local authorities now appealed for advice. He suggested that under the circumstances they opt for discretion as the better part of valor and accept Tamerlane's terms of surrender.

During the negotiations, Tamerlane heard about Ibn Khaldun's presence in Damascus and asked the Damascene ambassadors about him. When Ibn Khaldun got wind of Tamerlane's inquiries, his vanity flexed itself. The historian was gripped by a sudden and overwhelming compulsion to meet the conqueror—to meet history itself, as it must have seemed—face-to-face. At the same time, he feared for his safety in the city at the hands of the faction opposed to surrender.

And that was how, as dawn broke over Damascus early one January morning in the year 1401, Ibn Khaldun, nearing seventy and one of the greatest historical thinkers of all time, found himself dangling high off the ground on the end of a rope, being slowly lowered to earth outside the city walls. He showed up at Tamerlane's camp unannounced, without even the customary gifts, which was at best thoughtless and at worst dangerous. But the historian and the conqueror seem to have hit it off. They were rough contemporaries, Ibn Khaldun being a few years older. At Tamerlane's invitation, Ibn Khaldun stayed in the Mongol camp for just over a month.

The celebrated encounter that took place during this time unfolded over many long conversations between the two men. It held elements of mutual flattery, veiled threat, genuine intellectual discussion, and high-stakes strategic sparring. Quick-witted and curious, Tamerlane had many questions about history. No doubt he enjoyed being compared with such illustrious figures as Caesar and Alexander the Great. But there was also a deadly cat-and-mouse aspect to the interaction, as Tamerlane questioned Ibn Khaldun about the Maghrib, patiently but persistently trying to seek out the weak spots. Ibn Khaldun had to keep his wits about him, crafting responses that satisfied the questioner while actually giving very little away. If Ibn Khaldun had any doubts about Tamerlane's ruthlessness, which he probably didn't, they would have been dispelled when Tamerlane broke the terms of surrender and allowed his army to pillage and destroy Damascus.

Pushing the relationship as far as he could, Ibn Khaldun succeeded in securing from Tamerlane safe passage back to Egypt for himself and a number of his friends. On the voyage home, he met up with the ambassador of yet another fierce conqueror, the Ottoman sultan Bayezid, who was called *Yilderim*, "Thunderbolt." Bayezid had spent more than a decade conquering lands in Asia Minor and the Balkans for the Ottoman Turks, who would ultimately make more of a mark on history than Tamerlane. But neither his flashy nickname nor his dynasty's future imperial might would be much help to Bayezid the following year, when Tamerlane annihilated his army at the battle of Ankara. Bayezid was taken prisoner and died in captivity.

As for Ibn Khaldun, he lived out five more productive years in Egypt, adding to his autobiography, continuing work on his history (including Tamerlane and his conquests), and being appointed to and dismissed from his grand judgeship several more times. He died peacefully in 1406, and was buried outside the two massive rectangular towers of Cairo's *Bab al-Nasr*, or "Gate of Victory," one of the city's three main gates.

Ibn Khaldun tends to leave modern historians somewhat at a loss. He stands out with irremediable starkness, a jutting spike on the flat-lining graph of Islamic historiography. Just as he lacked any real predecessors, so too did he lack any real successors, and both absences cry out for explanation.

Perhaps part of the explanation lies in the origins of history itself. History, we have suggested, is the energetic and unruly love child of a union between two mutually attracted but ultimately incompatible partners, the scientist and the storyteller. In the ancient Greek world, where storytelling about the past took the form of epic poetry, the two came together relatively quickly. There were no walls between them.

In the Islamic world, one of those parents was different: Islamic history, at least as conceived by Ibn Khaldun, is the stillborn half-sibling of the Herodotean tradition. The parent they share is science. But with Islamic history, in the place of the epic storyteller we have the prophetic storyteller. Because Islamic history was born into a monotheistic culture, rather than preexisting the rise of one, Muslim interest in the past was shaped not by epic poetry but by prophetic poetry, and by those who interpreted a single prophetic life. For Muslims, God literally came first—in time, as well as in priority. The past was the ward of this jealous God, who guarded it long and hard behind a wall of faith. And there it languished.

By the time Ibn Khaldun finally broke through the wall of faith to bring science and storytelling about the past together, the Islamic world had suffered its setbacks and begun its cultural decay. Even during the early days of confidence and cultural openness, there were those among the Muslims who accused their philosophers and scientists of pursuing an agenda that was foreign and un-Islamic. As it had already in Byzantium and the West—and as it periodically does in all cultures that have joined the long, unwinnable tug-of-war between Athens and Jerusalem—waning confidence gave the enemies of reason the traction they lacked in more-optimistic times. When confidence ebbs, certainty offers better comfort than curiosity, nativist appeals trump disinterested assessments, and authoritarian inquisitions win out over authoritative inquiries. In Ibn Khaldun's day, reason was already on the defensive in the lands of Islam, where the past just didn't have much of a future.

SIX

History Reborn

Sometime around the end of January in the year 1337, a young Italian named Francesco di Petracco set out for Rome on horseback from the hilltop fortress of Capranica, a journey of about thirty miles. Francesco had long yearned to see Rome. He was an aspiring poet in his early thirties, whose childhood reading of Cicero and Virgil had stirred a passionate interest in the classical past, and he'd already made a point of visiting Roman ruins closer to his home in southern France, where his family had settled when he was a boy. But Rome itself! "What do you think I would not give to see the walls and hills of the city," he'd written with self-conscious allusiveness to a friend, "and, as Virgil says, the 'Tuscan Tiber and the palaces of Rome'?"

He'd started calling himself Francesco Petrarca, presumably because it sounded better than Petracco, his father's name. In English, we know him as Petrarch. Traveling with Petrarch this winter day were his hosts at Capranica, members of the powerful Colonna family, along with a hundred mounted soldiers to protect the party from the Colonnas' deadly enemies, the Orsini. This was the period of the papacy's residence in Avignon, where, like his father, Petrarch worked for the papal curia, and of the long contest between Guelphs and Ghibellines that had caused Petrarch's family, allied with the Guelfs, to be exiled from their native

Florence before the poet's birth.* Wracked by factional strife, Rome itself was a prize in this complex international power struggle, in which the Colonnas and the Orsini stood on opposite sides.

Arriving safely in Rome, Petrarch spent an unknown number of days walking around the city with his older friend and host Giovanni Colonna, stopping at the end of a day's wanderings to admire various views of its ancient ruins and discuss the history that saturated the place. He wrote later that "every step brought some suggestion to stir the mind and loose the tongue." But not all his thoughts could be put into words quite yet. "You may well be looking for an outpouring of eloquence now that I have arrived in Rome," he wrote to a friend at the time. "Well, I have found a vast theme, which may serve perhaps for future writing; but just now I dare not attempt anything, for I am overwhelmed by the miracle of the mighty things around me . . ."

One "vast theme" that emerged from Petrarch's visit to Rome was nothing less than a polarization of the past, a perceptual reversal, a real revolution in the sense of an over-turning. Before Petrarch, people looked at the past and saw an age of pagan superstition that had been succeeded by the light of Christian revelation. Petrarch flipped this idea like a pancake: The enlightenment of ancient Greece and Rome was followed by an age of ignorant superstition in which ancient knowledge disappeared and culture decayed. It was Petrarch who first used the terms Dark Ages and Middle Ages, and who ushered in the "rebirth" or Renaissance

---

* The so-called "Avignonese captivity" of the papacy lasted from 1309 to 1377.

of ancient culture and learning that became known as humanism.

Though he wrote a work of history (about Rome, naturally), Petrarch wasn't really a historian at heart. He was first and always a poet. A high point in his life came four years after his first visit to Rome, when Petrarch returned to the city to be "crowned with the laurel" in a ceremony that revived the ancient institution of poet laureate. His interest in the past was more passionate than analytical, more enthusiastic than detached.

But he brought a quality of inspired imagination to his musings on the past that had been sorely lacking in the stiff and narrow writings of medieval chroniclers. And he treated the past as something to be approached on its own terms. He divorced classical antiquity from its anachronistic union with a God who had supposedly put Plato, Socrates, and Augustus on earth merely to prepare the way for Jesus.

Petrarch wrote a long epic poem, *Africa*, that celebrated the exploits of one of his heroes, Scipio Africanus, the Roman general who defeated Hannibal (this is probably the actual "vast theme" he had in mind in Rome). He composed letters to others, including Homer, Virgil, Cicero, and Livy, writing to them as if they were close friends. It was Cicero above all who inspired him, and another high point was his discovery, in 1345, of a manuscript containing Cicero's *Letters to Atticus*, in which the Roman orator displayed the virtuoso epistolary style that Petrarch emulated. But Livy, too, was on Petrarch's list of correspondents, a choice, no doubt, far more consonant with Petrarch's own romantic and epic tendencies than, say, the bitter and hypercritical Tacitus.

Petrarch was a big one for heroes, finding many in Livy's text and, apparently, one more in the historian himself.

The revival of the literature and the literary interests of antiquity that Petrarch started in Italy eventually spread to northern Europe. Petrarch shows us that a shift in historical understanding was at the root of this movement, even if its earliest interests lay more with authors such as Virgil and Cicero than with the ancient historians themselves. Earlier writers had tacitly assumed that preserving the past was the best we can do. In his passion for reviving the values of antiquity, Petrarch reshaped our attitudes to embrace the idea that even once lost, the past can be recovered. Though it took a while, history gradually lost the "hourglass" shape that had marked it since ancient times: big on the mythic past, thin in the historical middle, and big again on contemporary events. By championing the possibility of recovery, Petrarch radically enlarged history's scope, its potential, and its ambitions.

Petrarch gave us the idea of being modern. He also gave us the idea that each age amounts to a distinct civilization, which must always look back on other distinct civilizations in endless succession. And while it was new at the time, his perspective on the periodization of Western history is the one that we have kept.

Though few of us know it, he is our quiet but ever-present companion when we stop to take things in after wandering through history ourselves. At the end of the day, we all end up sitting there with Petrarch, sharing his view on the past.

Petrarch, whose sense of historical change is exactly the sort of thing Ibn Khaldun hungered for, died in 1374, just as Ibn Khaldun was embarking on the *Muqaddimah*. It's a shame that Ibn Khaldun, struggling to cultivate a new sense of history in Muslim North Africa, never knew that Petrarch had already sown similar seeds on more-fertile ground in Christian Europe. How Ibn Khaldun would have loved the Renaissance. We can picture him relishing its complexities with gigantic gusto, tossing the bones of digested facts over his shoulder, loading his plate with mighty slabs of continuity, gulping great drafts of refreshing novelty.

In the decades after Petrarch's death, humanism was taken up by a new generation of Italian writers and scholars. Many of the best could be found in vibrant Florence, the ancestral home from which Petrarch's family had been exiled. They were led by men such as Coluccio Salutati, chancellor of Florence from 1375 to 1406, an influential disciple of Petrarch's and a renowned teacher with a substantial following of younger Florentines. Among Salutati's many students was the brilliant Leonardo Bruni, who eventually followed in Salutati's footsteps as chancellor of Florence. Salutati and Bruni were inspired by Petrarch, but their interests lay less with poetry and more with political science and history itself. With this generation, history moves from the periphery to the center of the humanistic curriculum. Leonardo Bruni would be the first Westerner to write full-blown secular history in the classical tradition since ancient times.

One thing that helped this process along was the recovery of Greek. While Bruni remained primarily a Latinist, entranced (like Petrarch) by the intricate beauty of the formal Ciceronian period, he and his contemporaries were the first generation of humanists who had the chance to learn ancient Greek really well. This was an attainment that had eluded Petrarch and Salutati, despite their best efforts. Bruni was in his late twenties when Salutati arranged for the remarkable Byzantine scholar Manuel Chrysoloras to come to Florence and teach ancient Greek. Chrysoloras stayed in Florence for three years, from 1397 to 1400, and his inspiring teaching allowed the study of ancient Greek finally to put down permanent roots in the West, which it did first with Bruni and his friends.

Many of these young Florentines were wealthy aristocrats, but Bruni, the most gifted of them, was not. He had to make a living by his pen, and he was lucky that the times he lived in brought rich financial rewards as well as social advancement to people with talents like his. He'd been born in Arezzo, a Tuscan town about fifty miles southeast of Florence, and for that reason he is sometimes known as Aretino. When not in Florence, he spent much of his career working at the Vatican, which employed many of these early humanists in secretarial and other positions, and which became a major center of humanist learning. Bruni used his newly won expertise in Greek to render works by a variety of Greek authors into Latin, including Xenophon, Polybius, and Plutarch, as well as Plato, Aristotle, and the Athenian orators Aeschines and Demosthenes. He was selective with Plato and Aristotle, focusing on works that had something to say about politics or history, ignoring the metaphysics. For most of these works, Bruni's translations were the first versions available to a Western readership.

His output as a translator alone would have been enough to secure his reputation, but Bruni went further than simply translating these works. He imbibed the thinking of their authors, and he used them as models that he could imitate in putting forward his own ideas. In 1401 he published an encomium, *In Praise of Florence*, that was based on Greek encomiums of Athens. Salutati had compared republican Florence with republican Rome. Bruni went further and compared Florence with Athens. His exaltation of democratic political values would be taken up by thinkers like John Locke, and so Bruni can be regarded as the father of modern political philosophy.

In 1415, Bruni quit the Vatican after a decade and returned to Florence, where he began work on his groundbreaking *History of the Florentine People*, the work in which he revived the critical, secularizing methods of the ancient historians, and upon which he would labor until his death nearly thirty years later. Basing his account on close scrutiny of the ancient sources, Bruni was able to expose a number of myths about the city that had been cherished by the chroniclers. Florence was founded by Julius Caesar. Florence was destroyed by the Goths. Florence was refounded by Charlemagne. Wrong, wrong, and wrong again! The chroniclers had anchored Florence's past to popes and emperors. Bruni threw all that away. Instead, he polished for the ages the picture of Florence that Salutati had sketched out, tracing the growth of a republican city-state rooted in secular, democratic values. He also reinforced the periodization implicit in Petrarch's approach, of "ancient," "medieval," and "modern."

For Bruni and others, history came first among the humanistic disciplines. It kept that place as more Byzantine scholars arrived in Italy with their manuscripts, and a number of Italians went to Constantinople to study ancient Greek and look for manuscripts to bring back on their own. Under Byzantine tutelage the Italians rediscovered and translated Herodotus, Thucydides, Xenophon, Polybius, and Plutarch, among other historians. Still, the Italians saw the Greeks as mere beginners compared with the Romans who followed them. Even when they translated the Greeks, they looked to Livy, Sallust, and Caesar as the models they followed most closely when they wrote history themselves.

One who did both was Lorenzo Valla, a Roman who wrote a history of the Neapolitan king Ferdinand of Aragon, studied Greek under the Byzantine expatriate Cardinal Bessarion in Rome, and was the first to make complete translations of Herodotus and Thucydides into Latin. But Valla's history is a rather tepid business, and he's best known for other achievements. He may have been only a mediocre historian, but he was a linguist of genius and is lionized today as the founder of modern philology.

Valla's most famous achievement (though hardly the one for which modern specialists accord him such respect) was his demonstration that the Donation of Constantine, the document on which the papacy staked its claims to temporal power, was no more than a medieval forgery. To prove it, Valla used his intimate knowledge of classical

Latin, showing conclusively that the language of the document placed its composition in the late Middle Ages, not in Constantine's time. Despite his skepticism of such papal claims, Valla was welcomed at the Vatican, where he contributed to the humanistic program of the extraordinarily broad-minded Pope Nicholas V, himself a humanist and the founder of the Vatican Library.

Another Roman humanist, and more of a historian than Valla, was his contemporary, Flavio Biondo, who played a big part in the development of Renaissance historiography after Bruni. Lorenzo Valla had enlisted linguistics in the service of history. Flavio Biondo enlisted other new areas of knowledge, such as archaeology and epigraphy, which would prove even more essential to history's future.* He wrote a number of pioneering works on Roman, Italian, and European history, but two of them stand out, though albeit in different ways.

The title of the first one, *Decades of History from the Decline of the Roman Empire*, might have a familiar ring about it, and for good reason, since it was a major source for Gibbon. Departing from the standard humanist emphasis on antiquity, in this seminal work Biondo gave a coherent and remarkably well-informed account of European history from the sack of Rome by the Vandals in 410 up to his own era. He did more than anyone else to change the "hourglass" shape of history into something closer to a straight-sided cylinder, shifting the emphasis from the near to the

---

* *Archaeology* can be defined as the study of humanity's material remains, in all senses of the word, from preserved corpses and bones to artifacts and refuse. *Epigraphy* is the study of inscriptions, which are usually but not always found on stone tablets. We shall hear more about these two disciplines in future chapters.

more-distant past, for which service to history he has been called the first historian of the Middle Ages.

His other major work, *Italy Illustrated*, incorporates topographical and historical information gleaned from Biondo's own travels (shades of Herodotus!) to tell the story of Italy's eighteen regions, again from antiquity right up to his own times. In other works, *Rome Restored* and *Rome Triumphant*, he had already done the same for the eternal city itself.

The big watershed for Italy during the Renaissance era came at the end of the fifteenth century, when Italy was repeatedly invaded by French armies, which effectively broke the system of independent city-states that had arisen starting in the Late Middle Ages. Italians know this as *la Calamità*, "the Calamity," and for the first half of the sixteenth century, Italy reverted to its earlier role as a battlefield for the conflicting dynastic claims of outside powers—in this case, France and Spain. Political survival in Italy during these years depended on sniffing out new scents on the wind and on sensing how and when the wind was about to shift. The powerful had to be able to switch sides at a moment's notice if they hoped to keep their power.

In Florence, traditional republican rule was contested by the dominant Medici family, which allied itself most often with the papacy and Spanish arms. Against that alliance the republicans usually threw in with the French, whose arms they relied upon. Florence seesawed between Medici and republican regimes with French or Spanish armies looming. Somehow, the peculiar Florentine alchemy kept on transmuting dire uncertainty into outstanding works of history, with the result being that Florence stayed at the vanguard of historical and political thought for a few more decades, until the decisive Spanish victory around the middle of the century. Two Florentine writers capture this world compellingly, one of them so memorably that his name, Machiavelli, has become a byword for cynical political maneuvering, though the other, Francesco Guicciardini, is generally counted the better historian.

Niccolò Machiavelli was born in 1469, into a poor branch of a prominent bourgeois family which could not afford to educate him with the fashionable humanist tutors of the day. Instead, he seems to have largely educated himself, with help from his father Bernardo, a bibliophile, who if poor in cash still possessed a rich humanistic library. The young Machiavelli read widely in the classical authors, especially the historians, although he never learned Greek. His writing style was always forceful and direct, and he wrote in vernacular Italian.

By the time Machiavelli was thirty he had risen to a fairly high position in the republican government at the time, and he soon gained the confidence of Florence's *gonfaloniere* (chief magistrate), Piero Soderini. Soderini sent him on numerous diplomatic missions to the powerful rulers who constantly threatened the republic's independence, as well as to other less powerful ones whose orbits in some way crossed Florence's. Soderini also took up Machiavelli's suggestion that Florence end its reliance on mercenaries and go back to its old practice of raising its army from among its citizens. It was at the head of such a citizen army that

Machiavelli himself oversaw the successful siege of neighboring Pisa, Florence's one-time rival and, for fifteen long and irritating years, its rebellious subject.

Pisa had been a constant thorn in Florence's side. Every red-blooded Florentine had fire in the belly on the subject of Pisa. No republican regime could count itself secure until Pisa had been won. Pisa or bust! Machiavelli, still only in his early thirties, had covered himself and his republican government in glory.

Unfortunately, however, no republican regime in Florence could count itself secure anyway, Pisa or no Pisa. This turned out to be the high point of Machiavelli's career, and of the republic's. France and Spain remained on a collision course in Italy, helped along by Pope Julius II's campaign to liberate northern Italy from French domination, with the eager help of the Spanish. Against Machiavelli's advice Soderini insisted on honoring the republic's traditional alliance with France. When French power in Italy collapsed a few years later, the republic's enemies—the papacy, the Medici, the Spanish, and pretty much everyone else—held all the cards. In 1512 a Spanish army marched into Tuscany. Machiavelli's citizen militia crumbled with humiliating ease, and so did Soderini, who fled across the Adriatic. The republic was abolished, the Medici were brought back, and for a decade and a half Florence was controlled by the Medici-Vatican axis.

As a key official of the ousted regime, Machiavelli found himself stripped of influence. And when a man arrested for plotting against the Medici turned up a list of possible sympathizers that had Machiavelli's name on it, Machiavelli himself was arrested, imprisoned, and tortured. There was no other evidence against him, and he was eventually released. But he was effectively banned from all political activity, which was the only thing he cared about.

Withdrawing to the last remnant of his family's property, a small estate outside Florence, he turned to writing, and there, over the summer and fall of 1513, he produced that classic work cited by so many and read by so few, *The Prince*. In hopes of rehabilitation he dedicated it to Lorenzo de Medici, Florence's new ruler, but the offering failed to sway. When Lorenzo died a few years later, however, Machiavelli fared better with his cousin, Cardinal Giulio de Medici, who began using Machiavelli for small errands and appointed him, interestingly enough, as Florence's official historian. Machiavelli had already finished another book on a historical subject, his *Discourses on Livy*, and he now rather lackadaisically began a *History of Florence*, to which he applied himself with slightly greater zest after the cardinal became Pope Clement VII in 1523.

By that time Machiavelli had struck up a close friendship with Francesco Guicciardini, a politician and writer some fourteen years his junior. In many ways the two men present a study in contrasts. In their backgrounds and temperaments, certainly—Machiavelli, a republican commoner from an impoverished family, emotional and irrepressible; Guicciardini, an aristocrat, a snob even, a piece of cold fish who took every privilege as the unquestioned right of his exalted social rank, and whose family for generations had done very well by allying itself with the Medici.

Even in their interests, where they had much in common, they overlapped only to a limited extent. Machiavelli was all about politics, power, and prescription. Often credited as the inventor of political science, he strove to make human affairs rationally predictable. He took an interest in history, of course, but tangentially—and he wrote it mostly as a way of worming himself into the good graces of the Medici. Guicciardini was interested in politics and power, but he preferred explanation to prescription, which is another way of saying he was more of a historian. He had begun writing history as a young man, but he never published his early works, two separate attempts at a history of Florence. Rediscovered centuries later, they remain valuable largely for the way they reveal his growth as a thinker. Only his last work, the monumental and epoch-making *History of Italy*, was written for publication, and it was published decades after his death.

Two things they shared, and which seem to have lain at the heart of their odd friendship, were a deliciously black sense of humor and a near total contempt for organized religion. They met in circumstances that brought these qualities out and blended them together in a fragrant cocktail, and if those circumstances had been any less absurd, it seems likely they would have had little enough to say to one another.

It was the spring of 1521, and Machiavelli was on his way north to a meeting of Franciscan friars at Carpi, where his irksomely trivial mission was to negotiate for the Florentines on the status of Franciscan monasteries in Florentine domains. Carpi lies roughly between Florence and

Milan, just north of Modena. As part of the Papal States, it was controlled by the pope's governor of Modena, who at that time happened to be Guicciardini. The two met when Machiavelli stopped at Modena on his way to Carpi. We have no record of the meeting, but from the letters that soon began flying back and forth between them, we can imagine Machiavelli's sardonic heat on the subject of monks quickly melting Guicciardini's no doubt initially glacial reserve.

When he got to Carpi, Machiavelli found an even more surreal assignment waiting for him. Florence's influential Wool Guild had sent word requesting that he ask one of the monks to come and deliver a sermon for them on the coming Lent. As Guicciardini wrote him the next day with characteristic irony, "It was certainly good judgment on the part of our reverend consuls of the Wool Guild to have entrusted you" with this particular task. In short, Guicciardini continues, asking Niccolò Machiavelli to find a preacher for an important sermon was like asking a well-known pederast "to find a beautiful and graceful wife for a friend." We can only gaze in admiration. We might also keep an eye on the theater listings for word of a Tom Stoppard play based on this incident and the ensuing shenanigans.

The Wool Guild's woolliness set the tone, but it was only the beginning, the catalyst, perhaps, for what followed. Not to be outdone, Machiavelli wrote back right away, beginning his letter, "I was sitting on the toilet when your messenger arrived, and just at that moment I was mulling over the absurdities of the world; I was completely absorbed in imagining my style of preacher for Florence." But potty humor quickly gives way to the greater potential Machiavelli sees in the messenger himself, a mounted crossbowman dispatched by Guicciardini to hand-deliver the letter.

The messenger's galloping arrival had so impressed the monks that Machiavelli's status immediately shot up from backwater lackey to international VIP. Machiavelli reinforced the impression by dropping vague but portentous references to great personages and events supposedly implicated in the urgent missive,

> so that they all stood around with their mouths open and with their caps in hand. And even as I am writing this, I have a circle of them about me; to see me write at length, they marvel and gaze at me as at one inspired; and I, to make them marvel even more, sometimes pause writing and breathe deeply; then they absolutely begin drooling . . .

Please send another messenger tomorrow, he concludes: "let him gallop and get here covered in sweat so that this gang will be dumbfounded. By doing so you will bring me honor and at the same time give that crossbowman of yours some exercise—and it is quite healthy for the horses on these spring days." Guicciardini did so, with several added flourishes, including instructions to the crossbowman that he arrive in full emergency mode, talk loudly about how important Machiavelli is, and hand over an extra-fat packet of top-secret messages that Machiavelli can ostentatiously conceal or wave around as he sees fit.

All good fun, but the prank may have soured a bit for Machiavelli when Guicciardini's next letter came, for with it came some humanistic ruminations on history that can hardly have improved Machiavelli's self-image, even as his image with the monks was being so grossly inflated. The joke they were perpetrating had made Guicciardini think of the once-great Spartan general Lysander, whose unpopularity with his troops had brought him low:

> *My very dear Machiavelli. When I read your titles as ambassador of the republic and of friars, and I consider how many kings, dukes, and princes you have negotiated with in the past, I am reminded of Lysander, to whom, after so many victories and trophies, was given the task of distributing meat to those very same soldiers whom he had so gloriously commanded . . .*

Machiavelli's plight shows how the past repeats itself: "all the very same things return," Guicciardini says, but with the names, faces, and "extrinsic colors" changed, so that it takes wisdom to detect the pattern. "Therefore history is good and useful, because it sets before you and makes you recognize and see again what you had never known or seen." So, Guicciardini exhorts his friend, stay with your task of writing the history of Florence. The days seemingly wasted with the monks will no doubt contribute some insight of their own eventually.

Guicciardini is here referring to Machiavelli's own view that history is cyclical (which, we recall, goes back in one form or another to Polybius and the Hellenistic historians). With that advice given, Guicciardini turns back to the next installment of messages, but after the semi-serious note, the joke now seems a bit forced on his part. Machiavelli, for his part, shows no outward sign that he's tiring of it over his next two determinedly jocular letters. His only reference to Guicciardini's advice comes at the very end of his last letter from Carpi. He tries to turn that into a joke, too, but it clanks a bit.

Machiavelli was pretty much done by the time he blew into Carpi with his galloping messengers and top-secret letters. He lived six more years, during the last couple of which he succeeded in moving a bit closer to being a real international VIP again, rather than a phony one. But this was largely owing to his friendship with Guicciardini, and it hardly turned out well. Guicciardini and Machiavelli were Clement VII's main advisors in a diplomatic and military debacle that left Italy in chaos. It culminated in the horrific and protracted sack of Rome starting in May 1527 by the unpaid German mercenaries of the Habsburg emperor Charles V.* In the aftermath Medici rule was again overthrown in Florence, and Machiavelli returned to a republican Florence that same month. But he was kicked aside as a Medici collaborator. Within weeks, he fell ill and died.

In *The Prince* Machiavelli had done something truly original. Since ancient times, political theory had assumed that states should always act morally, though any reader of Thucydides knew claims of morality to be no more than a veil for self-interest. Machiavelli made the novel argument that the state's self-interest was a kind of morality in itself, and that this morality could trump conventional morality. He is often thought of as amoral, but that's wrong. Instead,

---

* Charles V (who ruled 1519–56) united Spanish and German dynastic realms inherited from both his parents, giving him a big edge over his French rivals.

he weighed one morality with another, concluding that sometimes it's desirable for the state to do evil in order to accomplish a greater good. The ends can justify the means, in other words, an argument his detractors have inveighed against ever since, while enjoying the benefits of living in nation-states that employ precisely Machiavelli's calculus.

Modern political science starts with Machiavelli. Modern history, on the other hand, starts with his friend Guicciardini.

As the pope's man, Guicciardini was exiled from Florence during the three years in which republicans again held power there. It's been suggested that the wounds of exile lay behind the implacable harshness with which Guicciardini persecuted the republicans after Clement's armies recaptured Florence in 1530 and the pope put him in charge of the city. Guicciardini had many of the republican leaders tortured and executed, driving others into exile. Whatever the reason for Guicciardini's mercilessness, it led to his being vilified by generations of Italian historians. Machiavelli, in contrast, has long been acclaimed as one of the fathers of Italian nationalism (which those doling out the praise have taken to be a good thing).

Guicciardini served Clement for several years as governor of Bologna, but he lost the position following Clement's death in 1534. After that he advised Florence's new ruler, Cosimo I de Medici, but Cosimo shut him out of public life for good in 1536. Like Machiavelli earlier, Guicciardini took advantage of his forced retirement to write, beginning work on his *History of Italy*. It would occupy him until his death four years later.

Guicciardini's *History of Italy* is contemporary history, covering the period from the first French invasion of Italy in 1494 to the death of Clement VII. The title was given to the work by its editors later, and it might almost (but not quite) have been called *A History of Europe*. Like Machiavelli, Guicciardini wrote in Italian, but within a few years of its publication the book was being translated into other European languages, starting with widely read versions in Latin (still the international language of European learning), French (which would replace Latin as the language of learning in the seventeenth century), and English. Discussed, critiqued, bowdlerized, and taken up as fodder in the unfolding struggle between Catholics and Protestants, Guicciardini's book did more than any other single source to shape our conception of his age. Poisoners, libertines, incestuous unions, "Machiavellian" politicians, sensual and indulgent "Renaissance popes"—the characters and set pieces are familiar to many who have never heard of Guicciardini himself. In his pages we find the racy portraits of the Borgias—Pope Alexander VI, along with his famous bastard children Cesare and Lucrezia—and other figures that have left such an indelible impression of this period on the popular consciousness.

Never mind that parts of this picture probably weren't true. Modern scholars, for example, doubt that the Borgias relied on poisoning to get rid of their enemies, although Guicciardini and virtually all of his contemporaries were certain they did, and Guicciardini says so explicitly in his history.

In general, though, Guicciardini gets high marks for accuracy. Still, it's not his reliability or his insight that has led modern authorities to call Guicciardini's book "the first great work of modern historiography," and the man himself "the greatest historian between Tacitus . . . and Gibbon." Nor is it how he wrote (in vernacular Italian), though that's part of it. Rather, it's how he conducted his research. Earlier historians had relied largely on, well, earlier historians, at least when writing about the distant past, and on firsthand knowledge or eyewitness accounts when writing about recent events.* Only sporadically had they turned to nonliterary sources such as documents or official records, and when they did so it was to pad out the other material. Guicciardini reversed this formula, relying on scrupulous examination of documentary evidence for the bulk of his narrative, and fleshing it out with observations based on his own experience or that of other eyewitnesses. And this is what the best historians have done ever since.**

Beyond his use of documentary sources, Guicciardini also put a new emphasis on the role of chance, or Fortune, as he calls it in the humanistic fashion. The goddess Fortuna, of course, had been around since antiquity (the Greeks had called her *Tyche*). For medieval thinkers, God controlled the world. Humanists, as their name implies, tended to replace divine control with human control. Both saw chance as supplementary—Fortuna reared her ugly head only now

---

* For this reason, ironically, modern historians often find humble chroniclers to be better historical sources than "literary" historians writing in the classical tradition. Occasionally a fuzzy-headed modern historian confuses the two roles, suggesting that because a chronicle is a more useful source, its writer is a better historian. A useful historical source is not necessarily a good work of history, nor is a good work of history on a period necessarily the best historical source for it.

** Of course, this step could occur because official documents were becoming much more plentiful than in the past, as the haphazard feudal kingdoms of the Middle Ages evolved into the efficient, centralized nation-states of modern times.

and then, on special occasions when normal control was suspended momentarily. Guicciardini put brute unpredictability at the heart of history, and, like his reliance on documentary evidence, there it has stayed.

In this he differed from his friend Machiavelli, who never gave up trying to make human events predictable and subject to human control. Both men suffered vicissitudes, but for Machiavelli the buffets of fate were a fact of life, and proper understanding combined with an iron will might overcome them. For Guicciardini, born to privilege, adversity came as a shock. His history has few heroes. Its narrative arc follows Italy's loss of independence and the fitful, restless demise of republican ideals. With Guicciardini, and Machiavelli too, humanistic history turns away from Livy and toward Tacitus.

This was oddly appropriate, given the sack of Rome by hairy unpaid Germans in 1527. Even as Guicciardini was writing his history, German writers had begun using Tacitus to establish German history on an equal footing with Italian. Germans, French, English, and others—the barbarians were restless again. "All the very same things return." In the coming decades of bloody conflict, much as it had a millennium earlier, the writing of history would once again help northern Europeans define themselves against Italy, and, above all, against Rome.

SEVEN

Point, Counterpoint

*I*f the Renaissance revived the secular ideals of antiquity, the Protestant Reformation recoiled from those ideals in disgust. What had all that humanism led to, after all? Corrupt, secular popes with corrupt, secular preoccupations!

But like the Renaissance, the Reformation had history at its heart. No less than Petrarch, Martin Luther based everything on a radical reinterpretation of the past; in this case, the traditions of the Christian church. His followers yearned to resurrect the earliest forms of Christian worship, to scrub off the dirt that centuries of human interference had deposited on the church's original shining face. Fundamentalism is always a historical project. Or at least it masquerades as one.

While humanist historians had sought to remove God from history, the new zealots from the north itched to put Him back into it. Having done that, they used history itself to advance their cause.

This entailed a bit of a contradiction, since history was part of the humanist package that the reformers seemed to be rejecting. But many of the reformers, like Luther's lieutenant, Philip Melanchthon, were humanists who used their learning in the service of reform. (Melanchthon even affected the humanist trick of rendering his original name into a "classical" form—*Schwarzerd*, German for "black earth," became *Melanchthon* in Greek.) There was really nothing new about all this. Early Christians, too, had embraced contradictory attitudes toward the classical inheritance, using what worked for them and rejecting the rest. Or, as in the case of history, adapting it to suit their needs.

Nor, for that matter, was humanism itself exclusively and purely, or even primarily, secular. Many humanists were devout Christians who worked to reconcile classical learning with Christian revelation. Like most broad movements, the currents of Renaissance, Reformation, and Counter-Reformation had countless side branches and eddies, in which secular and religious streams fed into each other.

Nothing illustrates this better than the strange phenomenon that modern scholars call "Tacitism," which refers to the international vogue that Tacitus enjoyed starting around the time of Machiavelli and Guicciardini.* To stay with our river metaphor, we might say that encountering Tacitism is like coming across maps of two different islands, each with a large stream running through it in twists and turns. By accident we happen to lay one map on top of the other. Naturally, the shapes of the islands are different. The startling part is that, when we superimpose one map on the other, with all their twists and turns, the two streams meet in the middle and merge seamlessly into one.

We recall Tacitus as the historian of Roman moral decay, of absolutism's dire consequences in all their corrupt splendor. This Tacitus was a brilliant political psychologist,

---

* See Arnaldo Momigliano, "Tacitus and the Tacitist Tradition" in *The Classical Foundations of Modern Historiography* (Berkeley, 1990), to which I'm indebted here.

a purveyor of trenchant insights in a famously biting style. He's the Tacitus that Machiavelli and Guicciardini found so apposite as a model in writing about their own disillusioned times. He would continue to find followers into the seventeenth century and beyond.

But there's another Tacitus, who shows himself in the works written before the *Annals* and the *History*, above all in the *Germania*. We skipped lightly over this short book earlier, but now it comes to the fore in quite a dramatic and unexpected way. In the *Germania*, Tacitus presents what is on the surface a rich and very Herodotean ethnographic account of the German tribes who lived north of the empire's borders. Yet, being Tacitus, he also has a moral message for his Roman readers, and this is where the two Tacituses meet and become one. In painting the Germans as noble savages—fierce in war, pious in their simple folk religion, direct in their tribal politics, and brimming with manly vigor—Tacitus implies, though he doesn't come right out and say so, that Germans are everything Romans used to be but aren't anymore.

And didn't the Germans just love that when they started reading Tacitus in the late fifteenth century. Right when they're on the point of forging a new national identity, along comes a highly respected ancient historian to tell them how wonderful their roots are. And how pure! "I agree," Tacitus writes, in blissful ignorance of how his words would help poison the future, "with those who think that the tribes of Germany are free from all taint of intermarriages with foreign nations, and that they appear as a distinct, unmixed race, like none but themselves."

The descendants of these primitive untainted Germans showed their appreciation a few centuries later by giving Tacitus refuge. Many of the best manuscripts of Tacitus's works survived the Middle Ages because they were copied by German monks in German monasteries, where they were eventually turned up by early Italian humanist book-hunters who brought them back to Italy. Then, completing the circle, Germans who came later to study at the feet of the Italians rediscovered these works all over again.

One of those German humanists was Conrad Pickel, who studied in Italy in the 1480s and Latinized his last name to Celtis. By the early 1490s, Celtis was lecturing on Tacitus in German universities, and in 1500 he published an edition of the *Germania*. It's been claimed that Celtis's lectures were the earliest example of a historical subject being taught in a university. This would make Herr Pickel, technically, at least, the first history teacher. A fierce patriot who would become best known for his lyric poetry, Celtis was determined to show that Germany could outdo Italy in its history and culture. He delved into medieval German literature, publishing (among other works) the plays of the tenth-century woman poet Hroswitha, and leaving an unfinished work, *Germania Illustrata*, which was modeled on Flavio Biondo's *Italia Illustrata*.* And this is how modern Germany got its name, from Tacitus through Celtis, though it would be several centuries yet before Germans had a unified "state" to reflect their unified "nation."

Biondo had seen the Middle Ages in humanistic terms, as a dark age in which culture was lost. This picture, you'll

* Mentioned in the last chapter.

132

recall, resulted when Petrarch "flipped" the medieval conception of a pagan dark age followed by Christian enlightenment. Celtis and his many followers in Germany essentially "flipped" the picture back over again, so that the Middle Ages appear as a period of cultural birth, with Germans as the energetic, virile nation that had shaped Europe's destiny after the collapse of an attenuated antiquity.

The new German nationalism played a central role in the Reformation that began in Germany about a decade after Celtis's death in 1508. Martin Luther is usually remembered for his (possibly apocryphal) nailing of the ninety-five theses on the door at Wittenberg Castle Church in 1517. A more incendiary tract was his *Address to the Christian Nobility of the German Nation*, published a few years later, which detailed the German people's long list of grievances against the papacy and called on Germany's secular rulers to revolt against Rome. This was a German "Declaration of Independence," cast in religious terms. It fed popular patriotic sentiment in a way that soon got completely out of hand. Having triggered a national revolt, Luther rapidly found himself trying to contain it.

Patriotic histories began appearing all around Europe, as the Spanish, French, British, Polish, and others got in on the act. Like the German efforts, some of these new historical enterprises intertwined themselves with the religious reaction against Rome sweeping the north. But while the others all had their special stories, Germans hearkened to a distinguished and authoritative voice proclaiming their uniqueness from the distant mists of antiquity. Tacitus—and

Tacitism—gave German pride a validating boost that lasted centuries.

Looking back on all this a century later, in a widely read satire called *Reports from Parnassus* (1612), the Italian writer Traiano Boccalini has the Greek god Apollo identify Martin Luther and the text of Tacitus as the two greatest evils Germany ever produced. If only. But the link was not a fanciful one. By Boccalini's time, German Protestants had rewritten the history of Christendom so that it focused on a single dominant theme: the age-old struggle of tyrannical, demonic Rome to enslave noble, pious Germany.

The Reformation was helped along, of course, by the invention of printing with movable type in Germany around the middle of the fifteenth century, which allowed the Protestants to spread the Good News with unprecedented effectiveness. And the Catholics wasted little time in firing back bombastic broadsides of their own. The ensuing war of words (or Words) was the incidental music for the actual wars that convulsed Europe during this period.

The main salvo from the Protestant side is known as the *Magdeburg Centuries* (1559–74). Compiled by various Lutheran scholars, this massive collection of articles on ecclesiastical history was planned and edited by a Croatian theologian named Matija Vlacic, which he Latinized to Matthias Flacius after settling in Germany. An inveterate controversialist (he wrangled with Philip Melanchthon many times over points of doctrine), Flacius had come to Wittenberg as a young man in 1541, five years before Luther's death, and he began work on the *Centuries* in the 1550s. He hoped to endow Lutheranism, whose greatest vulnerability was its novelty, with a shield of historical legitimacy, and he based the whole argument on Germany's divine destiny. Flacius's authors, whom posterity, predictably enough, has dubbed "the Centurions," raked over the entire history of Christian doctrine in minute detail, century by century, seeking to prove that everything good and true in it was really Lutheran and everything bad and false was really Catholic.

Even more tendentious was the Catholic answer, the *Annals* of Cardinal Cesare Baronio, whose name, naturally, was Latinized to Caesar Baronius. But this Caesar failed to live up to his famously concise namesake. Flacius and his flacks had churned out thirteen volumes; Baronius single-handedly filled twelve. Published over two decades, from 1588 to 1607, the year Baronius died, the *Annals* were riddled with errors and blatantly deceptive argumentation. Protestant critics got especially good mileage out of Baronius's poor knowledge of Hebrew and Greek, among numerous other shortcomings.[*]

Yet all the propagandizing wasn't entirely without its benefits. Both efforts involved the close examination of huge amounts of previously unpublished material,

---

[*] In its entry on Baronius, the online version of the Catholic Encyclopedia maintains of the first volume, published in 1588, that it "was universally acclaimed for its surprising wealth of inforomation [sic], its splendid erudition, and its timely vindication of papal claims. The 'Centuries' were eclipsed." The Reformation era remains a fairly cheesy corner of historical studies, owing to the high proportion of confessional participants.

especially the *Annals*. In his day job, Cardinal Baronius ran the Vatican Library, so he had unrestricted access to a treasure trove of historical documents stretching back centuries. He made heavy use of it, quoting freely and dumping entire documents unabridged into his text. However biased in their arguments, however uncritical in their marshaling of "facts" to support those arguments, these religious partisans served history by taking Guicciardini's innovation—the reliance on documentary evidence—at least a baby-step further. And if they proved nothing else, both sides performed the always-useful service of demonstrating that brevity is the soul of wit.

There were others whose work reached a higher level in quality, if not in quantity. On the Protestant side, the diplomat and lawyer Johannes Sleidanus (Johann Philip von Schleiden to his friends) wrote a political history of the Reformation that was well informed and comparatively balanced, though he followed it up with a simpler and far more partisan work of Lutheran "universal history" that was used in German schools for generations. Writing for the Catholic Counter-Reformation, the Venetian friar Paolo Sarpi pinpointed papal corruption as a major cause of the Protestants' disaffection, leading to physical attacks on his person by the ardent defenders of papal purity. Both Sleidanus and Sarpi have been praised by later historians, but all things are relative. This was an age of extreme partisanship, and for these writers as for many others of lesser stature, bias ruled in the end.

Though lacking a Tacitus to meld their glorious national origins with anti-Roman sentiment, other countries followed the German example and found their own patriotic histories soon enough. At the same time, just as movable type helped Protestants disseminate their sacred texts, it also helped humanists spread their secular ones. Printed translations of ancient historians, as well as editions in the original Greek and Latin, began appearing across Europe. Their historical lessons could always be applied to local conditions, though sometimes a little bending was required to fit the patriotic mold.

Perhaps not wholly unexpectedly, the oddest story is that of Britain, where patriotic history, like the Reformation itself, arrived in a typically eccentric fashion. The man who wrote Britain's first patriotic history wasn't British at all, but Italian. Polydore Vergil, a young Italian humanist and priest, was in his early thirties when he arrived to help collect taxes—the so-called "Peter's Pence"—on behalf of the Vatican in 1501 or 1502. Henry VII, the Tudor king whose victory over Richard III at Bosworth Field had ended the Wars of the Roses, was aging. He commissioned Vergil to write a history of his reign, but died in 1509, long before it was completed. The throne passed to the young Henry VIII, under whose royal aegis Vergil carried on his work, expanding it into a history of Britain from Roman times up to his own.

His history is insightful and critical, but Vergil also aimed to please his Tudor patrons. He went out of his way, for instance, to portray Richard III as a twisted, crippled, princes-in-the-tower murdering villain. A generation later, the English chronicler Raphael Holinshed took that and other historical portraits straight out of Vergil; shortly afterward they found their way into Shakespeare's history plays, for which Holinshed was the major source. Vergil also did us the favor of demolishing a twelfth-century pseudo-historical concoction that had been taken far too seriously for far too long, *The History of the Kings of Britain* by Geoffrey of Monmouth. While it's wonderful literature (it, too, would be a source for Shakespeare, and its Arthurian material helped inspire Thomas Malory), Geoffrey's fanciful "history" had little basis in reality.

Though he lived out nearly all the rest of his life in England, Vergil remained a good Roman at heart. He may have shown the Tudors in a positive light, but his history was of only limited use in justifying Henry VIII's split with Rome. Nor did the first humanist history written by an Englishman (another unfavorable portrait of Richard III, also used heavily by Shakespeare) help much in that regard, penned as it was by the equally loyal Catholic Sir Thomas More, whom Henry VIII executed for refusing to go along with the uncanonical royal divorce that initiated the English Reformation.

Polydore Vergil died in 1555. History's next big steps in Britain were taken by three heavyweights who were born right around that time: William Camden, born in 1551; Sir Walter Raleigh, born in 1552, and Sir Francis Bacon, born in 1561. The latter two, of course, are better known for other accomplishments and wrote history as a sideline to wide-ranging literary and intellectual pursuits. Camden is known primarily for writing scholarly history, which may be partly why he isn't much known at all, except by scholarly historians.

Not that he was negligible. Born in London and educated at Oxford, William Camden was a schoolmaster before the grant of two stipends—one from the Church of England, the other from the king (which after the Reformation technically amounted to the same thing)—freed him to write full-time when he was in his mid-forties. His two major works were *Britannia*, a topographical and antiquarian treatment of the British Isles in the manner of Biondo, and his highly patriotic *Annals of English and Irish History in the Reign of Queen Elizabeth*, on which most later accounts of the Elizabethan Age have been founded.

Camden was a learned and groundbreaking antiquarian, but he lacked Raleigh's personal and literary flair or Bacon's restlessly probing intellect. Raleigh's sensational *History of the World*—written in the Tower of London as the fallen courtier awaited execution—was far more widely read by contemporaries than either of Camden's books, while Bacon's *History of the Reign of King Henry VII* possessed a philosophical dimension that was missing from Camden's erudite but partisan disquisitions, and which saved it from being merely a rehashing of a by-now-familiar story. With his lively wit and astringent judgments, Bacon, not Camden, was the English successor to Machiavelli and Guicciardini.

In the meantime, French historians had found their own patriotic approach to the past in the rapidly growing area of legal history, as they struggled to clarify the tangled strands of French law. German and British law had remained unencumbered by the Roman tradition, which was embodied in the ponderous sixth-century compilation known as the Code of Justinian, after the emperor who commissioned it. The Code officially governed the south of France, while unwritten provincial custom generally held sway in the north. The very practical need to reconcile these disparate legal systems provided an impetus for scholarly historical inquiry in France, but as that inquiry revolved around Roman influences, it lent itself quite easily to the same sort of patriotic and religious controversy sweeping the rest of the continent. And if the path the French historians took was different, they shared with their German and British counterparts the same point of origin in the humanist scholarship of the Italian Renaissance. Once again, all roads lead to Rome. Or away from it, as the case may be.

EIGHT

New Worlds

A couple of decades before Catholics and Protestants began rioting against each other in Europe, America discovered Christopher Columbus, who rowed ashore on an island he called San Salvador with large amounts of undeclared baggage that started detonating almost immediately. Nor was landfall in America entirely unconnected with the religious struggle that broke out in Europe a generation later. As it turned out, Columbus brought undeclared baggage home, too.

Rarely has anything been so revealingly named as the New World that Europeans now began plundering, infecting, and occupying, although, as often happens in such cases, the name tells us more about the namers than it does about the named. About the named, sadly, we know all too little, lacking a clear understanding of even such basic matters as population levels in the pre-contact Americas.* The vacuum is in part accidental, but, substantially, also quite deliberate. Although dwarfed by the untold human suffering it helps to hide, the effacement of that world as it existed before being crushed beneath the horrifying burden

---

* The population of the Americas on the arrival of the Europeans has been a subject of controversy in recent years, owing largely to new research suggesting that it was much, much larger than earlier assumed. For a summary, see chapters 2 and 3 of James W. Loewen's superb analysis of American high school history textbooks, *Lies My Teacher Told Me* (1995; rev. ed. 2007).

of someone else's newness still constitutes a grievous loss to history.

In other ways, however, Europe's invention of the New World boosted history vigorously, much as it invigorated Europe and European culture in general. For a start, it shook the Old World to its core, rattling ancient certainties, overturning previously unnoticed assumptions, widening pinched outlooks and perspectives. So when we go to grasp the implications of Columbus's landfall for Europeans, we find not the monolithic block of a single new world but a leafy proliferation of them that gives the impression of spilling copiously over our narrow retrospective horizon. More probing than the roots of climbing ivy, these new worlds insinuated themselves into venerable edifices of belief, implacably and relentlessly prying them apart.

And one of the first edifices to crumble was the immense and imposing slab of church authority. For a millennium the church had jealously affirmed its exclusive knowledge of the world. Over the course of the sixteenth century, two vast continents' worth of previously unknown peoples, animals, plants, mountains, lakes, rivers, forests, and coastlines gradually took shape in the European imagination, where they asserted a compelling hold. Yet no passage of scripture, no prophet, no pope, no visionary saint had ever hinted at their existence. America gave the lie to the aura of omniscience and infallibility on which the medieval church had staked its claims to be the last word on everything. No less than humanism—maybe more—the shock of the "new" cast doubt on virtually every major aspect of Catholic teaching. Simply by existing (and, more importantly, by being shown to exist), America constantly ratified the impulse to question authority, to investigate, to look and think for oneself.

In this basic way the navigators and the humanists pushed out together. Geographical and intellectual exploration fed into each other, creating a globally consequential feedback loop that spun into being not just new empires and new worlds, but also, a new cosmos. The ancient authority Ptolemy, whose church-sanctioned geography specified an earth with three continents and whose church-sanctioned cosmology put that small earth at the center of the universe, was the biggest casualty of this dual revolution. At almost exactly the time Columbus proved Ptolemy wrong about the earth's size, a young Polish astronomer, Nicolaus Copernicus, began the studies that would also prove him wrong about its place. One of Copernicus's inspirations was the humanistic curriculum of Italy, where he spent several years studying Greek philosophy around the turn of the sixteenth century.

That coming century saw rapid advances in secular learning, as these discoveries stimulated inquiry across the board, not just in the broad realms of geography and cosmology, but also in smaller scientific niches such as biology, botany, and zoology, as well as what would eventually be called the social sciences, primarily history. This included legal history, but also ethnography and nascent disciplines like anthropology, political science, and political philosophy. Historians today call this process "the Columbian exchange," noting the many good things—gold, potatoes, corn, democratic values—that crossed over to Europe from the Americas, though that begs the question of what exactly the Americas got in return.

With its new ways of looking outward, what Europe really discovered was itself. That may sound grand, but such processes are never easy. This age of exploration, colonization, and secular learning was also an age of turbulent self-redefinition. Physics would soon advance to the point where it could tell us that for every action there is an equal and opposite reaction. Perhaps a historical equivalent of Newton's dictum can be applied to the progress of such secular understanding itself. It would help account for the grim, often desperate, ferocity with which the backward faithful sought to defend or to assert their threatened identities at home and overseas. As we saw in the last chapter, the writing (or rewriting) of history emerged as one of the most attractive ways of justifying this struggle. For better or for worse, history was now taking on the part it so often plays today, as the trampled and torn-up turf over which we fight our bitterest culture wars.*

For better and for worse, since this role can be both fractious and fruitful. If the genocidal treatment of America's original inhabitants represents a crime against humanity with only a few rivals (one being the contemporaneous enslavement of millions of Africans meant to replace the dying "Indians" as a source of labor), the horror did not go as unobserved—or, for that matter, as uncondemned—by

---

* Culture warriors, we might observe in this context, tend to enslave history as an identity-buffer, with "buffer" being taken in two senses—either as a spongy partition between impossibly self-contained and eternally clashing entities, or as a device for artificially polishing something dull to make it more attractive to oneself and others.

Europeans as we might imagine. Even at the very beginning. The Spanish conquest of the Americas was not the unified national killing and looting spree we tend to see it as now. Almost from the start, the conquest was powerfully contested by Spanish voices. These voices asked the same basic question as everyone else—Who are we, really?—but they refused to settle for the common answers.

As we've seen, history often stands in the mainstream of such answers. Yet to its everlasting glory, it can also stand at the cutting edge of the refusal to accept them, though in this case it's only fair to insist that religion deserves much of the credit, too. While the backward faithful were busy rousing each other to slaughter, the enlightened faithful could still put together a strong case for brotherly love. The campaign to stop the Spanish conquest was led by a writer who may be the most remarkable figure we'll meet in these pages, a man most readers have probably never heard of but who has been called "the first great historian of the Americas": the Dominican priest Bartolomé de Las Casas, who fused history and Christian morality in a distinctive and compelling way that's all his own. That Las Casas wrote what he did when he did is impressive in itself. What's more impressive still is how close he came to altering history rather than merely writing it.

Bartolomé de Las Casas was a boy of eight when he first laid eyes on Christopher Columbus in the streets of Seville. It was April 1493, just a few weeks after the suddenly famous navigator's triumphant return from his first voyage. With

Columbus were the seven surviving Taino of the original ten to twenty-five he'd captured. The exotic party caused a sensation as it passed through Seville, where Bartolomé's father scraped a living as a merchant. Decades later, when Las Casas was writing his *History of the Indies* as an older man, the thrill was still fresh. The newly minted Admiral of the Ocean Sea "left Seville with as much finery as he could gather," including "beautiful green parrots," "masks made of precious stones and fishbone," belts "of the same composition admirably contrived, sizable samples of very fine gold, and many other things never before seen in Spain. The news spread over Castile like fire that a land called the Indies had been discovered, and that it was full of people and things so diverse and so new . . ."

That September, when Columbus embarked on his second voyage to the Indies, Las Casas's father and two uncles sailed with him. The father returned five years later, with a young Taino whom he handed over to be Bartolomé's slave, though Queen Isabella would eventually order the man to be freed and returned to the Indies. And in 1502, Las Casas joined his father in the fleet of the newly appointed governor, Nicolás de Ovando, which was carrying Spanish colonists to Santo Domingo, the port city on the island of Hispaniola that was Spain's first colonial capital.

Las Casas was eighteen at this point, and still very much the enthusiastic young colonial. He became an *encomendero*, owning and running a large estate (or *encomienda*) that relied on the labor of Indian slaves, and began moving up in the secular religious orders as well. He returned to Europe for a couple of years, and in 1507 he was ordained as a priest in Rome, though he did not yet join the Dominican order. He made his way back to Hispaniola and his estate, where he tried to treat his slaves humanely but did not, by his own unsparing account, trouble himself too much about the issue.

Then, just before Christmas of 1511, he heard a controversial sermon by a Dominican priest named Antón Montesino, who unequivocally condemned the ongoing massacre and enslavement of the Indians as a hideous sin and demanded that the Spanish recognize the Indians' equal rights as fellow human beings.* Montesino's passionate pleas on the Indians' behalf drew the colonists' ire, but Las Casas doesn't tell us much about his own immediate reaction, if any. Though he didn't join the angry calls for Montesino to retract his words—demands the Dominican spurned—neither was he ready to abandon his participation in the system.

Yet the arguments stayed with him, percolating quietly over the next few years, as did similar encounters with other Dominicans, who impressed Las Casas but still failed to sway him to action. Then two events combined to bring Las Casas's inner conflict to a head.

---

* It's a fascinating window on the complexity of historical perspective that the highly respected Las Casas scholar Lewis Hanke, in his revisionist book *The Spanish Struggle for Justice in the Conquest of America,* would call Montesino's sermon the "first cry on behalf of liberty in the New World" (p. 17). I'm indebted to Hanke's book, which revolutionized our picture of the conquest on its publication in 1949, for much of the information in this chapter. But his claim about Montesino shows how unconscious assumptions can create blind spots in even the best historiography. By ignoring the possibility of any previous cries from the Indians themselves, either during the conquest or, indeed, before it (can we really assume that thousands of years of human habitation in the Americas would have witnessed no cries for liberty?), Hanke unwittingly dehumanizes the very people whose defense by Montesino, Las Casas, and others his book so compellingly recounts.

The first was the conquest of Cuba, where Las Casas, who was acting as a military chaplain, witnessed Spanish soldiers indiscriminately cutting down Indians in the hundreds. He tried to stop the slaughter, managing to save a small group. But when he confronted the commander, the man just sat on his horse, "without speaking, acting, or moving any more than if he had been marble." The man's stony coldness obviously hit a nerve, a little detail in the midst of the bloodletting, perhaps, yet one that suggests the high value Las Casas placed on simple human warmth.

The second precipitating event occurred shortly afterward, as Las Casas was reading scripture while preparing a sermon for Easter. He was struck by one passage in particular: "Tainted his gifts who offers in sacrifice ill-gotten goods. . . . Like the man who slays his neighbor is he who offers sacrifice from the possessions of the poor" (Ecclesiasticus, chapter 34). His reading caused him "to reflect on the misery and servitude that those peoples suffered," and as he did so the words and actions of the Dominicans he had met came back to him with renewed force. As Las Casas himself presents it, he was converted.

Indeed, his change of heart clearly represents an affirmation of his deepest religious values, and we should keep in mind that his political activities would always be subordinated to the missionizing goal of saving the Indians' souls. The stand he took now was on how that aim should be accomplished—not by bloody coercion and empty mass baptisms, but by reasoned persuasion and respectful compassion. The Indians must be accepted as equals who were free to choose for themselves and, he would eventually demand, to govern themselves.

Vigorous at forty, Las Casas possessed formidable legal and religious book learning as well as wide practical experience. The first step was to put his own house in order, by renouncing his estate and giving up the enslaved Indians that came with it. He did this with some hesitation, knowing full well that a new owner would likely treat the Indians more harshly than he himself had. He saw, though, that credibility plainly required it. He also saw that challenging the *encomienda* system from the Americas was out of the question, and so in the fall of 1515 he went back to Spain and secured an audience with the elderly and failing King Ferdinand, who was too close to death for the meeting to bring any results.

The king died soon after, and the Spanish throne passed to the Habsburg king of the Netherlands, Ferdinand's young and inexperienced grandson Charles, who would soon be elected emperor of the Holy Roman Empire as Charles V.* Many Spanish were suspicious and resentful of the new king, and a period of instability ensued. Officially, at least, power resided in two men: the influential Francisco Cardinal Jiménez, Archbishop of Toledo, and the Dutch religious scholar Adrian of Utrecht, Charles's teacher, and later, Pope Adrian VI. They acted as co-regents until Charles's much-delayed arrival. Writing alternately in scholarly Latin (to Adrian) and the purest Castilian (to Jiménez), Las Casas besieged both men over the next couple

---

* Readers will recall Charles V from chapter 6, where we saw his German mercenaries sacking Rome in 1527.

of years with a series of letters in which he condemned the colonials' treatment of the Indians and suggested several ways of improving their situation.

Among those proposals was one that Las Casas would very quickly find reason to regret, but which would be linked to his name, perhaps unfairly, forever afterward. This was his suggestion to free enslaved Indians and replace them with enslaved Africans, which later writers seized on to condemn Las Casas as the founder of the African slave trade to the Americas. But that trade was already under way by the time he first came to America in 1502.

Las Casas had hastily assumed that the Africans so enslaved were prisoners of a just war, whom sixteenth-century European mores held might justifiably be enslaved. When he realized that this was not the case, he immediately took back his proposal. As he writes in his *History of the Indies* (referring to himself in the third person, as was his habit):

> When the cleric Las Casas first gave that advice—to grant the licence to bring black slaves to the islands—he was not aware of the unjust ways in which the Portuguese captured and made slaves of them. But after he found out, he would not have proposed it for all the world, because from the beginning the black people of Africa were enslaved unjustly and tyrannically, exactly as had happened to the Indians.

In his zeal to protect the Indians, he had overstepped. He knew it, he admitted it, and after this he became one of the very few voices from his age to cry out against the universally accepted practice of chattel slavery.

The other main proposal called for the resettlement of freed Indian slaves in planned communities, networks of small agricultural villages, which Las Casas hoped might act as labor-supplying suburbs for major Spanish towns and cities. The Indians would share in the profits of their labor, and would be looked after by their Spanish employers, who would be legally bound to supply medical care in hospitals that they would fund. As Las Casas still envisioned it, the Indians would be Spanish subjects, owing tribute and obedience to the Spanish monarch; they would be joined by Spanish farmer-colonists, who would teach them farming techniques and treat them as equals. Eventually, Indians and Spanish would intermarry and create a new American civilization.

Las Casas laid out this utopian scheme in a treatise entitled "Petition on Remedies for the Indies" in 1516, the same year—not entirely coincidentally—that Thomas More published his own original and more radical *Utopia*, also set somewhere in the New World. However, it was not for nothing that More coined the word *utopia* from the Greek for "No Place." Despite the support of Jiménez and Charles V, like so many similar plans, Las Casas's crashed and burned when put to the test of reality. In 1520 Las Casas sailed from Spain to establish a community in what is now Venezuela, but the project was crippled by a dearth of Spanish participants and opposition from the *encomendero* establishment. After an attack by the now-hostile Indians themselves, the community disbanded.

Deeply demoralized by this utter failure to realize his vision, Las Casas backed away for nearly a decade from further efforts at reform. Retreating into spiritual contemplation, he joined the Dominican order and became a monk in Hispaniola. There he stayed, despite letters of ongoing support that reached him from Adrian of Utrecht, now Pope Adrian VI. About this period he tells us little except to say that for several years "he, to all appearances, slept," and that only after this prolonged slumber did he slowly begin to rouse himself.

He did so first by starting work on the introduction to a history of the Spanish presence in the Americas. Focusing on the geography and culture of the Indians themselves, this ethnographic survey eventually grew to such a size that he split it off from the main work, publishing it separately as *The Apologetic History of the Indies*. The other he left, deliberately, to be published after his death as *The History of the Indies*. This is the work in which he described the early voyages of Columbus and the subsequent colonization of the Americas. It is notable not only for its richness of detail and narrative, but also for its verbatim inclusion of Columbus's own journal record of the voyage, which would otherwise have been lost to posterity.

These two monumental works, along with many smaller ones along the way, consumed a large part of Las Casas's energy over the remaining four decades of his life. But before much time had passed, he also returned to the political struggle with which all of his writing would always be intertwined, and of which he now became the acknowledged leader.

This phase of activism carried Las Casas through the 1530s and culminated, after many debates and much lobbying on both sides, in what appeared to be a great victory for Las Casas and his allies in the Spanish justice movement: the passage of the so-called New Laws of 1542, under which both Indian slavery and the *encomienda* system itself would be abolished within a generation.

Except that it never happened. Once again, despite the full support of Charles V—who was, on paper at least, quite possibly the most powerful man in the world—Las Casas's lofty ideals settled with the weight of a down feather on the rock of entrenched interests. Las Casas himself was elevated to the rank of bishop and charged with enforcing the New Laws in the New World. The infuriated *conquistadores* and *encomenderos* would have none of it. Faced with their obstinate noncompliance and even outright rebellion, Charles had to back down, and the New Laws were gutted just a few years after being enacted.

This time, however, Las Casas met defeat not by withdrawing but by renewing the attack. He immediately produced a set of twelve rules to guide priests in giving—or, more to the point, not giving—confession to *conquistadores* and *encomenderos*. The denial of confession had long been a powerful lever for priests who hoped to improve the treatment of the Indians. Indeed, before his "conversion," Las Casas had himself been refused confession by a Dominican, and this had been one of the memorable encounters that had helped sway him all those years ago.

Now Las Casas took it to a whole new level. His rules demanded that all penitents be denied absolution until they had provided restitution to the Indians, including restoring their freedom and all property. It was a blatant attempt to revive the New Laws almost literally by divine fiat. On top of that, Las Casas included in his rules explicit rejections of the pope's original right to donate the Americas to the king, and thus of the king's own sovereignty over them.* The conquest itself, in other words, was illegal.

Returning to Spain in 1547, Las Casas was challenged by the man who had, during Las Casas's absence over the past few years, become his strongest opponent—the formidable humanist scholar Juan Ginés de Sepúlveda. Sepúlveda seized on the radical provisions in Las Casas's rules that undermined papal and royal authority, denouncing him to the Inquisition for heresy and high treason. Although the Inquisition does not seem to have acted against Las Casas, the ensuing contest between Las Casas and Sepúlveda lasted years and reflected deep ideological and political divisions in Spanish society. It reached its climax—or, rather, its anticlimax—in the celebrated dispute they conducted before a panel of theologians at the Council of Valladolid in 1550–51.

Las Casas and Sepúlveda never actually faced each other at Valladolid, but instead made separate appearances before the judges. Sepúlveda went first and spoke for three hours. Las Casas's answer took up five days, and consisted of his reading aloud from a painstakingly prepared 550-page tract in Latin. As Sepúlveda joked, it seemed Las Casas's testimony would last either until the whole thing had been read, or until the judges couldn't take it anymore. An outside expert had to be called in to summarize Las Casas's

---

* The papal "donation" of the Americas to Spain and Portugal was formalized in the Treaty of Tordesillas (1494).

main arguments (there were no fewer than twelve of them) for the gobsmacked panelists. Sepúlveda got a rebuttal, Las Casas responded with a rebuttal of his own, and that was that. The judges went off and tried their best to forget the whole thing. They never rendered a decision. Perhaps by then everyone realized that what was decided in Spain mattered less than what was decided on the spot. Those who held the whip hand were Sepúlveda men all the way.

Even if Las Casas hadn't been so long-winded, the judges might still have been nonplussed. The two learned rivals focused largely on their differing interpretations of a single passage of Aristotle, in which the Greek philosopher had suggested that some people were suited by nature for slavery. In fact, it's entirely unclear exactly what Aristotle meant—he doesn't elaborate—and modern scholars suspect that neither Sepúlveda nor Las Casas had a proper understanding of Aristotle anyway.

Beneath the tedious wrangling over Aristotle, however, lies the wicked question that had been dividing the Spanish all along, but that had been articulated only in fits and starts up to then: Were the Indians fully human, or were they somehow less than human, inferior or bestial creatures who could justifiably (the thinking went) be murdered, enslaved, dispossessed, plundered, and otherwise abused?

Aristotelian speculation aside, Las Casas not only affirmed the Indians' humanity, but he went even further by turning the question back on the people who were posing it, to ask what it revealed about the Spanish themselves. Not in the way we might expect, however. Characteristically, he did this by combining a historical outlook with a religious one. In brutalizing the Indians, Las Casas argued, the Spanish were sealing their own historical fate, because God would surely lay waste to them and their empire for such a horrific crime. What goes around comes around, as today's pop culture might put it.

Despite the anticlimax at Valladolid, Las Casas emerged, if anything, stronger at court than before. Sepúlveda's supremacist tracts were officially banned from publication, some for centuries, while Las Casas, in contrast, shortly afterward published his strongest defense yet of the Indians, an abridged version of the *Apologetic History* that he had composed a decade earlier. Titled *A Short Account of the Destruction of the Indies*, this is the book modern audiences are most likely to know.

As a historian, Las Casas has some gaping holes, especially in his black-and-white treatment of the two sides. The Indians, who can do no wrong, are uniformly presented as gentle, meek, rational, and submissive, an undifferentiated mass of Christ-like sufferers. Even Las Casas's voluminous ethnographic screed reflects little cultural variation among the various native peoples, though it did much to establish the soon-to-be-commonplace cliché of the "noble savage." It's as if someone writing about Europeans lumped them all together, Irish and Greeks, Slovenes and Scots. By the same token, the Spaniards are all bloodthirsty oppressors, driven only by greed, lusting for gold, and caring nothing for Christian compassion.

On the other hand, Las Casas's writing has some curious strengths, not least of which is that he finally freed Christian historical writing from its ancient ecclesiastical straitjacket. Temporarily, to be sure, but for once, an avowedly "Christian" historian is concerned with actual human suffering, instead of with glorifying the worldly church, defending dogma, and condemning everyone else as heretics. Las Casas was the anti-Eusebius. We might say that he put the Christ back in Christian history, if it had ever been there in the first place, which it hadn't. This is all the more striking because he wrote during a period when other Christian historians were more concerned than ever with sectarian propagandizing.

Likewise, if Las Casas broke away from the pack of church historians, no less did he move beyond those previous secular historians who had written overtly moralizing history. Whether bluff, hearty soldiers or learned scholars, most had viewed morality in shallow terms that were limited to politics and war: good king Richard versus bad king John. Machiavelli, as we've seen, twisted moralizing history into a more-sophisticated shape, yet still molded it from the same political material. Again, Las Casas's originality, and his astonishing modernity, lie in the deceptively simple step of focusing on human suffering.* If Las Casas was the anti-Eusebius, he was also the anti-Machiavelli.

In neither capacity, we might add, did he have any real successors until the rise of the abolition movement in the nineteenth century. Indeed, a figure such as John Brown, though not a historian, offers some interesting parallels. We observe, for example, that both were accused of religious

---

* It would take secular philosophy two centuries to catch up with Las Casas, which it finally did in the writings of David Hume, who defined morality as concern for the well-being of others.

insanity by their many detractors, and even by some of their ideological allies.

Las Casas's profound outrage at the deliberate infliction of suffering gives him his modern feel, but he has another quality that commends him to us just as much. We admire his indignation, certainly, then so unpopular but now so "politically correct"; we applaud his uncompromising commitment to doing the right thing, the Christian thing; we celebrate his wide-ranging if rather superficial curiosity about the indigenous peoples whom he championed so tirelessly. Yet Las Casas was more than a sixteenth-century avatar of humanitarian values prized more highly today than in his own time (if indeed that's what he was at all, and if indeed we prize those values more than Las Casas's contemporaries, both of which claims should perhaps be treated with skepticism). He must also be counted as one of the most unflinchingly honest writers of all time, always as hard (or harder) on himself than on others.

In describing his own conduct before his "conversion," for example, Las Casas refuses to soft-pedal his complicity as an *encomendero*, owning and profiting from Indian slaves. Nor does he try to let himself off the hook for his brief and limited support of African slavery, or for a share in the collective guilt of belonging to a slave-owning society. With regard to his suggestion that African slaves could replace the Indians, "he was not sure that his ignorance in this matter and his good intentions would excuse him in the court of divine justice." We are all guilty, he continues, of the sins committed by the slavers, "not to mention our own sin of buying the slaves."

While his outrage may make him feel modern, it's his honesty that lends his books their immense gravity. Without it, he's nowhere, and he knows it. All historians, of course, lean on our trust, but Las Casas does so to an unusual degree—one that corresponds to the unusual nature of his subject. Like the Jews who wrote under the leading edge of another genocidal wave four centuries later, resolutely recording names, dates, every grim detail they could—as much hard information as possible before they themselves were erased from the world—Las Casas writes to commemorate events whose horrific reality he knows will be hard to accept for those who did not witness them. He says as much, over and over, desperately. A pose of honesty won't do. The stakes are too high. So he gives us the real thing.

His openness about his own behavior inclines us to accept his basic historical point that the root cause of the genocide was simple greed. But at bottom it's a visionary's honesty, not a historian's:

> *Greed increased every day and every day Indians perished in greater numbers and the clergyman Bartolomé de Las Casas, whom we mentioned earlier, went about his concerns like the others, sending his share of Indians to work fields and gold mines, taking advantage of them as much as he could. He always tried to maintain them well, treat them mildly and pity their misery but, like everyone else, he neglected the fact that they were infidels in need of indoctrination into the Christian fold.*

To a modern secular reader, at least, the last part jars a bit—we expect a ringing declaration of the Indians' equal

rights as human beings, not a call for their religious indoc-
trination. And elsewhere Las Casas does make such declara-
tions. But this passage reminds us of the religious impulse
behind them.

Though he never returned to America, Las Casas lived
another decade and a half after his inconclusive contest
with Sepúlveda at Valladolid, dying at the age of eighty in
Madrid in 1566. During this time, he remained an influential figure at the Spanish court, where he continued to
produce long speeches and dense treatises in defense of
the Indians. Sepúlveda was eclipsed in Spain, his writings
banned, his arguments against the humanity of the Indians
ostensibly discounted by the elegant courtiers and coun-
selors who tugged at the strings of empire, and who now
replaced the term *conquest* with the much-copied imperial
euphemism, *pacification*. Overseas, on the other hand, the
conquistadores and *encomenderos* held Sepúlveda up as their
hero and carried on pretty much as before. In Mexico City,
the Town Council voted to thank him officially with a gift
of two hundred pesos' worth of jewels and clothing. Only
much later would Las Casas, who would be idolized by
revolutionary leaders such as Simón Bolívar, have statues
erected to him in town squares throughout Central and
South America.

In the meantime, other historians on both sides followed up on Las Casas's example, with the predictable and
all-too-familiar result that this ideological struggle rapidly
took on the dimensions of a historical controversy. In 1571,
for instance, the indignant Spanish viceroy of Peru commissioned an assistant, one Pedro Sarmiento de Gamboa,

to write a history of Peru that would counter the ample documentation of Spanish brutality dating back to Francisco Pizarro's celebrated campaign against the Incas four decades earlier. Sarmiento's history painted the Incas as bloodthirsty tyrants whose unmitigated cruelty entirely justified the Spanish takeover. When it was ready, the viceroy commanded the "principal and most able descendants" of the Incas to gather, along with the few wizened surviving *conquistadores* who had accompanied Pizarro, so that the history could be read to them and they could solemnly approve its veracity. Yet when the viceroy sent it back to Spain, the king and court ignored it, despite the fact that one of its main points was to reinforce royal title to American lands. It was never published.

In one form or another, the "black legend" of Spanish cruelty has been the central issue in Spanish and Latin American historiography ever since Las Casas. Even during the late twentieth century, academic historians of all ideological stripes bristled at each other in print over Las Casas and Sepúlveda, Sarmiento and the Incas, gold and civilization, cruelty and tyranny. Las Casas has cast a long shadow.

But perhaps a strangely narrow one. Desperation to tell one big truth seems to have prevented Las Casas from seeing smaller, discordant truths. And small discordant truths make up the fabric of history no less than big harmonious ones—even more, many historians would argue.

Still, if modern readers may doubt his black-and-white portrayal of noble Indians versus rapacious Spaniards, we cannot doubt that black-and-white was how Las Casas saw his moral environment. However simplistic, however rooted in faith, his vision possessed power enough to seek out and explore human territory that earlier historians had never suspected lay over the horizon. How sad that no one rushed in to exploit *that* new world for history.

NINE

The Challenge of Reason

In 1657, an English bookseller named William London published a reference guide entitled *A Catalogue of the Most Vendible Books in England*. In the fashion of the day, London's directory carried on its title page the lengthy subtitle *Orderly and Alphabetically Digested Under the Heads of Divinity, History, Physick and Chyrurgery, Law, Arithmetick, Geometry, Astrology, Dialling, Measuring Land and Timber, Gageing, Navigation, Architecture, Horsmanship, Faulconry, Merchandize, Limning, Military Discipline, Heraldry, Fortification and Fire-works, Husbandry, Gardening, Romances, Playes, & c.* Of this imposing list, only the first three—divinity, history, and "physick and chyrurgery"—got large print the same size as the title itself, while the subsequent lesser "heads" got smaller print.

From three and a half centuries' distance we may have difficulty putting our fingers immediately on the meanings of some of these terms, but their inclusion on London's charming title page means that they represented subjects of considerable interest to English readers.* And the ranking of "history" at second place (after "divinity," no less, suggesting that history, not cleanliness, is next to godliness) reflects

---

* *Dialling* refers to the construction of sundials, *gageing* to gambling, and *limning* to painting. *Physick* refers not to physics—which, interestingly, is not represented—but to medicine, while *chyrurgery* (from the Greek for "laying on of hands," as in the more-familiar "chiropractor") refers to surgery.

the large proportion of history books in London's catalog of best-sellers. Literature and literacy were about to embark on a period of explosive growth in Britain and elsewhere—coffeehouses and the earliest newspapers and magazines were just around the corner for London's London—and history would be right there at the center of it. Ancient historians—Herodotus, Plutarch, Livy, Tacitus, Suetonius—were being translated and gobbled up eagerly; the first scholarly achievement of the young Thomas Hobbes was a translation of Thucydides, published in 1629. Meanwhile, humanistic historians carried on the tradition of colorful if often unreliable narratives of more-recent events.

Paradoxically, however, even as historians ancient and modern were connecting with a wide new readership, history itself was subjected to renewed attacks by those who, echoing Aristotle's indictment of two millennia earlier, questioned its very legitimacy as a branch of knowledge. Herodotus, who stoutly maintained that success incurs the envy of the gods, might have enjoyed the irony.

And there is a distinctly Greek flavor to the whole situation, arising as it did out of the rebirth of secular reason in the Scientific Revolution and the Enlightenment that followed.* History's new critics may have been the heirs of Aristotle in their dislike of history, but they were also the

---

* The Scientific Revolution is generally held to have begun in the mid-sixteenth century, when Copernicus proposed that the earth revolves around the sun, and to have culminated in the work of Isaac Newton, who proposed his theories of gravity and motion in the late seventeenth century. The Enlightenment (also called the Age of Reason) is considered to have built on these accomplishments, beginning with writers such as Rene Descartes (d. 1650) in France and John Locke (d. 1704) in England, and to have ended, rather abruptly, one might feel, with the French Revolution (1789).

ones who overturned Aristotle as the eternal, unquestioned authority in all things. Of course, with its Oedipal overtones, that's a rather Greek-flavored irony, too.

The role of nemesis in this drama is played by that archrationalist, Rene Descartes, whose celebrated dictum *cogito ergo sum* ("I think, therefore I am") set the world of thinking on its ear in the first half of the seventeenth century. That world was dominated by the resurgence of Skepticism, which when we write it with a capital "S" denotes a specific philosophical school that questions the possibility of certain knowledge. Because Skepticism was originally a strand of ancient Greek philosophy, its resurgence was part of the larger rediscovery of ancient thought that began with the Renaissance.

The most influential champion of Skepticism in the Renaissance had been the sixteenth-century French essayist Michel de Montaigne, a great fan of the ancient historians, whom he cites constantly (along with other classical authors from Homer to Marcus Aurelius). Montaigne didn't think very highly of thinking. He described the mind as "all the time turning, contriving, and entangling itself in its own work, like a silk-worm; and there it suffocates, 'a mouse in pitch.' "

Descartes wanted to cut through the entangling silk, to unstick the mouse, to show that there was, after all, a high ground of certainty and clarity that thinkers could aspire to. Though he died in 1650, his dialogue with the Skeptics lasted the rest of that century and beyond. Descartes built a scaffold that he hoped would allow him to bypass the carping Skeptics and scale the summit of certainty. One certain truth could be known, Descartes proclaimed: the fact that I think proves that I exist. (Not really, the Skeptics responded; it just proves that you *think* you exist!) And if thinking proves my existence, then the things I think about must also exist. (Think of a unicorn, then, said the Skeptics.) On this basis, Descartes believed he could establish, for example, the existence of God and of the soul.

But not history. Descartes' obsessive appetite for certainty led him not only to trash historical knowledge as invalid, but also to deny the significance of the past entirely, since any perception of it (he claimed) was based solely on faulty human memory. And memory, he said further, was precisely where human thinking about the world most commonly went wrong.

Ironically, this extended the same line taken by Thucydides himself, who anticipated Aristotle in suggesting that because the distant past was unrecoverable, he would focus on the immediate past, for which he presumed the evidence would be firmer and more reliable. He did this, we recall, in the guise of the objective, scientific reporter. But in donning a scientist's lab coat, Thucydides opened the door to a perpetual fancy-dress ball in which historians could never compete on an equal footing. Subsequent thinkers like Aristotle and Descartes could always outdo them with more-authentic scientific getups that put the historians' clownish costumes to shame.

This is the historian's eternal insecurity, which we might call "test-tube envy." Nothing in the past is recoverable with absolute "scientific" certainty, so the insecure historian suspects deep down inside that the whole enterprise of history might be useless. The answer for many has always been to add flourishes to the Thucydidean disguise—graph paper, calculators, pocket protectors—in a strained and (I would argue) gratuitous attempt to legitimize their endeavor.

In reaction to the rise of modern science, in other words, with all its awe-inspiring explanatory power, we have the at least partly defensive rise of so-called "modern scientific history." Optimistic, ambitious, and often quite powerful itself, this immature impostor nonetheless stands revealed in the end as a naive, overconfident, and somewhat pathetic creature, a child dressing up as one of its parents, to stay with our central metaphor. It will assume an increasingly prominent place in the rest of our story, until history finally begins to grow up in the denouement.

Graph paper and calculators put us in mind of numbers, and it is to numbers that science now turned decisively. In his *Discourse on Method* (1637), Descartes had argued that mathematics was the purest form of reason, that reason was the sole path to certain knowledge, and that such knowledge could occur only in science. In focusing on math, Descartes was anticipated by figures such as Galileo, who a century earlier had taken the revolutionary step of introducing quantitative measurement to the scientific method. "The book of nature," he pronounced famously, "is written in the language of mathematics." Galileo, too, scorned history, disparaging historians, in terms Descartes would echo, as mere "memory experts." Their books, he might have said (but didn't), were written in water.

At the same time, however, it was growing clear to some that even squeaky-clean numbers might fail to endow scientific knowledge with the crystalline certainty that Descartes craved above all else. Descartes' older contemporary, Pierre Gassendi—a brilliant mathematician as well as a priest, scientist, and Epicurean philosopher—argued that all knowledge is probabilistic rather than certain. Even at the high point of Cartesian rationalism, Gassendi and others were transforming mathematics from a language thought fit for expressing only certainty into one that could also articulate more nuanced shades of probability.

And there was the rub. Descartes notwithstanding, it was Gassendi's vision that would ultimately carry the day as modern science unfolded. His innovative emphasis on probability made mathematics a much more flexible tool, and one far better suited to scientific investigation. As the new experimental science took shape, one of its key features was a gradual but unmistakable movement away from presenting its findings as certain facts. Instead, scientists began growing increasingly comfortable with probable explanations, based on conclusions which were testable and even confirmable for all immediate purposes, but whose provisional nature was still recognized in the final analysis.

This remains a core concept in science—despite the persistent image of the scientist as a person who deals exclusively in cold, hard facts. Scientists now accept that the world is a slippery place, and that reason and the senses are easily fooled. In modern science we see this most clearly with quantum theory, which is profoundly counterintuitive and entirely probabilistic.

For centuries historians have dreamed of settling in the coveted terra firma of science. Had they but scouted out the territory, they would have seen their promised land revealing itself to be every bit as unstable as the ever-shifting landscape they so desperately sought to leave behind.

But this is good news, historians! You've had to grapple with probabilities from the start, always envying the scientist's perceived certainties. Now you can take heart that those certainties never really existed for scientists, either, and rely instead on the hard-won skills you've been developing all along. Even as you struggled so hard to emulate the scientists, the "cold, hard fact" is that all the time, they were becoming more like you.

Yet we should also acknowledge that this fact would be cold comfort, indeed, to those poor historians who smarted under Descartes' stinging lash.

Others, for what it's worth, had thicker skins. One of the most robust responses to Descartes—on many fronts, including history, where it was perhaps a little too robust— came from no less eminent a rationalist than Gottfried Wilhelm Leibniz, who was a little boy of three in Leipzig, Germany, when Descartes died.

Highly regarded today as a metaphysical philosopher and mathematician, Leibniz is best remembered for his independent co-discovery, with Isaac Newton, of the calculus; while Newton had priority, Leibniz published first, and it is Leibniz's superior system that is still in use. But despite his undoubted brilliance, and his best efforts to make sure that everyone else knew about it in great detail, Leibniz never secured a position that would bring him an income from philosophy or mathematics. Instead, his bumpy career as a courtier encompassed stints as diplomat, political operative, technological advisor, librarian, mining engineer, and, finally, official historian of the German house of Hanover.

Leibniz noted the mutual disdain in which philosophers and historians commonly held each other and hoped to reconcile the two pursuits. Like others, he put an especially high value on eyewitness accounts and archival sources, but he went a bit further in defending history's verifiability, by suggesting that historical knowledge could be proven. This, of course, would have been heresy to Descartes, and indeed to most mathematicians, in whose discipline the whole idea of "proof" had originated.

At the heart of Leibniz's philosophy was the idea of the *monad*, which he proposed in order to explain the relationship between consciousness and matter, the old problem that Descartes had tried to solve by asserting that (with humans, at least) an immaterial soul dwells in a material body. The big objection to Cartesian dualism had always been Descartes' ultimate inability to explain how the two interacted: How could an immaterial soul exert any influence on a material body?

Leibniz circumvented dualism's dead end by suggesting that all matter is organic if you look closely enough (the recent invention of the microscope helped him here, though not enough, apparently), and that monads are the building blocks. A monad was essentially a convergence of perspectives, a "point of view" that could both act on the world and be acted upon by it. A consciousness, in other words. Everything is made up of monads, in layers, with sets of monads making up other monads, and those in turn forming other ones. I'm a monad, you're a monad. We're each built out of other monads (kidney, brain, skin), each of those is built out of others, and so on and so on. That rock is a monad, and so is that tree, as well as the forest of which it's a part. Furthermore, locked within each monad is a holistic impression of the entirety of all monads (the universe in a grain of sand, as William Blake would put it more poetically a century or so later). The book in which Leibniz laid all this out, we're not too surprised to learn, was entitled *Monadology*, and it, presumably, was a monad, too.

Leaving aside the obvious objection that not all matter is organic, and the less obvious question of whether monads might help solve the problem of matter and consciousness anyway (most philosophers think not), Leibniz's approach has interesting implications for historians. For one thing, because Leibniz emphasized the importance of perspective in shaping how we see the world, his philosophy encourages historians to think long and hard about their sources, especially written accounts of events. More generally, the reminder that multiple perspectives always exist urges them to broaden their outlook, to resist the claims of parochial narrowness.

A true polymath if there ever was one, Leibniz himself had breadth galore. No area of knowledge, it seemed, was off limits to his frenetic if oddly unfocused curiosity. He was Leonardo da Vinci, without the art. He designed water pumps, hydraulic presses, carriages, clocks, submarines, gears, lighting systems, heating systems, canals, windmills. He came up with new techniques for the desalinization of water, the separation of chemicals, the casting of iron, and the production of valuable phosphorus (from distilled human urine). He belonged to the cutting-edge scientific associations of the day: the Royal Society in London, the Paris Academy. He corresponded with everyone—some 15,000 of his letters survive, on subjects from science, mathematics, and philosophy, to politics, religion, literature, and history. When he visited Amsterdam in 1676, he peered at bacteria with Antonie van Leeuwenhoek, and he sat down to talk philosophy for four days straight in the cramped garret where Benedict de Spinoza eked out a living polishing lenses.[*]

Leibniz brought this expansive outlook to the writing of history. That might have been more profitable for him, but for the inconvenient fact that his aristocratic employers didn't want expansive. They wanted straightforward and stirring, a nice flattering account of their clan's noble origins in Italy and its subsequent glorious ramifications in Germany. Despite the two decades that Leibniz spent working on the project, they never got their book, because he never wrote it. What they did get was thousands and thousands of published pages of archival research and erudite scholarship, comprising no fewer than nine massive volumes. They said start at the beginning, so he did, with an introductory sketch entitled *Protogaia*, which was—well, perhaps you get the idea.

* We are lucky now to have Matthew Stewart's thought-provoking and highly readable meditation on that fabled meeting, *The Courtier and the Heretic: Leibniz, Spinoza, and the Fate of God in the Modern World* (New York, 2006).

Strangely, though, for someone who began his intellectual career arguing for the importance of individuals (his baccalaureate thesis was entitled "On the Principle of the Individual"), Leibniz makes little attempt to treat historical figures as if they were actual human beings rather than abstractions. His is very much one-damned-thing-after-another history, an endless parade of facts, facts, facts, with little or no interpretative glue or explanatory insight to hold them together. And in marshaling his facts, Leibniz sticks largely to war and politics, like Thucydides (who seems all warm and fuzzy by comparison).

Yet there are some notable strengths. It's a bit of a cheap shot to snicker at *Protogaia*, for example, since here we have Leibniz incorporating into history the knowledge of fossils and other geological phenomena that he'd encountered as a mining engineer. If the state of that knowledge was rudimentary, that's hardly his fault. The effort itself is impressive, and represents one of several ways that Leibniz appears to have been rather astonishingly ahead of his time. Not until the age of Darwin would a serious attempt be made to fit human history into a geological time scale (though church historians did it regularly, so perhaps we should say a serious *secular* attempt).*

And if it lacks strongly drawn characters, Leibniz's history doesn't at all lack for individualistic depictions of historical events. By the same token, if readers yearn for Leibniz to throw them an interpretive bone once in a while, they don't have to put up with grand theories that attempt

---

* For Darwin and the linking of human history to deep time, see chapter 15.

to reduce everything to a single principle or cause. Leibniz, modern historians have observed gratefully, doesn't posit sweeping "laws of history" or indulge in gross generalizations. Each war and each political contest is treated as its own phenomenon, shaped by its own particular set of circumstances.

This deceptively simple clarity of vision, it's been suggested, may be Leibniz's most positive legacy to historical writing. It would appear to stem from his transcendent and nearly forgotten philosophy, with its delicate interplay of the individual and the universal, and so it may be that philosophy's most positive legacy, too.

Leibniz was hardly alone, for history was finding other effective responses to Descartes. Around the same time that Leibniz was so frustrating his Hanoverian patrons, two of the strongest came from historians who occupied opposite ends of the epistemological spectrum—a radical skeptic and a pious monk. In a strange way, however, skeptic and monk arrived at the same place, as if their unusually powerful minds possessed enough strength between them to actually bend the spectrum itself with sheer intellectual force, joining the two ends together in a seamless loop.

The skeptic was the formidably learned Pierre Bayle, whose *Historical and Critical Dictionary* (1697) offered such a scathing condemnation of historical credulousness that Bayle is sometimes portrayed as an enemy of history itself, in the Cartesian mold. Nothing could be further from the truth. Bayle was the enemy not of history, but only of bad history, which makes him good history's good friend. His dictionary represented not a defeat for history, but a victorious holding action that prevented what could easily have turned into a rout. His motto might have been, "Historians, choose your battles."

Few today have heard of Bayle or his dictionary, but it would be hard to overestimate the book's impact both when it first appeared and for generations afterward. Indeed, it's been called the most popular book of the eighteenth century.* Leibniz certainly read it, for it stimulated him to take up a correspondence with Bayle on philosophy and history. But virtually every one of the Enlightenment's leading lights was influenced by it, including Voltaire, David Hume, and Thomas Jefferson. Diderot and his fellow Encyclopedists modeled their own works on it, while others from Samuel Johnson to Ambrose Bierce and beyond soon copied Bayle's catchy gimmick, which was to present more or less learned disquisitions in the form of ironic, witty, and frequently irreverent definitions, organized alphabetically.

Bayle's bugbear was the supernatural. He saw the breathless retailing of miracles as a pox upon the past, and he loathed it with an intensity that crackles off the page. But other forms of historical gullibility also evoke his wrath. The ancient historians, Bayle says, reported only great events and ignored details, often relying on nothing more than hearsay and invention. The more recent humanist histories avidly read by the educated, he asserts further, similarly hold little more than rhetorical trickery and more

* By the *Stanford Encyclopedia of Philosophy*, in its article on Bayle.

invention. He rakes his contemporaries over the coals for uncritically accepting this or that unsupported commonplace about the past.

Bayle takes Montaigne's already low opinion of human reason and lowers it even further. He loves shocking his readers with frank discussions of the roles that sex, murder, and general depravity have played in history. He rails against euphemism, hypocrisy, intolerance. And he's very funny, as when he weighs the offenses against propriety of Hipparchia (who was supposed to have had sex in the street with her husband, the philosopher Crates) and Diogenes the Cynic (who was supposed to have masturbated in the street). "Those who will find it strange that I relate obscenities as horrible as those above," he intones solemnly, "have need of being told that they have not considered carefully enough either the rights or the duties of a historian." *

The big surprise with Bayle—and this is where he loops the spectrum, as it were—is his strong and repeated endorsement of blind, unquestioning faith. It's probably safe to say that few of his rationalistic Enlightenment followers found this to be quite the thing. He's against superstition and repeatedly denounces the credulousness of Christians, but he seems to make a distinction—possibly an overfine one, some might feel—between those things and faith per se. Be that as it may, Bayle was one of the first to perceive that religion represents a basic human instinct, and that this instinct—regardless of whether God "exists" or not—has helped people live well and do good things.

---

* On that note, so to speak, we observe that an estimated 95 percent of the dictionary's text comes in the form of bloated, endless footnotes. Hilarious.

That certainly doesn't discount the horrors it also helps them perform, horrors that haunted Bayle's age and his own life. A French Protestant, he was forced by Catholic persecution to take refuge in the tolerant Netherlands. Yet Bayle's experience of religious intolerance made him hate intolerance, not religion. There we might have no trouble following him.

Like God, though, Bayle moves in mysterious ways. In the same entry cited above ("Hipparchia"), he appeals to faith, tongue seemingly only partly in cheek, in defending his use of strong language and obscenity. The argument is that the stronger the language, the stronger the shock in the reader:

> *This can humiliate and mortify our reason, and convince us of the infinite corruption of the human heart, and teach us a truth that we ought never to lose sight of—that man has need of a revealed light, which might make up for the defects of the philosophical light . . .*

Bayle is often called an atheist, but, in fact, he plays his cards so close to his chest that it's hard to tell what he believes, exactly. Perhaps he himself wasn't sure. Or perhaps, as a bipedal primate whose brain encompassed both human instincts and a fine, discerning mind, he was content to recognize both and embrace any apparent contradictions arising from the conjunction.

While Bayle's own religious convictions, if any, remain obscure, we can hardly say the same of our monk, the redoubtable and reportedly quite charming Jean

Mabillon. Older than Leibniz and Bayle by about a decade and half, Mabillon belonged to the Maurist congregation of the Benedictine order, which had been founded a couple of decades before his birth to conduct historical research on all things Benedictine. A similar group of scholarly Belgian Jesuits also formed in Antwerp around Jean Bolland; together, the Maurists and Bollandists took Counter-Reformation historiography to new heights of thoroughness and, yes, objectivity.

Of course, those new heights were relative, and they look (from our perspective, at least) more like hills than mountains. In the first place, despite their innovative methods, these scholars stood firmly in the old Eusebian territory of church history. Then, as Catholic historians, they also had to stay within the barbed-wire fence of Catholic doctrine, which further narrowed their range a bit, bless them.

Mabillon, the fifth son of a peasant farmer, is generally considered the best of them. Educated by his uncle, a priest, and then at the university in Reims, he took vows in the Maurist abbey at Reims in 1564. A decade later, by then in his early thirties, he arrived at the Maurists' Paris headquarters, St. Germain-de-Prés. There he lived out the rest of his life, which he devoted to strict monastic discipline and his studies.

Mabillon edited his share of the obligatory multivolume archival compilations—saints' lives, commentaries by medieval authorities, monastic annals, and the like—that these scholars saw as their bread and butter (and upon which historians today still frequently rely). But the outstanding ones were those who took a step further, to contribute something original of their own. Mabillon's contribution was spectacular, since he invented a whole new discipline that has long stood at the center of medieval studies, and has since expanded to include classical antiquity and, more recently, non-European literate cultures. It's called *paleography*—from the Greek for "ancient writing"—and it deals with the problem of figuring out when and where anything written was produced. In short, it's the study of old handwriting.

Earlier scholars had vaguely understood that different ages and places had their own styles of penmanship and manuscript production, and that medieval scribes working in their monasteries, while showing some degree of individual quirkiness, followed the style particular to their age and region. Any scholar could have told us that a ninth-century British manuscript of the Venerable Bede uses a different style of lettering from that of a twelfth-century papal bull. Mabillon told us that such differences are predictable and regular, and he defined many of the styles that the scribes used. The ninth-century Bede, for example, would be in *transitional insular minuscule*, while during the twelfth century any papal bull came in the shape of carefully formed *later curialis*.*

Mabillon published his findings in *De Re Diplomatica* (1681), "On Diplomatics," a landmark textbook that

---

* These examples come from the excellent Web site of Dr. Dianne Tillotson, "Medieval Writing," found at http://medievalwriting.50megs.com/writing.htm (from the site map, click on "The History of Scripts"). With respect to the discussion of "modern scientific history" earlier in this chapter, while most authorities still refer to paleography as a science, I'm happy to report that Dr. Tillotson calls it "fundamentally an art, with some scientific props."

founded not only paleography but also the closely related discipline of *diplomatics*, or the study of documents.* The book also sparked a heated controversy with the Jesuits, since it refuted the claims of the leading Bollandist that some early medieval Benedictine charters were forgeries. It dealt exclusively with Latin manuscripts; a quarter of a century later, in 1708, the year after Mabillon's death, Mabillon's Maurist colleague Bernard de Montfaucon put Greek paleography on an equally sound footing.

The era of Mabillon and Montfaucon was the Maurists' golden age. It included many figures who never took vows with the Maurists but were closely associated with them. One of Mabillon's friends was Charles du Fresne du Cange, a pioneering Byzantinist (and the first to use the term "Byzantium" to refer to the later Roman empire), who compiled valuable handbooks for the study of Latin and Greek; another was Sebastian de Tillemont, who wrote a groundbreaking *History of the Roman Emperors*. Both would be important sources for Gibbon later in the eighteenth century.

For the first time, organized ranks of scholars were combing through the archives—even if just the religious ones—of Europe. They produced volume upon volume of carefully edited documents that continue to be of great use. Their heirs would be the "scientific" historians who dominated history in the nineteenth century, who saw archival documents as the timeless repository of cold, hard facts, and who insisted that nothing else mattered.

---

* In this context, *diploma*, literally "double-folded," means document; a *diplomat* in the modern sense is someone who carries a lot of them.

We've seen a mathematician answer Descartes' challenge with document-based facts; we've seen a radical skeptic adopt a defensively minimalist approach to historical knowledge, furiously assailing the fabulous; and we've seen industrious religious scholars further advancing the cause of faith-based "documentary" history. Surely all this ought to be enough to knock Descartes out of the ring.

So why do we have the feeling that something's missing?

TEN

Reason and Imagination Pass Each Other in the Night

illiam London's *A Catalogue of the Most Vendible Books in England* (1657), with which we began the last chapter, lists numerous varieties of reading matter in its long subtitle (putting history second among them, it's worth recalling). For the modern reader in particular, the absence of one kind of book from London's title page stands out: There are no novels. The novel had not yet been invented. Still, it's not a strictly nonfiction catalog, since the headings include (at the very end) "Romances" and "Playes." In the usage of the day, "Romances" would have included extravagantly exotic tales in both poetry and prose, which were the ancestors of what was about to take shape as the *novel*, or "new thing."

New or old, such entertainments were hardly the thing a serious scientist should be caught dipping into. London was not alone, it seems, in putting romances next to plays, especially after the Restoration of Charles II in 1660 pushed the Puritans out of power and ushered in a period of famously bawdy theater. By the middle of the decade, the upright Robert Boyle, father of modern chemistry and a founder of the Royal Society, was sternly denouncing "those numerous Plays that daily imploy [sic] the Stage, and those voluminous Romances that are too often the only Books which make up the Libraries of Gallants and fill the Closets of Ladies."

The idea that Gallants and Ladies were filling their Libraries and Closets with Romances goes against the impression we get from London's subtitle that Romances weren't selling well enough to rate a spot further up the list. Perhaps London had some other reason than their commercial prospects for putting "Romances" second from last. Social propriety? Status? Even his particular market niche as a bookseller, at least if the list was based on his own sales? (The list appears to be tilted toward a readership of country squires, a practical, non-Romance-reading clientele if ever there was one, and as socially remote from Boyle's Gallants and Ladies as Boyle himself.) London's list, Boyle leads us to suspect, took its order not from commercial viability alone, but also at least partly from social considerations.

One thing Boyle and London seem to agree on, then, is that Romances are less than totally respectable as reading material (the same could be said today, it occurs to us, although the label has changed its meaning). We don't know how Boyle, the hardheaded scientist, felt about history, but London's list appears to put History and Romances at opposite ends of the spectrum, with History at the respectable end (next to godliness, no less, after all).

There's another undercurrent flowing here, however. Romances and Playes have a different quality from the no-nonsense nonfiction items that make up the rest of London's list. They feel tacked on at the very end, fanciful confections less than completely at home in workmanlike company. By contrast, the other categories register as distinctly masculine: medicine, the construction of sundials, land management, gambling, husbandry, heraldry. Military discipline. History. Timber. Hey, this is virile stuff! Manly reading for manly men.

That points to something we've known all along, of course, which is that history has so far been almost entirely a man's game. Don't expect to find Thucydides or Polybius on the shelves of Boyle's sissified Gallants and romance-reading Ladies.

Which brings up another interesting point. Science itself has always been a man's game, too. There's a tinge of something butch about reason, just as there is of something effeminate about fancy. Here, perhaps, is the secret of Thucydides' success in linking the pose of "scientific" rationalism with those other manly pursuits par excellence, war and politics. By simultaneously narrowing his focus to war and politics, donning the scientist's lab coat, and rejecting the storyteller's appeal to the fabulous, Thucydides offered the male historians who came after him an irresistible way to reaffirm for themselves the masculine, rational nature of their pursuit.*

If history is the scientific study of war and politics, what room could it possibly have for imagination? That would be the province of those who write for Gallants and Ladies. Especially Ladies, who were now beginning to read widely for the first time, and, at last, to write.

---

* The word Thucydides uses for what he rejects is *mythodes*, "the mythic," which Rex Warner tellingly translated as "the romantic element" for Penguin in the mid-twentieth century. Thucydides is from Mars, Herodotus is from Venus—whether he likes it or not.

After hearing Boyle on the subject, we're hardly surprised that the earliest audience for novels was made up largely of women. It is somewhat more surprising, though, to learn that the first novel was itself written by a woman, that she was also the first professional woman writer in England (she wrote plays as well), and that, apparently, as a woman working in a man's field, to give her story credibility and appeal she disguised it as a work of history.

Most surprising of all, however, is the possibility that it might actually have been a work of history, one that only later came to be perceived as a novel.

Aphra Behn is believed to have been born around 1640 in a small town near Canterbury. Not much is known about her life, but if the events she narrates actually happened, when she was in her mid-twenties—about the time that Robert Boyle was peering disapprovingly into Ladies' Closets—she accompanied her father to Surinam, the British colony on the northern coast of South America, where he was to take up the position of lieutenant governor. The story she wrote and published two decades later is set there. Its main characters are the young Englishwoman who is the narrator—and who may represent Aphra Behn herself—and an African slave whom she encounters soon after arriving in Surinam. His name gives the book its title: *Oroonoko, or The Royal Slave: A True History.**

The story itself is fairly straightforward. The narrator arrives in Surinam, where English colonists have established sugar plantations worked by slaves imported from

---

* There's an excellent Norton Critical Edition of *Oroonoko*, edited by Joanna Lipking and published in 1997, to which I'm indebted here.

Africa. There she meets Oroonoko, a warrior-prince in line to succeed to a West African kingdom, who had been treacherously captured by an English slave trader with whom Oroonoko himself had previously done business, and with whom he was dining on board ship. After being sold to the owner of Parham, the plantation close to the narrator's own quarters, he is reunited with the woman to whom he had been betrothed in Africa, who unbeknownst to him had also been enslaved. She becomes pregnant, and Oroonoko, wanting his child to be born in freedom, leads his fellow slaves in a revolt, but the whites capture him through trickery. After his failed suicide attempt, his captors hack him to pieces. He dies without uttering a sound, enduring his brutal dismemberment with the same stoic nobility he has shown throughout.

Oroonoko and its enigmatic author together amount to one of the most intriguing puzzles in the history of English literature. The big question for many, of course, is "Is it true?" The narrator repeatedly affirms that it is. And her main characters, as far as we can tell, did exist with the names and positions she gives them: the owner of Parham was Lord Willoughby, the overseer was John Trefry, the colony's deputy governor was William Byam, all as given in the book, and—again, as far as we can tell—all drawn true to life. But there's no record of any lieutenant governor who might have been the author's father, and the details of life in Surinam might have come from the ample description in George Warren's widely read *An Impartial Description of Surinam upon the Continent Guinea in America*, which was published in 1667. (Such accounts from the New World were popular; others were coming back from places like Virginia and Massachusetts.)

Because they seem to bind together topics of compelling ideological interest to many postcolonial academics—the big three, no less: race, gender, and power—book and author have enjoyed a recent vogue in academic literary criticism. But it's all too easy to forget that, like Anna Comnena, the history-writing Byzantine princess whom we met earlier, Aphra Behn wasn't a modern academic, and her book is not a tract against slavery or racism, as it is sometimes taken to be. The idea of race as we now understand it didn't exist yet—it would be created and molded by the succeeding long centuries of American slavery.

And Aphra Behn (or at least her narrator) never objects to slavery. What she does object to is the unnatural enslavement of a king, and it is this crucial distinction that clues us in to her primary concern, which is not race, or gender, or power, but royalty. For Behn, Oroonoko is not first and foremost black, a man, or a slave. He is a king, and it is as a king that she is most interested in him.

That realization, in turn, adds a further historical dimension to the mix, in addition to the tale's intrinsic interest and potential veracity. Aphra Behn was a staunch royalist, a Tory who held fast to the principle of the divine right of kings. In the mid-1660s (probably after returning from Surinam), she had served the newly restored king of England, Charles II, as a spy in the Netherlands. When the government failed to reimburse her for her expenses on assignment, she is thought to have ended up in a debtors' prison. It was to get out of debt that she began her unusual, and unusually successful, writing career. She was respected for her poetry, much of it frankly erotic, and even more celebrated for her plays, some fifteen to twenty of which were produced on the London stage. The best known of them was *The Rover* (1677), which entertainingly deploys the bawdiness and intrigue that makes Restoration drama so lively.

In 1688, however, the Glorious Revolution brought the curtain down on the Restoration, as the antiroyalist Whigs instigated the removal of Charles II's younger brother, James II, who had succeeded to the throne after Charles's own death four years earlier. James had made the mistake of being a Catholic and then, after coming to power, producing a male heir, who embodied the threat of another Catholic king. The bloodless coup replaced him with his Protestant daughter Mary and her Dutch husband, William of Orange, who ruled jointly.

Behn wrote *Oroonoko* just before the Glorious Revolution, as it was becoming clear that James had lost support even among many Tories for his pro-Catholic policies. Unlike those weak-kneed Tories, Aphra Behn was having none of it. A king is a king is a king—only God can decide who gets to be one—and a king's divinely bestowed inner nobility cannot be eradicated by any human deed.

The parallels with her story are clear. James was one of the "black Stuarts," so called because of their dark hair and swarthy coloring. In poems honoring Charles and James, she addresses both royal brothers as "Caesar," which is the pointedly regal slave name given to Oroonoko in Surinam. In both reality and story, a potential heir sparks a revolution. To pound the point home, "the frightful Spectacle of a mangl'd King" at the end of the story would have inescapably reminded Behn's readers of the beheading of James's father, Charles I, in 1649, and warned them against committing the same crime all over again.

Aphra Behn died in 1689, the year after the Glorious Revolution. To this day, scholars are divided about how to classify her book. Absent much evidence one way or another, most settle for calling it an autobiographical novel. Yet the enticing possibility exists that she did her best to write about things that happened as they happened, and that she was moved to do so by their bearing on the historical situation in which she found herself.

Traditionally, credit for writing the first novel goes either to Daniel Defoe, whose *Robinson Crusoe* (1719) came three decades after *Oroonoko*, or to Samuel Richardson, whose *Pamela* (1740) came more than half a century after it. But confusion over genre should not be allowed to efface Behn's achievement. Even if it's as true to life as she could make it, a "history," at least in a loose sense, *Oroonoko* also rises to the level of a richly imagined work of stunning originality (if not depth), opening the way not just for Defoe and Richardson, but also for Jane Austen and George Eliot.

Two and a half centuries after Behn died, Virginia Woolf suggested that all women should throw flowers on Behn's grave for securing them the right to self-expression. But it's the men who should be grateful, really. Defoe, Richardson, Henry Fielding—over and over again, the words "true" and "history" pop up in their subtitles and mock-documentary introductions just the way they did in *Oroonoko*'s subtitle, and the stories they tell purport to be true, just like Aphra Behn's. Such authors, who wrote largely for women and often about them, hoped to capture both the cachet of a true story and the enchanting allure of an imaginary one. It became a literary convention, but it wasn't yet one when Aphra Behn invented it.

We can never know, but it seems just possible that Aphra Behn was in earnest, that she did her best to relate events that actually happened, as closely as she could to the way they happened. The melding of imagination into the meaning of those events in no way detracts from that effort. If anything, it makes it more original.

If its author had been a man, we wonder, would the book have been taken as nonfiction? And would that have delayed the rise of the novel, or changed its form? Could posterity have insisted on perceiving Aphra Behn's book as fiction for no other reason than its clear imaginative power, denying its "historicity" simply because she was a woman?

The answer to those questions is most likely no, and some will find the questions themselves a bit overimaginative. Yet the chance remains, however slender, that the accident of Aphra Behn's sex not only shaped the future course of world literature, but also stole something real from history.

In 1668, when Aphra Behn is thought to have been stuck in an English debtors' prison, a boy was born in faraway Italy who would spend his life struggling to reclaim history from those who would bleach imagination out of it. Giovanni

Battista Vico, called Giambattista, was the son of a poor Naples bookseller. He did not do well in school, educating himself instead in his father's one-room bookshop, where the family also lived.

When Vico was seven he fell off the ladder leading up to the sleeping loft, taking a wicked blow to the head. So bad was the injury that the doctor predicted the boy would at least suffer severe brain damage, and quite possibly die. He didn't die, but some observers, themselves concussed by Vico's explosive ideas, which burst abruptly out of his blazing prose before being sucked back into the inferno, have suspected brain damage.

Whatever the truth, there's no one who writes or thinks quite like Vico. His thoughts can feel disordered, and occasionally they seem to float unanchored. It's often difficult to figure out what he means. Reading Vico is like climbing a sheer rock face without a rope, a dizzying and often disorienting experience, but if you make it to the top, an exhilarating one.

In some ways, Vico resembles no one so much as Ibn Khaldun, the fourteenth-century Arab historian who labored so hard to put history on a sound theoretical footing. Like Ibn Khaldun, Vico aspired to explain history's largest outlines, to grasp the overall patterns of history, and to see beneath them to the underlying structure. Also like Ibn Khaldun, he never for a moment entertained the possibility that history might not actually have such patterns or structure. Both men, too, were largely ignored by immediate posterity, their complex thought hidden in relative obscurity until being "discovered" much later, when it came into its own in a big way, resonating with modern thinkers as it never did with contemporaries.

But at least Ibn Khaldun enjoyed success and fame during his own lifetime. Poor Vico just spun his wheels. Self-educated, plagued always by poverty, he worked as a tutor in his twenties and then secured a low-paying professorship of rhetoric at the University of Naples. He married an uneducated childhood friend, Teresa Destito, with whom, scrounging every penny, he would have eight children, three of whom died young. Professionally, his biggest heartbreak came in 1723, when he was turned down for a much better paying job as a law professor at the same university. It was this frustration that pushed him to begin the work now recognized as his masterpiece, *The New Science*. He worked on it for the rest of his life, publishing three editions: the first in 1725; the second in 1730; and the third, now viewed as the standard one, in 1744, the year of his death.

Naples, where Vico lived nearly all his life, was enjoying something of a renaissance at the time. Some forty bookstores could be found on the short Via di Biagio dei Libri, where Vico's father had his own small shop. As a young man, Vico tells us in his *Autobiography* (written just after the first edition of *The New Science*), he hung out with his fellows in the city's lively salons, discussing cultural and intellectual topics and chewing over the newest ideas. Other cities, of course, shared in the excitement of the age's intellectual ferment. But Naples possessed a special pedigree that set it apart from larger hubs like Rome, Paris, or London. Ever since antiquity, Naples had been a leading center of Epicureanism, the ancient Greek philosophy that espoused a number of ideas, including atomism, which were being picked up on by the new scientists.

Lucretius, the Latin poet who was a contemporary of Julius Caesar, is thought to have lived and taught in Naples. His darkly powerful epic poem *On the Nature of Things* did more than any other single work to disseminate Epicurean scientific and philosophical ideas, which Lucretius loved deeply. (Read the poem—it's a passionate exposition of a dispassionate, very rational philosophy, which is a neat trick.) Recently translated into Italian, it was widely read and discussed by young intellectuals around the time Vico was in his teens and twenties, though Vico taught himself Latin and would have read the original. From Lucretius, Vico took the Epicurean view of early human history as bestial, savage, and dominated by fear of nature and of the gods. (This sounds very much like Hobbes, which it is, except that Hobbes's primitive humans were afraid of each other, not of nature and the gods.) Vico may have picked up a certain flair for dramatic imagery from Lucretius as well, for his writing, like the poet's, is heavily punctuated by lightning, thunder, and other crashing sensual chords.

More recently, Pierre Gassendi, the French scientist whom we saw in the last chapter advocating a probabilistic approach to knowledge, had also been an Epicurean. Gassendi had visited Naples, where he became the first person in history to observe and record the transit of a planet, Mercury, across the sun. (Or, at least, *probably* the first, as we suppose he'd say.)

Vico was not yet twenty when Isaac Newton electrified the European intellectual world with the *Philosophiae*

Naturalis Principia Mathematica, or "Mathematical Principles of Natural Philosophy," in which he lays out his theory of gravity (what we now call "science" was then known as "natural philosophy," and was still, as the name implies, considered a branch of philosophy). This was the purpose for which Newton developed the calculus, which can mathematically describe the motion of bodies like planets. Leibniz came out with a better version, we recall; honoring the power of mathematics, Vico calls Leibniz and Newton "the two foremost minds of our age" in *The New Science*. Another topic Vico discussed with his friends was Descartes, whose reverence for pure reason was still doing much to shape the intellectual landscape. At first, Vico was impressed by Descartes, but slowly, that began to change.

By about 1710, Vico had begun to formulate his own audacious response to Descartes, one very different from the line taken by Gassendi, Leibniz, or anyone else. In claiming reason as the sole path to knowledge, Descartes had insisted that all real knowledge can be attained by reason alone, without the aid of experience. The English philosopher Francis Bacon (whose historical writing we encountered in chapter 7) had already sketched the opposite position: that experience, not reason, tells us what we know about the world. Called *empiricism*, from the Greek word for "experience," this would become the characteristically British answer to Cartesian rationalism. Isaac Newton took it up enthusiastically, and Newton's friend John Locke developed (and somewhat modified) it in his influential *Essay Concerning Human Understanding* (1690). Vico, too, approved of Bacon's empirical approach, venerating Bacon as one of his "four authors," and calling Bacon's inductive method "the best method of philosophizing," by which he meant conducting scientific investigations.

As it turns out, however, on Vico's lips this was faint praise.

As we've seen, other historians had always bowed to science, assuming that the best way to defend history was by giving it a scientific makeover: Only by being more scientific could historians hope to approach the high degree of verifiability that science enjoyed. Of course, they could never really get there, sad creatures; the most they could hope for was to come close. Vico's ingenious rhetorical stroke was to turn this thinking on its head. History, Vico argued boldly, is actually *more* knowable than science, and, if properly pursued, promises all the certainty of mathematics. It was science that could never hope to come close.

Vico based his argument on the principle that we can truly know only that which we have made ourselves. Cultures and their pasts are made by humans, so humans can know them; nature, the subject of science, was made by God, so it will always remain obscure:

> *But in the night of thick darkness enveloping the earliest antiquity, so remote from ourselves, there shines the eternal and unfailing light of a truth beyond all question: that the world of civil society has certainly been made by men, and that its principles are therefore to be found within the modifications of our own human mind.*

This is the case that Vico makes in *The New Science*. Unfortunately, the appearance of the word "science" (*scienza*) in the title and in the text has led to the mistaken impression that Vico's book is just one more attempt to legitimize history by dressing it in scientific garb. But *scienza* at the time merely meant "knowledge." In proposing a *nuova scienza*, Vico proposed not a new science in the sense we give the word in modern English (and Italian), but a whole new branch of knowledge. Far from merely trying to turn history into a science, Vico instead aimed to create an entirely distinct discipline to stand alongside science. While incorporating some useful elements of scientific thought, such as Baconian induction, Vico's "new knowledge" will embody methods and values all its own.

And those methods, he insists with equal originality, must be based on imagination as much as reason. According to Vico, after an initial primitive state of bestial savagery, all civilizations pass through three stages of development: an "age of gods," in which people are dominated by religion and the fear of the supernatural; an "age of heroes," in which societies divide themselves into a ruling upper class and a ruled lower class; and an "age of men," in which emerging political equality gives rise to commonwealths and limited monarchies. There's nothing especially original about that, nor about the celebrated idea of *ricorso*, "recourse," by which a new barbarism can descend on the age of men, starting the cycle all over again (as Vico suggests happened with the collapse of the classical world).* Polybius, for example, with his

---

* Most famously, Vico's *ricorso* inspired James Joyce, who begins and ends *Finnegans Wake* with it.

recurring cycles of three kinds of constitutions that Vico's ages paralleled, would be nodding sagely at this point. But Vico stepped into uncharted territory by stressing that in each of these three ages, and in each separate recurrence of them, people have thought and acted in ways that differed sharply. Therefore, to understand another historical age demanded a monumental, sustained, and disciplined effort of imagination.

In other words, we cannot assume that people in the past thought or acted the way we do. Only by applying our imaginations properly will we be able to use the best methods we have of entering the thinking of another age or culture. Those methods combine a variety of sources—"philosophic proofs" such as legal history and theology, and "philological proofs" such as mythology, heroic verse, and etymology (a favorite of Vico's)—but the important thing is the central role of imagination in approaching historical sources.

That basic point seems so obvious now that it's hard to grasp how novel it was. Grasping that novelty, in fact, requires precisely the sort of effort that Vico calls for—the imaginative leap of putting ourselves in the heads of people who operated on assumptions different from our own. That we are now willing to accept the need for such an effort (even if often unwilling actually to make it) is due to Vico, and it shows how deeply his ideas have shaped our own concept of history, even if few of us know Vico's name.

Vico was out of step with his times. Or rather, in many ways he was reacting against them. A devout Catholic, he disapproved of the skepticism and secularism he perceived in the writings of figures such as Pierre Bayle, who was one of his favorite targets. Wisdom, he said, required piety. Nor did his exaltation of imagination strike a responsive chord among the rationalistic thinkers who were coming into prominence as the eighteenth century wore on.

Not until the Romantic Movement, itself a reaction against Enlightenment rationalism, did Vico begin to come into his own. When Goethe visited Naples in 1787, a friend pressed Vico's book into his hand as if it were a precious secret; another German, Johann Gottfried Herder, already knew of Vico when he visited Naples two years later. It remains unclear whether Herder read *The New Science* before forming his own very similar ideas, but his works would be decisive in the growing call for historians to use their imaginative powers in trying to grasp past civilizations.[*] However, only when the influential French historian Jules Michelet translated *The New Science* into French in 1827 did Vico's ideas enter directly into European thought. If Vico gets many of his details wrong, modern authorities agree, he was right on target in many of his main points. It is to Vico that scholars now trace the idea that distinct civilizations and cultures have existed in history, each with its own set of values and attitudes.

In the meantime, the assumptions that Vico was attempting to dispel have persisted in much secular, rationalist mainstream history. Sometimes they're hidden, sometimes they're right out in the open: Human nature is unchanging and constant, with people in one age sharing the same basic values and attitudes as people in another;

---

[*] See Isaiah Berlin's classic essay "Vico and Herder," in his *Against the Current: Essays in the History of Ideas* (1980).

absolute, timeless truths exist in areas like morality and culture, and reason is the best or only way of seeing them; history books ought to illustrate those truths, as a moralizing lesson in the proper conduct of human affairs; secularism, tolerance, freedom, and learning stand in eternal opposition to religion, intolerance, tyranny, and obscurantism.

This tradition is still going strong, but never so much as in the century after Vico, when crowing reason ruled the roost and imagination was pushed firmly into the Closet.

ELEVEN

Making It (Sort of) in the Enlightenment

In 1744, the year in which Giambattista Vico died, the Academy of Sciences in France published a short work entitled *A Dissertation on the Nature and Propagation of Fire*, which had been written several years earlier by a leading French mathematician and physicist. The following year, the essay's author began work on a translation of Newton's *Principia* that remains the standard French version of that work even today, while the celebrated writer Voltaire—newly appointed royal historian to the court of Louis XV—published the first installment of his *Essay on the Manners and Spirit of the Nations*, a pioneering study of world history that he conceived expressly to persuade this illustrious scientist that history possessed every bit as much significance and intellectual interest as science itself.

It didn't work. In the brief time left to her—the author of the scientific works mentioned above, who was also Voltaire's lover and intellectual comrade, would die from complications following childbirth in 1749—Émilie du Châtelet doesn't seem to have modified, at least not much, her earlier opinion that history was meaningless drivel.

Naturally, we're tempted to imagine the expression on Robert Boyle's face had he lived long enough (and been so lucky) as to gain access to the Closet of this particular Lady. Having thus imagined, we might further note the various levels of irony at work in a female scientist's skepticism about history sparking in reply a major historical work by a rationalistic male writer best remembered today for a satirical novel about a credulous fool.* For it was precisely as credulous fools that Madame du Châtelet had condemned the historians whose work she held in such low regard.

We've got to admit she had a point. She was referring not to the dense scholarly treatises of Mabillon and his ilk, which fell out of the range of most general readers, but to the remnants of the once-formidable humanist tradition, the same uncritical histories that had so irked Pierre Bayle half a century earlier. Voltaire's first youthful work of history, *The History of Charles XII,* had been very much in this vein—kings, battles, and a properly classicizing moral (immoderate pursuit of military conquest will bring you down in the end). First published in 1731, when Voltaire was in his mid-thirties, it was revised constantly in coming years, as its already-famous author grew and responded to the many criticisms that other historians offered, not always in a helpful spirit.

We don't think of Voltaire as a historian. We don't associate him with any specific area of intellectual endeavor, really, but with intellectual endeavor itself. He possessed a prodigious mind, rivaling even Aristotle in the scope of his restless curiosity and powers of insight. He was a generalist, a simplifier, a synthesist, rather than a deep thinker, and the most specific label we can pin on him, if we must, is that of a writer. Voltaire wrote the way some people

---

* The novel, of course, is *Candide* (1759).

read. He wrote anything he could get his hands on. And he had wondrously prehensile hands: In addition to his histories, he wrote poems, plays (tragedies and comedies), novels, allegorical fables, philosophical tales and treatises, popular treatments of science, and reams and reams of letters. A public man, often an activist, he was intimate with kings and ministers, artists and intellectuals. More than any other single figure, Voltaire embodied his age, and history gained great intellectual credibility from his endorsement.

For a while, anyway. Inevitably, Voltaire's cultural leadership was challenged by younger figures such as Denis Diderot and Jean-Jacques Rousseau, whose opinions of history were closer to Madame du Châtelet's than to Voltaire's. By then, however, history's pen had been taken up by others. They included a much younger friend of Voltaire's, a man of equal or near equal intellectual vigor, whose narrower range of interest was more than compensated for by a willingness to give history everything he had, and who would become the Enlightenment's quintessential historian.

Voltaire's interest in history very much recalls that of Petrarch four centuries earlier. If, like Petrarch, Voltaire was seen by later observers as embodying his age, like Petrarch he also deliberately fostered that impression. Each believed that his own values broadened those of a previously narrower era, effecting a large-scale shift in historical consciousness. Both saw the writing of history as a way of serving that grand conception, and it's neither insignificant nor coincidental that both first approached historical writing not in prose but in epic poetry—Petrarch with *Africa*, which took as its subject the Second Punic War, and Voltaire with *The Henriade*, which celebrated the reign of Henry IV, who had ended France's disastrous wars of religion. Each obviously aspired to be a Virgil more than a Livy.[*]

Born François-Marie Arouet to a middle-class Parisian family in 1694, Voltaire was barely twenty when, having charmed Paris and the court with his epigrammatic wit, he went too far and insulted the Duc d'Orléans, the powerful regent for the young Louis XV. Thrown into the Bastille for a year, the young writer took advantage of his confinement to begin work on the poem that would become *The Henriade*. A year or so after regaining his freedom, and after winning his first literary success with an interpretation of Sophocles' *Oedipus*, he took the pen name Voltaire (thought to be an anagram of Arovet, the Latin for his surname, plus the initials of *le jeune*, "the younger").

Adopting the fashionable persona of the *Philosophe*, Voltaire struck up a friendship with the exiled English Tory politician and historian Lord Bolingbroke and began studying English. That came in handy soon afterward when, having once more (and not for the last time) pushed his luck at court, Voltaire himself was exiled to England, where he spent two and a half years hobnobbing with the likes of King George I, Lord Bolingbroke (back from exile), Jonathan Swift, and Alexander Pope. This was a period of intense intellectual excitement for Voltaire, who, intoxicated by the

---

[*] For Petrarch, see chapter 6.

comparative freedom of English society, devoured some of the works that would shape him most profoundly, such as Locke's *Essay Concerning Human Understanding* and the writings of the militant Deist Samuel Clarke.* He went to Isaac Newton's funeral and encountered the plays of Shakespeare for the first time, onstage in the original language, having previously seen only the cumbersome, lifeless versions current on the French stage.

Voltaire returned to France in 1729 and renewed his career as literary, intellectual, and social gadfly, stinging and biting the backs of the influential, pestering the establishment just enough to elicit a few idle and easily eluded slaps but carefully gauging his attacks to fall just short of the level that would provoke a concerted effort to crush him for good. He enjoyed further success in the theater and finished the first edition of *The History of Charles XII* (1731), chronicling the rise and fall of the militaristic Swedish monarch who met his nemesis in the form of the Russian tsar, Peter the Great. A few years later, he displayed the fruits of his English sojourn with the *Philosophical Letters* (1734), in which he compares Locke and Newton favorably with French thinkers such as Descartes and Pascal, and celebrates England's political and religious freedoms. This short but seminal book staked out Voltaire's position as the enemy of tyranny and religious intolerance and the champion of empirical reason, which he proclaimed as the

---

* Deism, a rationalistic religious outlook common among many leading figures of the Enlightenment, opposed revelation as a source of knowledge in favor of a "natural religion" that was thought to be inborn and accessible to reason. In the famous formulation, Deists viewed God as a "divine watchmaker" who created the world and the physical laws of nature, but did not interfere in their workings.

fountainhead of humanity's inevitable progress in science and the arts.

The book's subversive message caused a scandal. The publisher was thrown in the Bastille, public book-burning commenced, and an arrest warrant loomed. Voltaire found it prudent to leave Paris till the hubbub died down, and it was at this crucial moment that he had the extraordinary good luck to fall in with Madame du Châtelet, who would inspire and guide his emotional and intellectual life for the next sixteen years. Much of that time was spent at Cirey, her estate in northern Champagne, where the couple now took refuge.

A dozen years Voltaire's junior, Émilie le Tonnelier had married the Marquis du Châtelet at nineteen, borne him three children, and then, as he went off on long periods of military service, enjoyed that peculiarly French marriage arrangement that allows for domestic and social tranquility while permitting open dalliances on each side. For her and for Voltaire, Cirey now became the nucleus of a shared life that embraced the most exciting cultural developments of the day. Both loved theater, music, literature, and the arts. They built a theater and a laboratory at Cirey, and used them. If he defended history to her, she explained science to him. He wanted to write a work of popular synthesis on Newton, and she helped him explore nuances of Newton's science that had eluded him. She also gave him a new appreciation of the thought of Leibniz, among others. A stream of distinguished guests came and went, and the couple enlivened their enjoyment of each other with frequent trips to Paris and Versailles, as well as to cultural centers outside of France.

They both wrote steadily. Apart from more plays and the book on Newton, it was to history that Voltaire devoted the bulk of his energies during this period, beginning work on a second major historical work, *The Century of Louis XIV* (1751), and a third, the *Essay on the Manners and Spirit of the Nations* (1756). With these two monumental efforts—highly discursive, each runs to many volumes—Voltaire opened thrilling new perspectives for history.

In the introduction to the latter, he recounts how he was spurred by Madame du Châtelet's complaints. Not only are historians gullible and blinkered, but history itself is just plain boring. And so instead of rehearsing yet another arid and seemingly endless parade of battles and rulers, Voltaire will bring history alive:

> I would like to discover what human society was like, how people lived in the intimacy of the family, and what arts were cultivated, rather than repeat the story of so many misfortunes and military combats—the dreary subject matter of history and the common currency of perversity.

The intimacy of the family—we now call this *social history*, the "history of private life," to take the title phrase of a classic modern work.* And art! With deceptive casualness, Voltaire reaches in widely different directions at the same time. And he brings still another element into the mix. "Ideas," he writes, "have changed the world," and so his

---

* *A History of Private Life*, edited by Paul Veyne and translated into English by Arthur Goldhammer (1987). The editors and most of the authors of this collection are French; social history remains outstandingly practiced by French historians.

history of world civilization will also be a history of ideas, an area now known as *intellectual history*. So together, then, the main goals of Voltaire's new history will be "to know, so far as I can, the manners of peoples, and to study the human mind." Rulers and chronology, he continues, will provide merely the framework, not the main focus.

Like Vico's enlistment of imagination, Voltaire's enlargement of history feels rather normal to readers today, but at the time it was radically innovative. In one direction, Voltaire expanded history's turf toward the concrete, mundane external side of life; in another, toward the multifarious ways that we have expressed ourselves; in a third, toward the abstract concepts that rule both of these other realms. History was supposed to be about Great Men and Great Events, not regular people and their daily lives, and certainly not self-expression or ideas. Voltaire had suddenly and effortlessly broadened history's subject matter, claiming new territory in areas previously considered not just outside the historian's concern, but beneath it.

It's true that having declared these bold aims, Voltaire seems less than dedicated to following through. In fact, when we come right down to it, there's precious little of family life, art, or ideas in these books, and what there is often feels superficial and cursory to the modern reader. But at least the aim has been articulated, if not always fulfilled.

It would take other historians quite a while to make good on Voltaire's promise, proving that one doesn't have to labor in obscurity like a Vico to have one's ideas ignored. But nowadays, every aspect of human life and every area of human endeavor has a history: sexuality and theater, sleep habits and architecture, food and needlepoint, clothing and mountain climbing. It was not always so.

In addition to enlarging history's territory metaphorically, Voltaire also did so literally, by making his *Essay* the first attempt to write a truly global history. For the most part, the long tradition of "universal" history had been merely an outgrowth of church history, based narrowly on the Bible—start with the Jews, and then go all the way to the Christians. Hardly universal, as Madame du Châtelet observed acerbically.

Once again, though, we might feel that Voltaire fails to follow through fully on his innovative ambitions. He begins the *Essay* with an account of Chinese civilization, dwelling on its accomplishments from the Great Wall to Confucian philosophy, noting along the way the invention of the compass, gunpowder, and printing. He covers India and the Middle East, but then finishes this introductory section with an abrupt jump to Italy. From there we go straight to Charlemagne, who gets as much space as all the other stuff put together. Yet if this seems thin by modern standards, we might remember the novelty of the approach itself.

Voltaire's biggest weakness as a historian was that he lacked precisely the sort of imagination that Vico was calling for even as Voltaire began writing history. Voltaire makes no attempt to get inside the people he writes about. If including art and ideas seems to entail an effort of imagination, we should understand that Voltaire was attracted to these manifestations of the "human spirit" because they possess a dimension of timelessness. Vico, in contrast, wanted historians to inhabit the attitudes and values of other ages, and to trace the often-startling changes in them that take place over time. Voltaire's notion of historical change was limited to showing how reason has led to progress. It's a strangely static picture: Every age is populated with Enlightenment rationalists just like him, fighting with more or less success (depending on circumstances) to "crush the infamy" of the church and further the cause of progress. Either that, or they're hypocrites and scoundrels.*

But while noting his weaknesses, modern observers have found real strengths in Voltaire's historical outlook. In addition to his innovative enlargement of history's scope, for example, he brings out the role that economic factors play in political and social developments in a manner that once again points the way that future historians would follow. Above all, he is endlessly skeptical of all authority, which is perhaps the most valuable trait a historian can have.

Before the two books we've been discussing were finished, the tragedy of Madame du Châtelet's death derailed Voltaire emotionally and, for a time, creatively. (Both had engaged in other relationships, and the child whose birth killed her was not Voltaire's, but the result of a liaison with a young poet.) In Paris, several of Voltaire's plays flopped, and it was just at this time, too, that the younger generation of Diderot and Rousseau was coming to the fore, which added to his troubles. These writers, especially Rousseau, represented the first stirrings of the antirationalist reaction that would eventually culminate in the Romantic Movement. Voltaire left Paris, and, after

---

* See the discussion by J. H. Brumfitt, *Voltaire, Historian*, pp. 101ff., to which I am indebted here.

an unsettled sojourn in Prussia, moved to Switzerland, staying in Geneva and Lausanne. After a year or two he purchased an estate at a place called Ferney, just across the French border from Geneva.

At Ferney Voltaire recovered his energies and remained highly productive. But though he wrote several smaller works of history, including *A History of Russia* and *A History of the Paris Parliament*, he produced nothing on the scale of his earlier books. He was the most celebrated man in Europe and, as at Cirey, he entertained a steady stream of guests, some distinguished and some hoping to become so, but all admiring. He also worked tirelessly to better the lot of the village's residents, which brought protests from both government and church and affection from the townspeople, who adored him. There he lived out the last two decades of his life, returning for one last triumphant visit to Paris, where he died in 1778.

Among those who had attended Voltaire's famous parties and theatricals in the neighborhood of Lausanne in the late 1750s was a quick-witted and somewhat hot-blooded twenty-year-old English lad who had been sent to Lausanne to study—and to be shepherded back into the Protestant fold—five years earlier. He had done well in his studies, mastering the classics and eradicating the slothful habits and Catholic beliefs he had picked up earlier, during an abortive stint at Oxford. Recently, however, he had fallen hard for a Swiss girl, Suzanne Curchod, the vivacious and intelligent daughter of a minister. This, he suspected, was not what his father had in mind by finding his way back to the bosom of the church. It was just before his twenty-first birthday. His time abroad had matured and deepened him. Now his father decreed that it was time for him to come home. With no small measure of foreboding, Edward Gibbon packed his bags for England.

Getting there wasn't simple or even safe, since he had to go through France, and France and England were in the midst of the Seven Years' War. As Gibbon relates with characteristic understatement in his *Memoirs*, the hostilities "had rendered that polite nation somewhat peevish and difficult." English travelers were denied passage through France, but rather than take a roundabout route through Germany, Gibbon joined two Swiss officers he knew who were planning to travel to the Netherlands, where they were to serve on the French side. Thus disguised as a Swiss officer, Gibbon "passed without incident or enquiry through several fortified towns of the French frontier," noting dryly that in his youthful impetuosity he may have failed to "sufficiently reflect that my borrowed name and regimentals might have been considered in case of a discovery in a very serious light." In other words, he might well have been hung as a spy.

His homecoming, and his father's affectionate but obdurate refusal to countenance any "strange alliance" with a foreigner, combined to persuade Gibbon to abandon his romantic attachment to Miss Curchod, whom he had hoped to marry: "I sighed as a lover: I obeyed as a son," he tells us in his matchless style. "After a painful struggle I yielded to my fate: the remedies of absence and time were at length effectual, and my love subsided in friendship and esteem." They remained on good terms, and she later married Jacques Necker, Louis XVI's powerful finance minister. Gibbon, for his part, doesn't seem to have seriously considered marrying after this. The episode left a deep impression.

So did his earlier attachment to Catholicism, as he himself recognized. His father had sent him to Oxford at fifteen, which was a bit young even for that era. His teachers there had ignored him completely, and he returned the favor. He fell in with "Popish missionaries" who had been "suffered under various disguises to introduce themselves into the colleges of Oxford." They took advantage of his idleness and naiveté to fill him with talk of religious mystery. "Youth is sincere and impetuous," he writes, "and a momentary glow of Enthusiasm raised me above all temporal considerations."

Despite his later hostility to organized religion in any form, he never regretted his youthful "Enthusiasm," a word which in Gibbon's age still carried its literal sense of possession by a divine spirit. Quite the opposite, he says: "I am proud of an honest sacrifice of interest to conscience." As he observes further, he was in good company, for no less a hero to him than the great Pierre Bayle had benefited from a similar childish flirtation with the faith of Rome. "I can never blush if my tender mind was entangled in the sophistry that seduced the acute and manly understandings of . . . BAYLE, who afterwards emerged from superstition to scepticism."

Just as Gibbon succeeded by an act of will in quelling his emotional attachment to Suzanne Curchod, so did he soon (with the help of his tutors in Lausanne) find his way out of dark superstition, back into the sunlit realms of manly understanding, where he would live happily ever after. At least, that's the narrative he's left us, and it certainly does much to explain his enduring suspicion of both strong emotion and strong faith, both of which he now permanently abjured in favor of the clean, virile light of reason—an attitude characteristic of the age, of course, but strongly reinforced in Gibbon by his own history.

Gibbon's family was fairly though not extravagantly well off, and his father now provided him with an independent income. Having decisively curbed the main force of his threatening impetuosity, for the next five years Gibbon enjoyed the life of a gentleman of leisure, which allowed him to pursue his studies. His reading was somewhat interrupted by two years of service in the militia—England at this time being in constant fear of invasion across the Channel—but he would find later that the military experience more than compensated for the disruption in book learning when it came to writing of war.

No sooner was the end of hostilities in sight—in fact, two weeks before the treaty was signed—than Gibbon hurried off for the Grand Tour of the continent that traditionally completed the education of the well-to-do young Englishman. He went first to Paris, where he met the encyclopedists Denis Diderot and Jean Le Rond d'Alembert. Voltaire was absent, but Gibbon got the chance to renew that acquaintance soon enough. Three months in Paris was all he could afford, and he went on to Lausanne, where he spent the better part of a year visiting his old friends.

Then, in April 1764, Gibbon left Lausanne for Italy—
and Rome, for which his studies had long primed him. But
all in due course. First, Turin, Milan, Genoa, Parma, Modena, Bologna, Florence, Pisa, Lucca, Leghorn, Sienna—to the
reader of the *Memoirs*, Gibbon's impatience to reach Rome
is palpable, but is matched only by the mastery with which
he, equally palpably, has determined to defer that gratifica-
tion as long as possible.

"My temper is not very susceptible of enthusiasm," he
tells us, seeming to forget that we know all about his earlier
self, "and the enthusiasm which I do not feel I have ever
scorned to affect. But at the distance of twenty-five years I
can neither forget nor express the strong emotions which
agitated my mind as I first approached and entered the *eternal City*." Gibbon spent several exhausting months exploring
Rome, taking six weeks for a trip to Naples, then returning
for a second visit. And, like Petrarch, Gibbon found inspiration in the ruins. He recorded the moment in his journal: "It was at Rome on the 15th of October, 1764, as I sat
musing among the ruins of the capitol, while the barefoot
friars were singing vespers in the Temple of Jupiter, that the
idea of writing the decline and fall of the city first started to
enter my mind."

At least (once again) that's Gibbon's story, though as
scholars have observed, his journals in Lausanne suggest
that he was already considering a history of the later empire.
In deference to his achievement, however, perhaps we might
let him have the moment.

Like the moment, however, the achievement, too, was
also to be deferred for a while after its conception. Returning

to England, he published a book he'd written earlier, *Essays on the Study of Literature*, and he worked desultorily on other projects, including a history of the Swiss that he never finished. In 1770 he published *Critical Observations on the Sixth Book of the Aeneid*, in which he thoroughly demolished the Christian allegorical interpretation of Virgil recently put forward by an Anglican bishop. His father died that year, and Gibbon spent a couple of years dealing with the estate and selling property in the country before settling in a house in London.

But he read busily, and gradually he organized his sources and started planning his grand history of Rome's imperial decay in detail. In 1773 he began writing, and he doesn't seem to have been much distracted by running for and winning a seat in Parliament the following year. As a Tory, he backed Lord North, the prime minister, who was in charge of British policy in the Americas and was also working on imperial decay. Never insensitive to irony, Gibbon remarked in a letter that "for myself having supported the British I must destroy the Roman empire."

Gibbon's *The History of the Decline and Fall of the Roman Empire* was published in six quarto volumes over a dozen years, from 1776 to 1788. The first volume enjoyed immediate commercial and critical success, selling out the initial printing in fifteen days, and deluging the hugely gratified author with praise and calls for further volumes, which Gibbon commenced right away. Partway through writing it, he quit politics and moved back to Lausanne, which he'd long been hoping to do one day. It was there that he finished, characteristically recording the date and time of his "final deliverance"—"the day or rather the night of the 27th of June, 1787, between the hours of eleven and twelve." From conception to completion, then, took more than twenty-two and a half years. And the work itself covers a proportionately lengthy span of time: from the late second century AD, viewed as the empire's high-water mark, to the fall of Constantinople in 1453.

The coverage is weighted heavily toward the early period, with the first half of the text devoted to the first three centuries, leaving the second half to cover the remaining thousand years. Gibbon explains his reasons at the close of volume IV, two-thirds of the way through the text, by which point the reader has made it only to the seventh century. The western "Roman" empire has fallen, leaving only the eastern "Byzantine" portion. And the story of Byzantium, if he kept up the same level of detail, would bore the reader stiff and offer little in the way of instruction. "At every step as we sink deeper in the decline and fall of the Eastern empire, the annals of each succeeding reign . . . must continue to repeat a tedious and uniform tale of weakness and misery," he avers. "The scale of dominion is diminished to our view by the distance of time and place; nor is the loss of external splendour compensated by nobler gifts of virtue and genius." Whereas the ancient Greeks had lived in freedom and possessed "manly virtue" aplenty, "the subjects of the Byzantine empire, who assume and dishonor the names both of Greeks and Romans, present a dead uniformity of abject vices, which are neither softened by the weakness of humanity nor animated by the vigor of memorable crimes."

At this point, Gibbon seems to sense that we might well wonder why he bothered at all. "I should have abandoned without regret the Greek slaves and their servile historians," he assures us, "had I not reflected that the fate of the Byzantine monarchy is *passively* connected with the most splendid and important revolutions which have changed the state of the world." As the Byzantines declined and declined and declined, other peoples—Arabs, Slavs, Normans, Italians, Turks—took over their territory, and "the active virtues of peace and war deserted from the vanquished to the victorious nations; and it is in their origin and conquests, in their religion and government, that we must explore the causes and effects of the decline and fall of the Eastern empire."

Now, before we go any further, perhaps something in the way of disclosure is in order. I enjoy Gibbon immensely, but I am also a big fan of Byzantine history, and of Byzantium. So it would be less than honest to pretend that I'm at all impartial when it comes to Gibbon's verdict. Yet even those not so afflicted have detected a fundamental problem with Gibbon's famous thesis that Byzantium's long history constitutes an unrelieved story of decline. There's an irony here worthy of the master himself, for the problem is one of simple logic—of reason, in other words. And yet it never seems to have made its way to the cool, hyperrational surface of Gibbon's consciousness (though there are hints of disturbance under the veneer).

Gibbon's thesis of long decline refutes itself, because it begs the obvious question of how long any political entity can "decline" without disintegrating completely. If the Byzantines were so degenerate, in other words, so utterly weak and vitiated, how on earth did they last so long? We're talking about more than a thousand years! It's not as if the empire were surrounded by well-wishers who sought to support it in its senescence. Byzantium faced constant threats by powerful and aggressive neighbors on all sides. One by one it outlasted them all. All but one, that is—the Turks, a populous and militarily formidable people who took literally hundreds of years to get the job done. Gibbon never addresses this question satisfactorily, and he contradicts himself several times in trying to get around it.*

As is now widely acknowledged, one key to all this lies in Gibbon's attitude to religion. In the very last chapter of *The Decline and Fall*, he looks back with the reader over the landscape they have just traversed together. "In the preceding volumes of this History," he summarizes, "I have described the triumph of barbarism and religion." These are perhaps Gibbon's best-known words, and they draw a clear connection between the empire's external enemies and its internal transformation into a Christian society. A couple of pages before this, he even refers to "the attacks of barbarians and Christians," as if the Germanic tribes pressing on the empire's northern borders had been joined by similarly aggressive hordes of bloodthirsty Christians.

But the Christians were always inside the empire—and before too long, they *were* the empire. They didn't attack the empire, they saved it. Or so they themselves believed, putting their faith in God to keep the barbarians at bay.

* See the classic assessment of Gibbon by Speros Vryonis Jr., "Hellas Resurgent," in L. White (ed.), *The Transformation of the Roman World* (Berkeley, 1966). I'm indebted to it here. I'm also indebted to Professor Vryonis, my old teacher, for introducing me to Byzantium, and for much else besides.

By the end of the sixth century Byzantines were referring to Constantinople as their "God-guarded city." During sieges—and there were many of them—the patriarch could be seen up on the walls, parading around with the famous icon of the blessed virgin, which was thought to have the power to turn the enemy away. Religious faith and religious institutions, Byzantinists now agree, comprised the core of Byzantium's remarkable resilience through the centuries. One doesn't have to accept the Byzantines' claims about their faith to see the strength it gave them, and to recognize how that strength manifested itself in numerous ways over time. One does have to be open to seeing it, however, and that Gibbon clearly was not.

Like Thucydides, Gibbon possessed such a command of his material and such powers of insight and artistry that few who came after him were willing to question his assumptions. Predictably, the loudest objections came from religious authorities, but they decried his hostility to religion, not his analysis. Gibbon's assumptions stood unquestioned for more than a century, as today they still stand in the popular imagination. My teacher, the Byzantinist Speros Vryonis, wrote forty years ago that Gibbon "long put the kiss of death on Byzantine studies, even though these had already made remarkable progress in the seventeenth century." That progress had come from the efforts of du Cange, Tillemont, and others whom Gibbon used as sources.* Gibbon stopped it cold, and it was not resumed until the twentieth century. Even his famous wit helped, and not just by denigrating

---

* See chapter 9 for du Cange and Tillemont.

the object of study, which we might well feel is too high a price for fun anyway. But Vryonis notes that while Gibbon's engaging sarcasm and irony help lighten the burden of slogging through his several thousand pages, they also "contribute seriously to the distortion of the picture of the whole society which Gibbon presents."

Gibbon's thesis has now been decisively overturned by a century of scholarly research, but the prejudice against Byzantium lingers on, inside the academic world as well as outside it. We can't lay all the blame at Gibbon's door, however. The stereotype of Byzantines as cunning and effeminate goes back to the Middle Ages, where we find it alive and well in the writings of figures such as the vitriolic Liudprand, Bishop of Cremona, who visited Constantinople twice in the ninth century. It was immeasurably reinforced later, of course, by the Crusades. Gibbon merely bought into this long-standing hostility, but given his relentless skepticism on other matters, we might have hoped for better.

Despite his vast erudition, Gibbon's failure, like Voltaire's, was ultimately one of imagination. Not only did he fail to get inside the people he wrote about, but he also failed even to see that such an attempt could be made, and that it might be part of his job to make it.

Those ideas, already articulated by Vico, were about to be recovered and added to the historian's toolbox. Other tools would also be needed by the historians who rehabilitated Byzantium, and they too had already been invented, if not yet honed to their full sharpness. That story brings us yet again back to Germany, which as we've already seen had its own obsessive and ambivalent relationship with Rome.

TWELVE

History Goes to School and Gets a Job

O ur unlikely route to Germany and to the new German "scientific" history of the nineteenth century begins in, of all places, Scotland. This backwater kingdom in the farthest reaches of northern Britain has played no part in our story up to now, and for good reason. Before the eighteenth century, anyone's list of All-Time Great Scottish Intellectuals would have been quite short in all likelihood limited to one, the medieval philosopher John Duns Scotus. As it was his name that gave us the word "dunce," we might be forgiven for finding the prospects rather grim.

But suddenly in the middle of the eighteenth century the Scots burst into bloom. This Scottish Enlightenment remains unparalleled in its abruptness and extravagance— historians are still trying to explain it—and it involved a wide range of intellectual and artistic creativity. Works of history, as we might expect, were among its products, but ultimately so was a new kind of popular historical awareness that went beyond the writings of historians.

The Scottish Enlightenment's godfather was the philosopher Francis Hutcheson, who taught at Glasgow University and is best known for first formulating the concept of "the greatest good for the greatest number," thereby anticipating the Utilitarian philosophy of John Stuart Mill. Some of the movement's brightest stars were his protégés, including the empiricist philosopher David Hume, and the founder of modern economic theory, Adam Smith.*

David Hume may have considered himself a philosopher, and that's how we think of him today, but he didn't achieve fame in his own time until he tried his hand at history, producing a best-selling six-volume *History of England* (1754–62) that started with Julius Caesar's invasion of Britain and went up to the Glorious Revolution of 1688. Hume took a skeptical, rationalist approach, but although often accused of atheism, he was more open than Gibbon to seeing religion as a positive force in history as well as a negative one. For most of the reading public in Britain and abroad, he was David Hume the historian.

The other major Scottish historian, and with Hume and Gibbon one of the three most widely read British historians of the century, was William Robertson, who is largely unknown now but was probably more famous in his lifetime than either of the other two. A minister of the Presbyterian Church of Scotland, he wrote *A History of Scotland* (1759), which made his name and won him an appointment as royal historian. He then produced two far more ambitious works, *A History of the Reign of Charles V* (1769), which traced the rise of the modern European state in the mid-sixteenth century, and *A History of America* (1777), which limited itself to the European colonial experience.

These were all worthy achievements, and they quite rightly covered their authors in glory. But Scotland had

---

* Adam Smith's *The Wealth of Nations* was published the same year, 1776, as the first volume of Gibbon's *Decline and Fall*, and by the same publisher, who was having a good year.

something a lot juicier in store for history than dry Thucy-didean narratives about states and their activities. In the 1760s an obscure Scottish poet named James Macpherson published a series of epic poems that he claimed had been composed by the third-century Celtic bard Ossian, romantic verses that Macpherson alleged he had merely transcribed as they had been recited to him by the simple, rugged Highland folk who had preserved them over the centuries. The poems represented (or Macpherson represented that they represented) authentic Caledonian culture as it had happily existed before the arrival of Christianity. British critics, led by the ever-crusty Samuel Johnson, rapidly exposed Macpherson's fraud—for such it was, the young poet having authored the work himself—but not before "Ossian" had caused a literary sensation in Britain and abroad.

Of the European readers who embraced Ossian, none did so with more enthusiasm than the Germans, who as we've seen had long shown a special weakness for any-one peddling the glorious-national-past-shrouded-in-the-mists-of-time package. The young Johann Gottfried Herder (whose visit to Vico's home city of Naples lay more than a decade off yet) gushed with embarrassing credulity about "the Scottish bard" in a widely read essay. Herder also introduced Ossian to his friend Johann Wolfgang von Goethe, who in *The Sorrows of Young Werther* (1774) has his hero state that "Ossian has replaced Homer in my heart." Ossian thus became the Scottish centerpiece of the influential *Sturm und Drang* ("storm and stress") movement in German literature that these two writers were in the midst of founding, and which prefigured Romanticism in its rejection of reason and classical restraint in favor of emotions and primitive chaos.

Herder was formulating ideas about history that, like Vico's, exalted the role of imagination, but in a slightly different way. For Vico, various historical eras in various cultures differed, but analogies might be drawn between them. For Herder, the past was alien, but the changing spirit of each nation possessed a unique inner core that could help the historian feel his way into a particular period in that nation's history. Herder was fascinated by Ossian because in Ossian he saw the true, original "spirit" of Scotland. Where Vico's analogous relationships ran across cultures and were drawn through the use of imagination and reason, Herder's unique essences ran vertically through them and could only be grasped intuitively. Herder's emphasis on intuition left German Romantic historians more open to religious feeling than the secular Enlightenment thinkers they were reacting against, and it decisively influenced the course that history was about to take in Germany.

But the Scots weren't done yet. Two younger Scottish writers—Robert Burns, born just before Macpherson started publishing the poems, and Walter Scott, born a decade later, as Herder and Goethe were exalting them—now picked up the Scottish folk thread. With that thread, these two masters wove sumptuous fabrics of far greater suppleness and beauty than Macpherson's ostentatiously ossified Ossian. And in an odd North Atlantic feedback loop, Scott, who was influenced by Herder and Goethe, would return the favor to influence later German Romantics.

Walter Scott is well named. Almost single-handedly, this widely read and immensely influential poet, novelist, biographer, and historian invented the Scotland that now emerged as the world's first historical theme park. The Highland warrior wrapped in his tartan kilt, marching to the stirring sound of bagpipes—this iconic figure is a fantasy, and his associated emblems were either fantasies themselves (like the kilt), or at best marginally significant recent arrivals elevated to symbolic status only much later (like the bagpipe). They were not ancestral traditions. Go back a bit, and no tartan, no bagpipes. No Scottish Highlands, for that matter. Culturally, until a century or so before Scott, the "Scottish" Highlands were basically Irish. The whole thing was a gleeful concoction, and Scott was its principal author. Even a generation before, illustrations of Macpherson's Ossian, for example, showed him in a robe with a harp, far more authentic Scottish accoutrements than a kilt and bagpipe.*

To publicize Highlandworld, Scott also invented a new literary genre: the historical novel. The first was *Waverly*, which he began in 1805—the same year he wrote an essay for *The Edinburgh Review* in which, on the one hand, he quite correctly denied the authenticity of Macpherson's Ossian, while, on the other, he made the first reference anywhere to tartan as the supposedly ancient Caledonian costume. Almost a decade elapsed before Scott revived the unfinished tale, which is set during the Jacobite rebellion of 1745, the

---

* For the political and historical background, see Hugh Trevor-Roper's enjoyable and enlightening chapter on the invention of "Highland tradition" in Eric Hobsbawm and Terence Ranger (eds.), *The Invention of Tradition* (1983), to which I'm indebted here.

lost cause of Bonnie Prince Charlie that defined Scottish political identity. He finished *Waverly* in a summer and published it anonymously that same year, 1814.

Scott eventually wrote novels set in other times and places, such as *Ivanhoe* (fifteenth-century England) and *Quentin Durward* (fifteenth-century France), but *Waverly* and its Scottish successors—*Guy Mannering, The Antiquary, Rob Roy, The Heart of Midlothian, The Bride of Lammermoor, A Legend of Montrose*—were the first string. Hugely successful both commercially and artistically, these "Waverly" novels (as they're called) fictionalized various colorful episodes in Scottish history, sparking a fad for all things Scottish that reached a climax half a century later, when Queen Victoria and Prince Albert bought an estate, Balmoral, in the Highlands, for which the Queen's beloved Bertie designed a nice Balmoral tartan.

The Hanoverian British Queen and her Prussian consort were hardly the first Germans to succumb to the allure of Scott's historical fantasies. In the 1820s, a young German schoolteacher named Leopold Ranke read Scott's novels avidly and found that they stirred his own interest in the past. Up to then his awareness of history had been tangential to other disciplines, but his imaginative engagement with Scott was not unprecedented in his life. An accomplished classicist at an early age, he'd read Homer in Greek as a boy, and then gone off to play Greeks and Trojans. Ranke was also, and would remain, a devout Lutheran; most of his male relatives were either pastors or lawyers. At the University of Leipzig, he'd carried on both sides of this background by studying classical philology and theology.

His philology teacher, a leading German authority in a field that Germans now led, stressed the importance of technical linguistic knowledge in the study of the classics. Philology had come a long way since its origins with Lorenzo Valla, who had been the first to apply linguistic knowledge to the authentication of a text.* Widely variant readings in surviving manuscripts of ancient texts—mistakes by scribes, interpolations by later writers, gaps that may or may not have been filled by speculation—often made it difficult or impossible to know what the author had originally written. Intimate understanding of the author's linguistic context was a powerful tool for reconstructing the original text. Throughout the Renaissance, Reformation, and Enlightenment eras, scholars had increasingly subjected not just classical texts but also biblical ones to the closest critical scrutiny.

Much of this work had been done in Germany, and when Ranke was a young man, Barthold Georg Niebuhr, who had spent time in Scotland at the height of Ossian fever, applied the new methods to Livy with an eye to the light they might shed on the history of early Rome. The resulting book, *Roman History* (1811), was read and discussed excitedly not just in Germany but around Europe. Niebuhr shared the Romantic obsession with national origins, myth, and folk poetry that ran like an umbilical cord between Highlandworld and Teutonworld. He sifted through extant texts, like

---

* See chapter 6 for Valla and humanism.

Livy, on the assumption that they held nuggets of evidence from previous times that could be separated out from the surrounding fictional soil. His theories and findings have largely been discounted, but his methods caught on.

At Leipzig Ranke wrote his dissertation on Thucydides, applying the same techniques to problems in the text, and only secondarily discussing Thucydides' historical analysis of the Peloponnesian War. Thucydides would always remain his model, and once he took up history he would strive to emulate the Athenian's clinical detachment and penetrating political insight. His other big historical hero was Martin Luther, which would make for an interesting combination. After Leipzig he accepted a job as teacher at the *gymnasium* (secondary school) in the town of Frankfurt-am-Oder, where he carried on his studies, making frequent trips to Berlin to use the library at the new university there.

This studious young scholar-technician may not seem the most likely fan of historical novels, but we shouldn't forget the boy who played Greeks and Trojans. The two bumped up hard against each other when Ranke went to compare Scott's novels with the historical sources—and he found, to his profound shock, that Scott had taken unforgivable liberties with the historical record. "I read more than one of these works with lively interest," he wrote much later, "but I was also offended by them. Among other things I was hurt by the way in which Charles the Bold and Louis XI were treated in *Quentin Durward*, in full contradiction of the historical sources." Here we see the historian breaking out of the philologist's shell. Only an urgently proprietary sense of past realities could launch such indignation. It didn't just bother him, it *hurt*.

Worse yet, Scott not only included many "unhistorical" details in his story, but he also seemed to have done so deliberately, even though he knew they were wrong! For this, Ranke tells us, "I felt unable to pardon him."

Ranke's disillusionment with Scott turned him off to historical fiction, but it also turned him on to history. "In comparing the two, I found that the historical reports themselves were more beautiful and, in any case, more interesting than the romantic fiction. Thereafter I turned away from it altogether and decided to avoid everything fictitious and fanciful and to cling strictly to the facts." Ranke might have been channeling Thucydides, who attacked Herodotus in much the same rather humorless way for introducing "fanciful" elements into his history.

But what also strikes us about Ranke's reaction is its openly emotional embrace of beauty. Where Gibbon met emotion by bleeding it dry with irony, Ranke welcomed it. Ranke's personal engagement with history remained an emotional one. He always found history supremely gorgeous. As a mature historian he went to the archives the way a hot-blooded young man goes to a lover. And yet he did so in the name of facts. Like Scott, Ranke stands squarely within the Romantic Movement, but in this way he also reacted against it. It will help to keep this in mind as we try to grasp some of the hidden tensions beneath the smoothly rising arc of Ranke's long and extraordinarily influential career.

In 1824 Ranke published his first book, *History of the Latin and Teutonic Nations from 1494 to 1514*, which covered the French invasions of Italy during this pivotal period. Francesco Guicciardini, we remember, had narrated those wars in his *History of Italy*, which was still the standard account. Ranke's book went over well enough, but what really grabbed the spotlight for its young author was an appendix in which he thoroughly demolished his predecessor. Guicciardini, Ranke asserted, had misrepresented evidence, altered facts, and invented details. Moreover, he'd based his history on accounts recorded after the events took place, rather than on documents and other contemporaneous records—that is, in the historian's argot that Ranke would soon enshrine, on "secondary sources" rather than "primary sources." This was pretty devastating, and for many years Ranke's attack stood. Only relatively recently has it been shown to have been entirely baseless.

But it allowed Ranke to set himself up in Guicciardini's place, implying that where Guicciardini had relied on fluff, he, Ranke, would rely on the real thing: "memoirs, diaries, letters, diplomatic reports and original narratives of eyewitnesses; other writings only when they were immediately derived from the former, or seemed equal to them by virtue of their information." His job as a historian, Ranke stated further, was not to stand in judgment of the past, but to show the past as it really was—*wie es eigentlich gewesen* in the German.

This is Ranke's most famous phrase, and it suggested that there was a spirit, an inner meaning, to the past that lay under the surface of human affairs. Recovering that essence was the true task of the historian: Each age and each civilization, in another famous phrase, was "immediate before

God," and could only be grasped if the historian left himself and his own age behind. From Herder, Ranke took not only the idea of spiritual essences at work in history, but also the idea that intuition was the road to understanding them. "Everything, both general and individual, is an expression of spiritual life," he wrote. It was to understand the spiritual life of an earlier age that the historian accumulated facts. Rational inferences can help with the surface of history, but the inner meaning could only be grasped intuitively, once the historian had piled up enough facts to reach a threshold of understanding. Perhaps this mysterious process of osmosis helps explain why Ranke went to the archives each day with such joy and excitement.

The book, and its author's masterful self-presentation, won Ranke a position at the University of Berlin (it was said that bringing him to Berlin was easier than moving the university's library to Frankfurt). Ranke taught in Berlin for almost fifty years, all the while churning out history books based on tireless archival research. After retiring in 1871, he kept up a heavy schedule of research and writing despite his failing eyesight, producing eight volumes of a work he had long wanted to write, a history of the world. When he died in 1886 at age ninety, he was Europe's most famous historian, and he had utterly changed the face of history.

But history had also shaped him, and one problem with Ranke is that while he's eager to proclaim his own influence on history (Guicciardini might say a little too much so), he's entirely oblivious to history's influence on him, and on the German school of history that arose around him. In the end, Ranke shows us that historians cannot detach themselves from their own times, and his example also suggests that the ones who most loudly announce their success in doing so are precisely the ones of whom we need to be extra skeptical.

Ranke's life spanned a period in which Germany was cruelly buffeted between brief flashes of hope and long decades of despair. When he was born, Germans had ached for a century or more under the heavy burden of not being French. Herder and Goethe, with their energetic rebellion against the tyranny of the French Enlightenment, had thrown that weight off German culture, which was blooming at the time of Ranke's birth. But, oh, how shamefully German politics lagged behind! How that glorious French monarchy outshone the pathetically disunified German principalities, some three hundred of them! Then, adding injury to insult, during Ranke's childhood and youth Germany was invaded and conquered by the French, first by its revolutionary armies and then by Napoleon. With Napoleon finally dispatched, Germans' hopes for a unified state of their own were dashed by the Congress of Vienna, though the settlement at least reduced the number of states to some three dozen instead of three hundred. The resulting depression was psychological and eventually also economic. After festering for decades, it exploded in the revolution of 1848, full of sound and fury—including a parliament that was supposed to unite Germany under a new constitution— but signifying nothing. The revolution fizzled out the next year, and the Germans were right back where they'd started. Not until 1871, the year of Ranke's retirement, was the long desire for a unified state fulfilled in the person of Otto von

Bismarck, the "iron chancellor," who as an added bonus bloodied the noses of the French in the process.

It's not hard to see why, for Ranke and the other German historians, the state is the Holy Grail, the mystical chalice, the sacred repository of all the spiritual lifeblood of the Fatherland. Or, in Ranke's famous phrase, states were ideas in the mind of God. Culture, religion, civilization, national identity—all historical meaning was fused and embodied in the crystallized, diamond-hard, divine essence of everything that was the state. Hence Ranke's area of specialization, the rise of the nation-state in early modern Europe; hence, also, his Thucydidean treatment of it—war, politics, and (Ranke's personal emphasis) diplomacy.

Soon after arriving in Berlin, Ranke unearthed the greatest treasure of his career, the forty-seven volumes of reports by Venetian ambassadors that are called the "Relations" (*relazioni*), and that had been moldering unnoticed deep in the depths of his favorite library. These would be the major source for several of his books on European diplomacy. Their neutral tone and carefully guarded language seemed heaven-sent for the would-be objective scientist, who doesn't seem to have considered the possibility that diplomats might have an agenda. In assessing Ranke's writing, modern historians suggest that he was far less critical than he should have been with these sources, and that, indeed, his near-slavish reproduction of them, and of other such sources, was a big part of why he was able to write so many books so quickly.

While Ranke had many distinguished colleagues at the University of Berlin, he more than anyone is credited with establishing history as an academic profession, pursued mainly if not exclusively by professors who have been trained by other professors, and part of whose job it is to train yet more professors. It was Ranke, for example, who invented that eternal crucible of graduate students, the seminar, in which a select group of young professors-in-training meets to present papers revealing their findings, followed by discussion and critique under the benevolent guidance of an older, established professor. Ranke's students were among the most influential historians of the next couple of generations, and most of them were devoted to him. This is the more remarkable because in the lecture hall Ranke was, by all accounts, simply awful. "That was no lecture," complained one attendee in 1857, "but a mumbled, whispered, groaned monologue, delivered with arbitrary interruptions, of which we understood only individual words. Only the mimicry of the old gentleman was interesting," this observer concluded somewhat ambiguously, leaving us with the image of students imitating a doddering and oblivious old geezer, though we hope, perhaps too optimistically, that it was Ranke's own skills in mimicry which offered the sole source of interest.

The seminars inculcated Ranke's methods, which spread rapidly outward to become the new document-based "scientific" history of the nineteenth century. The basic idea was that the closer in time a document was to the event in question, the more reliable it was, though the researcher also had to weigh other considerations, such as bias or possible forgery, in assessing a document's worth. Mabillon and his colleagues had focused on the shape of letters in deciding when a document had been physically written down; Ranke and his disciples brought everything else into the picture to judge when it, or the original of which it was a copy, had actually been first composed, and to fill in as well the context surrounding its composition. Only when properly authenticated and assessed could the document be tagged, bagged, and added to the collection of historical facts. Called *quellenkritik*, or "source criticism," Ranke's method still comprises an important part of graduate programs in history in most universities.

Source criticism has proven to be an immensely powerful tool, and history has no doubt benefited greatly from Ranke's legacy. Yet some pitfalls await the incautious that seem obvious now, but weren't so obvious a century or so ago. It was easy to get carried away. "When all the documents are known and have gone through all the operations which fit them for use, the work of critical scholarship will be finished," two French historians declared toward the end of the nineteenth century. "In the case of some ancient periods, for which documents are rare, we can now see that in a generation or two it will be time to stop."

To be sure, scientists at the time were exhibiting the same overconfidence, which now seems equally naive as we look back on a century of startling scientific advances. When Max Planck was starting out in physics, for example, his teacher tried to warn him off, saying he'd be wasting his time because physics was almost over. A few years later, Max Planck discovered the quantum, and a few years after that Albert Einstein started putting out papers on relativity.

But for Planck and Einstein, intuition was a starting point, not a method, and scientific meaning, inner or otherwise, had to be reached rationally. History had no Plancks or Einsteins to overturn its classical paradigms while it entrenched itself as a solid professional pursuit in universities across Europe and in the Americas. Instead, for many academic historians a slow disillusionment set in over the course of the twentieth century, as they watched Ranke's goal of scientific objectivity take two steps away for each step they took toward it. Even in Ranke's time, however, there were those who declined to pursue the chimera—and even a few bold spirits who held out against the professionalization that seemed to go with that chase.

THIRTEEN

The Last Amateur

In 1828, *The Edinburgh Review* published an essay entitled "History," by a young but already celebrated writer named Thomas Babington Macaulay. At the time, *The Edinburgh Review* was Britain's preeminent journal of culture and politics, and the leading mouthpiece for the reform-minded Whigs. Macaulay's literary renown had come from a widely read essay on Milton he'd published in it three years before. Walter Scott had once contributed to the journal regularly (the 1805 essay on Ossian mentioned in the last chapter was published there), but had abandoned it as his Tory sympathies grew more pronounced. Only the previous year, 1827, had Scott come forward as the anonymous author of the "Waverly" novels, causing a literary earthquake of the first magnitude. Macaulay's essay now looked to Scott as a touchstone for the particular view of history that the younger writer wished to put forward.

Scott, Macaulay suggested, had woven his fictional accounts of the past out of parts of history that historians themselves had either scorned or overlooked completely. In particular, Scott had focused on the lives of common people, whom historians tended to ignore in the rush to dramatize Great People and Great Events. Macaulay called on historians to reclaim the overlooked common people. To make his point, he cited a piece of art:

At Lincoln Cathedral there is a beautiful painted window, which was made by an apprentice out of the pieces of glass which had been rejected by his master. It was so far superior to every other in the church, that, according to the tradition, the vanquished artist killed himself from mortification.

How radically Macaulay's response to Scott differs from Ranke's! At the very same time that Ranke is feeling wounded by Scott's flights of unhistorical fancy, damning a novelist for making things up, Macaulay finds in the novelist a model from whom historians might learn. In the story of the stained-glass window, Macaulay's sympathies clearly lie with the apprentice. Ranke, we suspect, would sympathize with the outdone master, though rather than killing himself he might have been more likely to go after the apprentice, at the very least banning him from the seminar room. When Ranke threw a piece of glass away, he expected it to stay thrown away.

If Ranke was the foremost professional historian of the nineteenth century, Macaulay was the foremost amateur, a politician, orator, essayist, and poet who was considered Britain's leading man of letters in his lifetime. His major work of history, *The History of England* (1849–61), reached a popular audience of Dickensian proportions in America as well as Britain.

He'd been born in 1800, of Scots descent on his father's side and English on his mother's, and lived for most of his life in London. As an adult, he would popularize the phrase "every schoolboy knows," sprinkling it liberally through his writings; as a child he seems to have left other schoolboys in the dust. By age eight, he'd outlined a history of the world, written compositions imitating Virgil in Latin and Walter Scott in English, and penned a tract for the proselytizing of heathen savages. The oldest of nine children, Macaulay was especially fond of two of his sisters, Hannah and Margaret, and would write to one or both of them almost daily throughout his life. He never married, and he loved Hannah's children as his own. One of them, George Otto Trevelyan, would follow in his uncle's footsteps as a historian (and the editor of Macaulay's letters, with an accompanying biography). In turn his son, George Macaulay Trevelyan, would carry on the family tradition, serving as Regius Professor of History at Oxford from 1927 to 1951.

The founder of this imposing dynasty was a short, somewhat pudgy, and prodigiously uncoordinated man, who was utterly lost if called upon to perform any physical activity whatsoever, including shaving himself or tying his tie. Educated at Cambridge, he was a lifelong lover of fiction (Fielding and Smollett were his childhood favorites) and poetry, but he had no ear for music, no interest in art, and no time for anything spiritual, religious or otherwise.

Macaulay held a fellowship at Cambridge in his twenties, but spent most of the time in London. The essays he contributed to *The Edinburgh Review* during this period brought him to the attention of the Whig leaders, and in 1830 one of them offered him a "safe" seat in the House of Commons. He soon made a name for himself as one of the strongest and most effective speakers in support of the much-contested Reform Bill of 1832, the first of several such measures that broadened voting rights in Britain over the course of the nineteenth century. After the success of the bill, he was appointed to a well-paid position in the colonial administration of India, which was about to be transferred to the Crown from the East India Company. In India he advocated equality before the law for Indians and Europeans and freedom of the press, and helped create a national education system. After several years in India, he returned to London and Parliament, where he served another decade, losing his seat in 1847.

The loss of his seat allowed Macaulay to devote himself to his *History of England*, in which he originally planned to cover the years from the Glorious Revolution of 1688 to the death of George III in 1820. He never got nearly that far. In the event, he covered only fifteen years, from 1688 to 1702, when the Parliamentary Whigs, as they had in the Glorious Revolution, again engineered the succession of a foreign sovereign (the first of the Hanovers) rather than face the possibility of another Catholic monarch. In 1852, by which time two volumes had come out, Macaulay suffered a heart attack that left him in declining health, and he died in 1859. He was able to publish two more volumes before his death, and his sister Hannah Trevelyan edited the fifth volume, which came out posthumously.

Macaulay's *History of England* puts into practice some of the ideas about history that its author had sketched out two decades earlier in his *Edinburgh Review* essay. It brings in everyday people and everyday life as well as (certainly not instead of!) Great People and Great Events, including significant passages of what we would think of as social history, very much the kind of thing that Voltaire had been groping toward a century earlier. Macaulay's essay had also argued strongly that history is a branch of literature, and should be practiced as such; in his hands *The History of England* unrolls with the supreme self-assurance and stately, measured progress of a Victorian novel.

In his essay Macaulay had also argued that history should combine reason and imagination, with the historian using reason to analyze the past, and imagination to interpret it and present it artfully to the reader. This supposedly clear-cut boundary would be a distinguishing feature of the "Whig" tradition of historical writing that Macaulay founded, and in which the two Trevelyans would stand as his epigones. We can readily see how this view of history differs from that of Vico and Herder, two strong influences on the German "scientific" school that Macaulay, by now, was actively writing against. For the continental historians, imagination was essential for understanding the past, though we've seen that they had differing ideas about how to use it. For Macaulay and the so-called Whig historians who followed him, imagination was necessary only for handing the past over to the present, as it were—not for grasping it in the first place. We can also see how restricting imagination to the dimension of presentation puts the Whig historians in line with Enlightenment predecessors such as Voltaire and Gibbon, rational analysts to be sure, but self-consciously literary men all.

This affinity is nowhere clearer than in Macaulay's evident, pervasive, and quite contagious delight in passing judgment on historical figures, an activity, of course, that

Ranke explicitly excludes from the job description of the "scientific" historian. Opening a page almost at random, we find him skewering the Earl of Clarendon, whom James II had appointed as Lord Lieutenant of Ireland:

> *he was, from temper, interest, and principle, an obsequious courtier. His spirit was mean; his circumstances were embarrassed; and his mind had been deeply imbued with the political doctrines which the Church of England had in that age too assiduously taught. His abilities, however, were not contemptible; and, under a good King, he would probably have been a respectable viceroy.*

Note that Macaulay isn't slamming Clarendon alone in this exquisitely compact bundle of slights. The Church of England and the king, the only other entities to make an appearance, receive casual yet forceful backhand blows in passing. To paraphrase Raymond Chandler, we could start counting the judgments in these few lines and give up at nine. The capper is hidden in Macaulay's faint praise of abilities that "were not contemptible" (though everything else clearly was): Macaulay doesn't think the man did such a bad job after all. A Rankean would have cut to the chase, but where would be the fun in that?

Having noticed Macaulay's sheer pleasure in passing judgment, we easily see another thing that separated the storytelling Whig historians from the fact-gathering scientific historians (at this point we may safely drop the scare quotes). In focusing his imaginative powers on the construction of artful, absorbing, and entertaining narratives,

Macaulay demonstrates his conviction that history's meaning lies not in the past but in the present. Passing judgment is how the historian fulfills the ideal of relating the past to that present. It is no mere sideshow, pleasant as it might be for historian and reader alike. It is a central duty, no less than getting the facts right. It also fed naturally into Macaulay's unshakable belief that history entails inevitable social progress, which came with the Enlightenment package, and which stood against the Rankean refusal to construct such overarching frameworks.

In his 1828 essay, Macaulay bows to the new scientific history even as he draws the battle lines: "The perfect historian," he writes, "is he in whose work the character and spirit of an age is exhibited in miniature. He relates no fact . . . which is not authenticated by sufficient testimony." But, he continues, "by judicious selection, rejection, and arrangement," the ideal historian reclaims for nonfiction narrative the "attractions" that novelists have "usurped." The important thing is that the historian's art serve his overall purpose, which is to "elucidate the condition of society and the nature of man."

This is hard to disagree with as far as it goes. What it leaves out, tellingly, is any sense of change over time. Whose society is the historian supposed to elucidate—the one that he's writing about, or the one he's writing for? One suspects the answer would be that they are the same. Macaulay gives us the same uniformity of texture that prevailed in the rationalist outlook of Voltaire and Gibbon: The past is peopled by the present. As a Whig writing in a time when Whigs were out of power, he chose to portray a moment from history that showed Whigs triumphantly and successfully wielding power. But the Whigs of 1850 weren't at all the Whigs of 1688. The party and its priorities (along with British society as a whole) had changed, in some ways beyond all recognition, but readers of Macaulay's history get no sense of that. Macaulay distorts the history of England no less than Gibbon distorts that of Byzantium—in much the same way, and every bit as enjoyably.

Ranke and Macaulay will forever be paired as opposites, and they were well aware of this, it seems, even during their lifetimes. Ranke would write his *English History* (1859-69) at least partly as a corrective to Macaulay's book. "We do not consider ourselves authorized," he pronounces, "to adopt the tone which English historians have borrowed from the proceedings of criminal courts; we have only to do with the contemplation of the historical event."

The two actually met in 1843, with highly amusing results. Macaulay had reviewed a book of Ranke's, and a breakfast meeting between them was arranged when Ranke was visiting England. It was recorded by the diarist Charles Greville, who as clerk of the Privy Council had access to many of the high and mighty:

> *I went prepared to listen to some first-rate literary talk between such luminaries as Ranke and Macaulay, but there never was a greater failure. The professor, a vivacious little man, not distinguished in appearance, could talk no English, and his French, though spoken fluently, was quite unintelligible. On the other hand, Macaulay could not speak German, and he spoke French without any facility, and with a very vile accent.*

Macaulay impatiently abandoned any pretense at French and, disregarding his interlocutor's own linguistic limitations, "broke into English, pouring forth his stores to the utterly unconscious and uncomprehending professor." A crescendo of mutual incomprehension having been reached, the party came to a rapid end, with the professor, characteristically, fleeing to the archives, "evidently glad to go off to the State Paper Office, where he was working every day."

In practice, though, differences between the two may have been less substantive than either would have been happy to acknowledge, a matter perhaps of style and ideology as much as anything else. Macaulay no less than Ranke wishes to get at the "spirit" of an age, and scholars have amply demonstrated that the deeply conservative Ranke has his own ideological axes to grind in his histories (especially after revolutionary turbulence swept Europe—and Germany, in particular—starting in the 1840s). Nor is Ranke's prose as neutral and colorless as he would have wanted to give out, and he stands out among his German colleagues in finding a large readership among the general public.

Not that sales of any of Ranke's sixty-odd works ever approached the 140,000 copies that Macaulay's book sold in Britain alone within a generation of its publication. Along with the inherent difficulties of viewing history intuitively through an objective scientific microscope, the fact that German readers in the nineteenth century were turning for pleasure to books by English historians made for no small amount of dissatisfaction in the Rankean camp. German professors may have approved the exaltation of the comforting Anglo-Saxon cultural values that came with the Whig outlook, but most of them were less enamored of its liberal political ideals. They could, however, take comfort from the fact that, at the very same time they were losing out on sales, they were taking over the study of history in Britain as well as on the continent—and soon, too, in the United States.

FOURTEEN

History Discovers Art and Culture

Around ten o'clock on the morning of June 8, 1768, a disoriented and profusely bleeding middle-aged man came staggering down the internal staircase in the Locanda Grande, a large and luxurious inn in the heart of the northern Italian city of Trieste. The inn was a busy place with a popular café, and several people ran to help the wounded man. As more bystanders and staff gathered, someone went to fetch a doctor. The man, who had been a guest of the inn for a week and was known to the staff only as Signor Giovanni—he had made clear his preference for anonymity—was helped back to his room, where he was laid on a settee.

The doctor could do nothing for him. As an autopsy would reveal, Signor Giovanni had been stabbed several times in the chest and abdomen. His lungs were filling with blood, and his diaphragm and stomach had been perforated, allowing contents of the digestive system to enter his chest cavity. He was told he didn't have long to live.

When the police arrived, the first thing they asked was his full name, but by then he was too weak to answer. He pointed instead to a corner of the room, where a folded document lay on his trunk. On examination the document proved to have been issued a couple of weeks earlier in Vienna. In bureaucratic Latin, it identified Signor Giovanni as Johann Winckelmann, "prefect of antiquities in Rome, on his way back to the city."

Winckelmann had been stabbed by a man named Francesco Arcangeli, an acquaintance he'd met a few days earlier at the inn, who later said he'd planned to rob him of some valuable medals that Winckelmann had shown him. In confessing to the crime, Arcangeli also said he'd thought that Winckelmann was poor; when Winckelmann had trouble figuring out which coins to use in paying for tobacco, Arcangeli decided he was stupid, too.

In fact, he was quite wealthy, and one of the most brilliant men of the century. In addition to his prefecture he had also served as director of the Vatican Library and secretary to Cardinal Albani, an eminent collector of classical art. A German, Winckelmann had lived in Rome for a decade and a half. Four years earlier, his book, *History of the Art of Antiquity* (1764), had revolutionized the way people viewed Greek and Roman art. Today, Winckelmann is considered the father of art history and one of the founders of modern archaeology.

Johann Winckelmann died that afternoon at four. He was fifty years old.

In its tawdry and sensational aspects, Winckelmann's murder bears an uncanny resemblance to that of the Elizabethan playwright Christopher Marlowe, almost two centuries earlier. Marlowe, too, was stabbed to death at an inn by a disreputable acquaintance, and both murders occurred under circumstances mysterious enough to later give rise to some highly speculative conspiracy theories, though in Marlowe's case these are perhaps better grounded.* Both men, too, were flagrantly, even exuberantly homosexual, walking very much on the Wilde side all their short lives. Predictably enough, it's often assumed that Winckelmann's liaison with Arcangeli was a sexual one. That's certainly possible, though we've no evidence of it, nor does Arcangeli's confession give any hint of covering up such a relationship.

When Winckelmann was born in the early decades of the eighteenth century, interest in the art of the ancient Mediterranean world—Egypt, Greece, Etruria, Rome—already had a long pedigree among the erudite antiquarians and artists who had been poking about in Roman and Greek ruins since the Renaissance. By midcentury, however, fascination was spreading to people who possessed less scholarship but equal curiosity. Each year, the Grand Tour brought growing numbers of wealthy young men and women to Italy, not only from Britain—the young Gibbon was touched by his muse in Rome the same year that Winckelmann's pioneering book came out, in 1764—but also from France, Germany, and other countries. Plenty of books had been written about Greek and Roman art, but they were generally inaccessible, unsystematic, and above all, passionless. It was Winckelmann's genius not just to put that art into an easily understandable narrative context—to give it a storyline—but also to write about it with a glorious, sensual passion that left readers almost panting.

* For a superb anatomy of Christopher Marlowe's murder, see Charles Nicholl's *The Reckoning* (Chicago, 1992).

The son of a poor cobbler from the Prussian town of Stendal, Johann Joachim Winckelmann had had only his wits to support him. He'd studied Greek with some enthusiasm as a boy, then turned to theology and medicine at the universities of Halle and Jena respectively. In his twenties he taught school in the tiny rural town of Seehausen, and then when he was thirty, he applied for and won a job as librarian and secretary to one Count Bünau, a retired diplomat-turned-historian, whose estate was near Dresden, the capital of Saxony. He got on well in Saxony, and his job there did three things for him: It gave him formidable research skills; it offered him the chance to read widely in history and other areas; and it exposed him to Greek art for the first time, since the Count's large library (which Winckelmann was tasked with cataloging) included many volumes on the subject.

In 1755 he brought his new learning to bear in a fifty-page essay, "Reflections on the Imitation of Greek Works in Painting and Sculpture." This first work of Winckelmann's was widely read and won him much celebrity, not least for a bold if possibly somewhat contradictory assertion: "The only way for us to become great, and, if possible, inimitable, lies in the imitation of the Greeks." The essay was also notable for an extended discussion of the famous sculpture of Laocoön and his sons, which Winckelmann extols as an ideal example of Greek art.* Not that Winckelmann

---

* Misattributed by Winckelmann to the classical period, this statue was made probably a bit later, in the first century BC. It was rediscovered with much excitement in Rome in 1506, whereupon it was purchased by Pope Julius II and placed in the Vatican. In Greek mythology, Laocoön is a Trojan commander who warns his fellow Trojans against letting in the horse offered by the Greeks. He is punished by Athena (or Apollo in some versions), who sends a sea-serpent that strangles him and his two sons. The statue shows the three male figures, with Laocoön in the middle, wrestling with the serpents.

was breaking any new ground with the observation; Pliny the Elder had praised the same sculpture in similar terms. But in the eighteenth century, Roman art, like all things Roman, was generally held to be superior to its Greek counterpart. This was Winckelmann's opening salvo in his campaign to reverse that hitherto conventional judgment. The essay also contains the often-quoted phrase "noble simplicity and quiet grandeur," which is what Winckelmann attributed to this sculpture, and to Greek art in general. Like Winckelmann's other work, the "Reflections" would influence fellow Germans particularly: Herder, Goethe, and Schilling read it, and Lessing wrote his own essay on Laocoön in response to it a decade later.

Various foreign dignitaries visited the estate where Winckelmann worked, and part of his job was to show them around the library. One of them was a papal nuncio, Alberico Archinto, who had befriended Winckelmann while visiting several years earlier. Now the papal governor in Rome, he arranged for Winckelmann to be offered jobs there as librarian and secretary. Winckelmann, raised a Lutheran but never terribly devout, had already converted to Catholicism under his friend's influence. Riding high on literary success, he moved to Rome.

If Petrarch and Gibbon found inspiration in Rome, Winckelmann found heaven. They visited; he took up residence, though at first he didn't plan to stay more than a year or two. Archinto died in 1758, and Winckelmann was offered a position as secretary to the great art collector Cardinal Alessandro Albani. None of these positions paid anything much, but that didn't matter. They offered him unparalleled access to a vast array of art, much of it classical, and much of which no one had bothered to look at closely before, and access as well to the books he would need to place that art in context. Much of his work for Albani was in the way of cataloging the collection, and it brought Winckelmann a deep mastery of his subject. It was now that his *History of the Art of Antiquity* began taking shape.

At the same time, Winckelmann was opening new vistas into a different but related area. Or rather, he was trying to; he met some pretty stiff resistance. The famous buried cities of Pompeii and Herculaneum, covered by volcanic ash in the same eruption of Mount Vesuvius that had claimed Pliny the Elder, had only recently begun to be excavated and explored, though ruins at Pompeii had been discovered in the late sixteenth century. Excavations at Herculaneum had begun in 1709, and at Pompeii only in 1748. Winckelmann had long been eager to explore the sites for himself and examine the many artifacts—vases, statues, jewelry, partly incinerated rolls of papyrus—that had been recovered. The sites are near Naples, then part of the kingdom of Sicily. With his papal connections and literary prestige, Winckelmann had no trouble securing impressive letters of introduction from Sicilian and Neapolitan bigwigs in hopes of getting in. But his plan backfired. His fancy letters antagonized the antiquarians in charge of the excavations, and they busily began throwing up bureaucratic roadblocks.

Testy egos aside, the people running the show at Pompeii and Herculaneum had good reasons to keep a knowledgeable outsider away. They were more concerned with influence at court than with scholarship, and their scholarship showed it. One of them, a professor of Greek from Naples named Jacopo Martorelli, took time out from lambasting his rival, another Greek scholar named Mazzochi, to write a 700-page work explaining his theory on the use of ancient inkpots, which might have been fine if the inkpot on which he built the theory had actually been an inkpot, not a jewelry box. Later in his career he proved that Homer had lived in Naples, founded the university there, and originated the same chair of Greek studies filled by Professor Martorelli himself.

Far worse than their questionable attempts to interpret the evidence they were uncovering was their incompetence in managing the process of actually uncovering it. Excavation was geared entirely toward filling museums and private collections, and even so, it was haphazard and reckless. The digging itself was done by chain gangs of convicts and Turkish prisoners of war. Soil and ash were shuffled from one spot to another instead of being removed, while the artifacts were rifled through for the best and most intact pieces, with the rest thrown to the side in heaps. The atmosphere was part prisoner-of-war camp and part treasure hunt, giving them another reason to view outsiders with misgiving.

This was the situation Winckelmann found in 1762, when he was finally able to push his way through the resistance and gain some access to Herculaneum. Outraged by what he saw, he wrote an "Open Letter on the Discoveries Made at Herculaneum" that he distributed to a select group of art collectors and other like-minded scholars he knew, most of them outside of Italy. After a second visit two years later, he followed up with a similar "Report on the Most Recent Discoveries Made at Herculaneum."

In these two scathing exposés Winckelmann not only shone a light on the self-aggrandizing foolishness of Martorelli and the others, but he also articulated with his characteristic blend of passion and precision exactly what their (and their patrons') shortsighted cupidity was costing the world. In addition, he made specific suggestions for how these and other important excavations might be put on a scientific footing. Like all his writings, the reports were read by the right people, especially after being translated into French, and those people brought increasing pressure to bear on the wealthy patrons who paid for the work. Though it took a few years, eventually Winckelmann's reports made it impossible for such excavations to go on as before. It is for this reason that Winckelmann has been called the father of modern archaeology.

All this time, Winckelmann was also working hard on what would become his magnum opus, the *History of the Art of Antiquity*—the first book of art history. Winckelmann divides the book into two sections: The first traces the history of art through the civilizations of the Egyptians, Phoenicians, Persians, Etruscans, Greeks, and finally the Romans, and the second looks more specifically at the historical evolution of Greek art. Throughout, he offers opinions that will strike knowledgeable modern readers as narrow or ill-founded, and assertions that were shown to be radically mistaken generations ago. Yet the basic storyline is one that's still familiar: Greek art developed during an "archaic" age, reached a peak during the classical age, and declined thereafter, whereupon the Romans picked it up and made sterile copies. Winckelmann also linked this arc to the rise and fall of political freedom—what we now call democracy—in Greek society. That arc was picked up on by political historians, and likewise remains a familiar, unquestioned parabola.

It's true that Winckelmann's fine observation and thrilling word pictures can, at times, bubble over the page a bit. "In the powerful outline of this physique," he writes, describing at sumptuous length the fragment of a statue of Hercules known as the Belvedere Torso, "I see the matchless strength of the conqueror of the mighty giants, who had risen up against the gods and were subdued by him on the Phlegrean Fields." But he can't help getting carried away, and we can't help getting carried away with him. "Ask those who know the best in mortal perfection whether they have ever seen a flank that can compare with the left side of this statue," he cries ecstatically. "The motion and counter-motion of its muscles is suspended in marvelous balance by a skillfully rendered alternation of tension and release," he adds, in case we thought he was just gawking. It's been said that all subsequent art criticism is a footnote to Winckel-mann; would that it rose to anywhere near the same level of clarity and delectation.

Winckelmann's book has had an incalculable impact. A rage for the "pure Greek spirit" swept Germany and much of the rest of Europe—but especially Germany—starting almost immediately after it was published, though, to be sure, European high culture was well primed. Codified by

Winckelmann and taken up by Herder, Goethe, and others, this mania would mutate into many strange forms: some Neoclassical, some Romantic, some domesticated, some horrifying. We've seen one of them already, in Ranke, whose crazy blend of intuition and professional stolidity (how German!) we contrasted with Macaulay's superbly condescending amateurism (how British!). Yet there's another historian, a younger contemporary of theirs, who was Ranke's opposite in different ways—and for whom we could make a strong case that he was Winckelmann's greatest heir.

Jacob Burckhardt was born in Basel, Switzerland, on May 25, 1818, a half-century almost to the day after Winckelmann's death, and in very different circumstances from those into which the cobbler's son had been born a half-century before that. The Burckhardts were one of the most solid bourgeois families in a city built of such families. The family fortune was based on trade and silk manufacture, and they had produced businessmen, civic leaders, doctors, academics, and clergymen since the sixteenth century.

After a youthful enthusiasm for classics—which he later said "enabled him at all times to live on terms of familiarity with antiquity"—Jacob dutifully planned to follow his father and grandfather into the Protestant ministry, devoting three years to theology at the University of Basel. But he couldn't stick it. No sooner had he won his degree than he lost his calling. It was history that had captured his interest, and with his father's approval in 1839, the young Burckhardt made his way to the most exciting place a historian could find himself in those days: the University of Berlin.

At that point, Ranke had been there for a decade and a half and was already famous. But he was only one star in an academic firmament that included many luminaries. Hegel, with whom Ranke had carried on a mighty controversy over structure in history, had died a few years earlier, having taught in Berlin for more than a decade. But the brothers Grimm, Jacob and Wilhelm—whose philological work was electrifying lecture audiences throughout Europe, though less well known today than *Cinderella* or *Hansel and Gretel*—arrived the year after Burckhardt. (They came as a unit.) And orbiting around Ranke like planets around the sun was a formidable array of historians: the sharp Prussian nationalist and biographer of Alexander the Great, Johann Gustav Droysen, a fiery Mars, who invented the notion of the Hellenistic Age, and who would soon disappoint Burckhardt by leaving Berlin for Kiel; classicist August Boeckh, a Venus, perhaps, whose research ranged from the poetry of Pindar to the emerging field of epigraphy, which would soon be recognized as a vital source for ancient historians; and, crucially, Franz Kugler, pioneering art historian, who was in the process of forcing his expertise into the professional realm of the academicians, and who qualifies as a Jupiter for his gravitational influence alone, at least on the young Burckhardt. He and Burckhardt soon became good friends. Burckhardt would dedicate his first book, a *Guide to the Artistic Treasures of Belgium* (1842) to Kugler, and would also edit revised editions of some of Kugler's books.

And then, of course, there was Ranke. "My eyes were wide with astonishment at the first lectures I heard by Ranke, Droysen, and Boeckh," he wrote to Heinrich Schreiber, an older historian who had encouraged him in his studies back home, in January 1840. "Unfortunately Ranke never lectures on Ancient History; nevertheless I shall go to all his lectures, for even if one learns nothing else from him, one can at least learn the art of *presenting* material." It seems a note of skepticism was creeping in even at this early stage, and we wonder what exactly Burckhardt had in mind when he hopes to emulate Ranke's presentation, which is the last thing we'd expect given the vast differences that would emerge between his own style of presentation and Ranke's.

A couple of years later, he gives us a couple of clues. By then, Burckhardt's personal attitude to Ranke has verged over into something closer to contempt. "Ranke is on close terms with hardly anybody here in Berlin; still, I have succeeded in gaining his goodwill," he wrote a bit smugly to Schreiber in the spring of 1842. "One day I shall be able to tell you quite a lot about that odd fish." He starts calling the odd fish "little Ranke" in his letters, making him the butt of gossipy stories of the kind favored by graduate students wishing to bring famous professors down a peg or two. But he still respects Ranke's literary style, for he praises it in a letter to another friend, taking pains to distinguish Ranke from "our donkeys of historians" who have alienated general readers with "dry narration of facts." Since that's exactly how posterity tends to see Ranke, Burckhardt's observations offer a valuable contemporary perspective. For his own part, Burckhardt vows "always to aim at what is interesting rather than at a dry, factual completeness."

Burckhardt returned to Basel in 1843, and for the next few years lectured on history, art, and art history at the university and to the public, who turned out in greater numbers than the students. Lecturing brought little income, and during this period Burckhardt also worked as a journalist. Political and social tensions now wracked the north; revolution would shortly sweep Germany. Burckhardt was exhausted by the inescapable " 'ists' and 'isms' of every kind" seething all around him—communists, industrialists, intellectuals, radicals, fanatics, idealists, everybody and everything. He needed desperately to get away, and February of 1846 found him excitedly preparing for a trip to Rome, "to the beautiful, lazy south, where history is dead, and I, who am so tired of the present, will be refreshed by the thrill of antiquity as by some wonderful and peaceful tomb." It's an interesting metaphor for such a lively historian to use, but Burckhardt lived in edgy times.

Rome he found "coarse and gaudy," but also enigmatic and thrilling. "Part of the pleasure of Rome," he writes, "is that it keeps one perpetually guessing and arranging the ruins of the ages that lie so mysteriously, layer upon layer." Its messiness offended his Swiss sense of order and its lassitude his Protestant work ethic: Romans must have "armed themselves against work for centuries" to let so many ruins pile up around them, and where are the shoe-cleaners? Still, he exhorts his correspondent: "Come here, say I. You can harvest such great and enduring gains in one month here that your life will be worth a good deal more to you." Rome, it seems, was exactly what he needed.

He spent about a year there before returning to Basel and his routine of lectures. But he had found a subject he wanted to write about—the rise of Christianity in the late Roman empire—and a few years later produced his first major work, *The Age of Constantine the Great* (1853). It was followed by the book that would enjoy the greatest commercial success during his lifetime, the *Cicerone* (1855), a travel guide to the art treasures of Italy, with extensive critical essays throughout.

That same year Burckhardt was offered a professorship of art history at the new Federal Institute of Technology in Zurich. The three years he spent there proved to be a turning point, for it was now that he began to articulate the cultural approach to history that he would pioneer for the rest of his career. Ranke's pigeons were coming home to roost. The student turned to the same time period treated by the master—Italy in the fourteenth and fifteenth centuries—but from a completely different angle. The result was one of the nineteenth century's landmark works of history, *The Civilization of the Renaissance in Italy* (1860), which would forever change our view of this period in much the same way that Winckelmann's *History of the Art of Antiquity* had changed our view of Greek civilization nearly a century earlier.

And as with Winckelmann, so completely have we absorbed Burckhardt's idea of the Renaissance that we've forgotten where it came from, and what it replaced. Before Burckhardt, the Renaissance was a purely literary phenomenon. It was Petrarch, and Boccaccio, and Bruni, and Poggio, and Niccoli, and the others who rediscovered ancient Greek and Latin literature. Today, we acknowledge their humanism as an important part of the Renaissance, perhaps even the heart of the movement, but hardly the whole thing. Burckhardt never finished the companion volume on Renaissance art that he had in mind as he wrote *The Civilization of the Renaissance in Italy*, and he doesn't have a section in the book on art per se. And yet the idea of art permeates the book; Burckhardt writes about the state, to be sure, but he writes about "the state as a work of art." When we think of the Renaissance, we see images, not letters, and we owe that to Burckhardt. He was hardly the first to notice the importance of Renaissance humanism, but he was the first to give it a living context, to paint it as part of a broader canvas.

And the first order of business is to reject the pose of Olympian objectivity adopted by the Germans. Burckhardt begins by telling us immediately that his book is just an essay, and that he's merely one interpreter of a large and difficult subject. In words that create visual images, he proclaims not objectivity but its opposite:

> *To each eye, perhaps, the outlines of a given civilization present a different picture; and in treating of a civilization which is the mother of our own, and whose influence is still at work among us, it is unavoidable that individual judgment and feeling should tell every moment both on the writer and on the reader.*

It's a big subject, the reader is told, and can be studied from many "points of view" (a phrase that recalls

Winckelmann); the author will be "content if a patient hearing is granted us, and if this book be taken as a whole."

Taking it as a whole is what Burckhardt is all about. Politics is only part of the picture. What we owe this book without realizing the debt is found in headings such as "The Development of the Individual," "The Awakening of Personality," "The Many-Sided Men," "The Discovery of the World and of Man." He shows us the costumes of women, the lovemaking of the courtier, the playing of music, the cultivation of superstition and faith in daily life. "We must insist upon it," he writes at one point, "as one of the chief propositions of this book, that it was not the revival of antiquity alone, but its union with the genius of the Italian people, which achieved the conquest of the western world." In this pioneer work of cultural history, Burckhardt gives us a Renaissance that invented not just modern nation-states, but modern Western culture as a whole. And that's the Renaissance we still have.

Burckhardt lived almost another four decades, and he wrote other books (including one on Italian Renaissance architecture), but nothing on the scale of *The Civilization of the Renaissance in Italy*. In 1871, he was amused to be offered the very chair in history being vacated by the illustrious Ranke. He declined the honor. "I would not have gone to Berlin at any price; to have left Basel would have brought a malediction on me," he explained, only half joking.

Burckhardt continued lecturing at Basel, where he grew increasingly pessimistic about the future of European civilization. He had little faith in democracy, which he saw as vulnerable to the depredations of commercial materialism and demagoguery. "In order to be reelected," he wrote in 1881, "the leaders of the people, the demagogues, must have the masses on their side, and they in turn demand that something should always be happening, otherwise they don't believe 'progress' is going on." It's a vicious circle, and Burckhardt sees no way out. Historians have a miserable track record as prophets, but more than one observer has seen the dark outlines of the coming century in Burckhardt's elegiac reflections on Western culture. Burckhardt died in 1897, just shy of that century's arrival.

FIFTEEN

Deep Time

In 1871, the year that Jacob Burckhardt didn't move to Berlin, a wealthy if somewhat shady businessman-turned-amateur-archaeologist named Heinrich Schliemann began excavations at a place called Hissarlik, a low nubbin of a hill rising from the plains near the northwestern coast of Turkey. In Hellenistic and Roman times, Hissarlik had been thought to be the site of Ilion, or Troy, the city against which Agamemnon had led the Greeks in the Trojan War of Greek legend. The weight of contemporary academic opinion put Troy, if it had existed at all, some five miles south of Hissarlik, at the more dramatic bluffs of Bounarbashi. But Schliemann had dug test trenches there and found nothing. Based on descriptions in *The Iliad*, he was convinced that Hissarlik was indeed the site of ancient Troy. And he was absolutely determined to prove Homer right by finding it.

The leading ancient historians of the mid-nineteenth century were divided about the value of myth and legend as evidence for the distant past. The great George Grote, the English historian whose twelve-volume *History of Greece* (1848–58) was widely regarded as the best work on the subject well into the twentieth century, did not think much of the idea. His German rival, Ernst Curtius, who came out with his own popular *History of Greece* in five volumes a decade later, was more optimistic. Unlike Grote, who never went to Greece, Curtius was actively interested in archaeology. In 1874 the German government sent him to Athens to negotiate a controversial deal giving German scholars exclusive rights to excavate at Olympia, the site of the ancient Olympic Games. Curtius led those excavations himself, and they signaled the beginning of large-scale academic archaeology in Greece.

But it seems doubtful that the German government would have been much interested in Greek archaeology if Heinrich Schliemann, after two fruitless years at Hissarlik, hadn't struck pay dirt in a spectacular way the year before. He tells the story in the book he wrote later about the discovery, *Ilios: The City and Country of the Trojans* (1881). By 1873, Schliemann, or rather his crew of 80 to 150 Turkish laborers, had dug a deep trench almost 100 feet wide right into the rocky hill itself, exposing layers upon layers of human occupation: foundation walls, stone floors and house blocks, stone tools, pottery. His equipment included 10 three-man handcarts, 6 horse carts, 88 wheelbarrows, 24 large iron levers, 108 shovels, and 103 pickaxes, "all of the best English manufacture." His second wife was with him, a young Greek girl named Sophia Engastromenos, whom the middle-aged Schliemann had found through an Athens marriage agency in 1869. They'd built a shack on the hill, but when they began that season's digging in February, the temperature inside was cold enough, despite the fire in the fireplace, to freeze water near the hearth. The wind driving through cracks in the walls at times prevented them from lighting their lamps, but to Schliemann this meant they were facing the same icy blasts of Boreas that Homer says afflicted the Greeks. The digging made the cold bearable by day, but at night "we had nothing to keep us warm except our enthusiasm for the great work of discovering Troy." We can only hope the warmth was shared equally between them, as this breathtakingly self-dramatizing but undeniably ingenious man assures us it was.

That May found Schliemann excavating along what he took to be a circuit wall around Priam's city, near a large gate, which he took to be the Skaian Gate referred to in Homer. Early one morning while digging at the foot of the wall, he "struck upon a large copper article of the most remarkable form, which attracted my attention all the more, as I thought I saw gold behind it." To keep the workmen away and "save the treasure for archaeology," he immediately called the break for the morning meal, though it was still on the early side. With the workers safely out of the way, Schliemann "cut out the Treasure with a large knife." It was a tough and dangerous job, he says, since the wall threatened to fall down on him at any moment. "But the sight of so many objects, every one of which is of inestimable value to archaeology, made me reckless, and I never thought of any danger." Still, he wouldn't have been able to do it "without the help of my dear wife, who stood at my side, ready to pack the things I cut out in her shawl, and to carry them away."

If this sounds too good to be true, it is. It turns out that Sophia was nowhere near the place at the time, having returned home earlier in the month after her father's sudden death. Schliemann included this detail in his published account, he explained privately, to make her feel better—and to encourage her interest in archaeology. That was Schliemann in a nutshell, casually playing fast and loose with the truth to make a better story, yet under the vainglorious self-presentation, a warm and emotionally generous man not entirely divorced from reality.

The treasure was packed together in a tight rectangle, as if it had been stored in a wooden chest, and next to it Schliemann found a copper key. The most valuable pieces were contained in a large silver vase, which Schliemann concluded had been placed upright inside the chest: some 9,000 pieces of gold jewelry—diadems, necklaces, earrings, and other items. Larger objects included numerous vessels of gold, silver, and copper; silver vases; weapons and helmet crests; and a fine if slightly bent shield. This, Schliemann concluded, must be the treasure of Priam, king of Troy, father of Hector and Paris.

He broke off work at Troy in June, amid difficulties with the Turkish authorities, to return to another site that he'd long had his eye on: Mycenae, on the Greek mainland. His reading of the second-century Greek travel writer Pausanias made him sure that inside the Acropolis at Mycenae he would find the tomb of Agamemnon, king of Mycenae and leader of the Greek forces in the Trojan War. Schliemann dug there for several years, and the results were, if anything, even more impressive. In November and December of 1876, *The Times* of London thrilled its readers with a series of telegrams it had received from Schliemann, describing the discovery of several large tombs. In one were found "human bones, male and female, plate, jewelry of pure archaic gold weighing five kilogrammes, two sceptres with heads of crystal, and chased objects in silver and bronze. It is impossible to describe the rich variety of the treasure." A later telegram informs *The Times*'s readers that Schliemann now possesses "the firmest conviction" that he has found the fabled tomb of Agamemnon. "But how different is the civilization which this treasure reveals from that of Troy! I write in the midst of the greatest turmoil."

Schliemann's confusion was well founded, and his forthright admission of it does him credit, however much later archaeologists have groaned over his violent methods. (In *Ilios,* he's forever describing how, in order to save archaeology, he happily smashed through this or that layer of ancient artifacts, since they obviously had nothing to do with Homer's Troy, which was the only thing he cared about. Whoops, there goes another one, he gives the impression of saying.) Subsequent research has shown that the treasure from Hissarlik is actually far older than the tombs at Mycenae, and predates the time in which the Trojan War might have taken place by about one thousand years.*

Schliemann went on to further glories, including more exciting discoveries at Troy and a brilliant new dig at Tiryns, a site near Mycenae, where he uncovered the remains of a large palace apparently from the same period as the tombs

---

* Scholars now believe that the Trojan War took place in the thirteenth century BC, if it took place at all, while the so-called Priam's treasure has been dated to c. 2200 BC. The tombs at Mycenae are still being interpreted, but also predate the (conjectured) Trojan War by about 300 years. The most famous artifact from Mycenae, the gold mask that Schliemann believed portrayed Agamemnon, is still disputed by archaeologists. See David A. Traill, *Schliemann of Troy: Treasure and Deceit* (New York, 1996), which perhaps overstates the case that Schliemann forged the mask. Schliemann's famous exclamation, "Today I have gazed upon the face of Agamemnon," is probably apocryphal.

at Mycenae. As he went, he made a real effort to improve his methods, turning more and more to qualified, trained experts for assistance and advice, so that his later excavations were more systematic and less destructive than the bull-in-a-china-shop approach he'd taken early on at Hissarlik, when the cold winds of Boreas were spurring him on. And he was thorough and timely in publishing his discoveries. His books—*Ilios* was followed by *Mycenae* (1878), *Tiryns* (1885), and others—are lavishly illustrated with finely rendered drawings of artifacts and sites, if equally lavish with self-praise.

Schliemann's discoveries at Troy and Mycenae brought him wealth and fame, but they also dramatically pushed back the boundaries of the known past. Suddenly, history was backed up by a concrete "prehistory," with tangible artifacts from an age that had previously been no more than a fabulous will-o'-the-wisp. And as part of his often-despised obsession with self-promotion—for which his talent rivaled his nose for buried treasure—Schliemann joyously invited the world to share his enthusiasm for an age of heroes. We now call that age the Mycenaean period, after Schliemann's discoveries at Mycenae. Whatever else we can say about this enigmatic man—and there's much to say, with more to suspect—we must accept his own characteristically immodest assertion that he had opened a new world for archaeology. And, we'd add, for history.

When the Greek government exhibited Schliemann's treasures at the Mycenaean Museum in Athens during the

1880s, thousands of excited visitors, laymen and experts alike, came to see them. One was a young British scholar named Arthur Evans, then only in his early thirties but already widely respected, who came in 1883. The son of a wealthy businessman with strong academic interests of his own, Arthur Evans was interested in numismatics, and within a few years he'd published important scholarly works on ancient coins in Sicily, Greece, and the Balkans. He also grew increasingly fascinated by the larger and related subject of ancient writing, especially writing that predated the use of an alphabet.

In 1892, Evans was visiting Italy, where he met the Italian archaeologist Federico Halbherr, who had carried out archaeological investigations on the island of Crete. Crete, the subject of rich tradition in Greek myth as the home of King Minos, now struck Evans as the most promising place to look for samples of pre-alphabetic writing. Friends had already shown him seal stones from Crete with what looked very much like such writing engraved on them, and he had seen other ones like them in several museums. And so on March 15, 1894, having survived rough winter winds during the twenty-four-hour crossing from Athens, a rather seasick Arthur Evans stepped gratefully ashore at the tiny port of Candia (now Herakleion), on the island of Crete.

Four days later, he made his first visit to Knossos, the ancient island's largest city, where the excavations of Halbherr and others had uncovered the walls of a palace thought to be that of Minos, along with fragments of some large pots and other artifacts. He also was shown several

seal-stones with engraved symbols that he set to work trying to decipher. But Crete was in the throes of gaining
independence from Turkey. Evans went home to England,
where he helped raise funds for his friends on Crete who
were working for independence. At the same time, together
with a Cretan archaeologist named Joseph Hatzidakis, he
arranged for the purchase of Knossos from the Turks.
With the island's independence secured, Evans returned
and began excavations at Knossos in collaboration with
the British School of Athens.

Over the next twenty-five years, Arthur Evans and his
coworkers at Knossos and elsewhere on Crete uncovered
extensive evidence of a wealthy and powerful civilization
centered on the island, which he called Minoan after the
legendary king, and which, as he had suspected early on,
had preceded the rise of Mycenaean culture on the Greek
mainland by many centuries.* The dates that Evans came
up with have been somewhat revised since then, so that
Minoan civilization is thought to have developed starting
around 3000 BC. It suffered a catastrophic collapse around
1450 BC, right around the time that signs of influence, and
possibly incursions, from the mainland Mycenaeans begin
appearing.

Among the celebrated objects found at Knossos is the
large, high-backed bench known, just a shade predictably,
as the throne of Minos. Evans also uncovered what he
called the Grand Staircase at the palace's entrance, which
he immediately began "restoring" to what he judged was its

---

* This, we might add, comports quite well with what Herodotus and Thucydides
have to say about Minos.

original appearance. Evans's extensive restorations would be the most controversial aspect of his work at Knossos; the visitor today enters a world that critics have suggested is as much of Evans's making as of the Minoans'.

But the biggest find, for Evans especially and also for us, was a deposit of thousands of clay tablets containing lines and lines of writing in what Evans called "the prehistoric script of Crete." "It is extremely satisfactory," he writes further, with distinctly un-Schliemannian (i.e., very British) understatement, "as it is what I came to Crete seven years ago to find, and it is the coping stone to what I have already put together." Ultimately, Evans found evidence of several scripts in use by the Minoans, though he was never able to decipher them.*

Together, Arthur Evans and Heinrich Schliemann played the leading roles in discovering the Bronze Age, as the Minoan-Mycenaean period of Aegean civilization is called (for its characteristic use of bronze in making weapons and other objects). Arthur Evans died in 1941, having quietly retired to the Oxford countryside. But his enthusiasm for Minoan civilization often brought him into conflict with other archaeologists who had begun intensive work in mainland Greece, and who resented the way he

---

* British cryptologist Michael Ventris, whose interest was aroused when he attended a lecture by Arthur Evans as a schoolboy, solved the puzzle of one of these scripts in the 1950s; see the classic account by his colleague, John Chadwick, *The Decipherment of Linear B* (Cambridge, 1967), which reads like a great adventure story (which it is). Ventris showed that Linear B, a script found at both Mycenae and Crete, was used to write an early form of Greek, thereby establishing that the Mycenaeans were Greek. Linear A, one of the other scripts found on Crete, has not been deciphered but does not seem to have been used for Greek. Scholars have concluded that the Minoans represent a population that predated the arrival of the Greeks in the Aegean area.

tried to make it appear as if everything Greek had Minoan origins. (Homer, Evans proposed, had basically translated a Minoan epic into Greek, a suggestion that classicists naturally found appalling.) Under the veneer of upper-class British restraint, so superficially different from Schliemann's habitual exaggeration, Arthur Evans had a little Schliemann in him after all.

Schliemann and Evans frequently made headlines, and much of their success came from their ability to popularize their work. This era of colonial enterprise, rising mass media, and increasingly rapid communication produced a plethora of intrepid white explorers heading off into the dark unknown, propelled by dreams of world celebrity; filling out "The Story of Civilization" was just one part of the picture. In the 1870s, for example, Schliemann competed for newspaper space with the sensational adventurer Henry Morton Stanley, who would have been able to teach even Schliemann a thing or two about self-promotion. Stanley had recently returned amid much hoopla from rescuing the lost African explorer Dr. David Livingstone. With equal verve he had just headed up the Nile—in search of its origins, and in the employ of *The New York Herald* and *The Daily Telegraph*—as Schliemann commenced digging at Hissarlik.

Even without such grandstanding to compete with it, by the early decades of the twentieth century, the ongoing discovery of Bronze Age Greece, well publicized as it was, was ceding space in the public eye to other, more dramatic, raids into the prehistoric past. Some of the biggest prizes were to be found elsewhere.

Since the beginning of the previous century, Greece's great rival for the attention of the West had been Egypt, which leaped into the European consciousness when Napoleon invaded it (with as much scientific as military fanfare) in 1798. The British stayed interested, even after their final defeat of the French expeditionary force three years later mollified their fear of a strike at India, the jewel in their imperial crown, through Egypt. The resulting fashion for things Egyptian was as much popular as it was academic, though archaeology did indeed make important strides as a consequence of it.

This Egyptian wave reached an early peak of sorts in 1822, with the decipherment of the Rosetta Stone, a four-foot-by-two-foot lump of black basalt that the British had captured in conquering Egypt from the French. Proud monument to several thousand years of Western cultural imperialism, the Rosetta Stone remains the most famous attraction in the British Museum (next to the Elgin, or rather Parthenon, marbles, about which we need say no more). Its face is inscribed with a text detailing the beneficence of Egypt's Ptolemaic Greek rulers in three languages: Egyptian hieroglyphics on top, a cursive form of hieroglyphics in the middle, and Greek on the bottom. Or, rather, we should say *two* languages, Egyptian and Greek, since the two forms of hieroglyphics represent different ways of writing Egyptian. Deciphering the Egyptian text took a couple of decades of work, first by an Englishman, Thomas Young, and then by a Frenchman, Jean-François

Champollion.* Champollion established that the Egyptian text had been translated from the Greek, not the other way around, as had been assumed. Using the Greek as a key, he was able to translate the hieroglyphics. This was a huge step for Egyptian archaeology, as we might imagine: It meant that Egyptologists could read hieroglyphics, which definitely helps if you happen to be one.

Encouraged by the fact that they could now understand all those droll little pictures, Europeans continued poking around (and more) in Egypt; the loot, or rather the results of their inquiries, may be seen in any of the continent's fine museums. Italians, French, German, British—all had their sites in the middle decades of the nineteenth century, where they busily dug, chipped, brushed, scribbled, sketched, cataloged, pondered, gazed, crated, and exclaimed learnedly before dressing for dinner.

In 1880 there arrived in Egypt a young Englishman with the prepossessing name of William Matthew Flinders Petrie, after his explorer grandfather, William Flinders, who had opened up parts of Australia and Tasmania for the white man. It was Flinders Petrie who would really put Egyptian archaeology on a solid academic footing, and he did much for the rest of archaeology at the same time. Still only in his twenties, he'd already published two pioneering books based on his examination of Stonehenge, in which

---

* Interestingly, Thomas Young, a physicist as well as an Egyptologist, also discovered the principle of interference of light—that light acts as a wave, so that light from different sources creates patterns of troughs and peaks that resemble similar phenomena observable on the surface of a liquid. Historically, this idea can be seen as a sort of "Rosetta Stone" for the quantum description of light that would emerge a century later.

he established the need for precise mathematical measurement in any understanding of that prehistoric monument.

During the next decade, Petrie began excavations of the Great Pyramid at Giza, discovered fragments of a colossal statue of the pharaoh Ramses II at Tanis in the Nile Delta, and proved (by discovering and analyzing fragments of pottery) that Naukratis and Daphnae, also in the Nile Delta, had been important trading centers for Greek merchants. He carried on active archaeological work for another three decades after that, both in Egypt and in Palestine. In the process of uncovering countless monuments, graves, tombs, and artifacts, Petrie pushed the time frame of Egyptian civilization back as far as 4500 BC. His seminal book, *Methods and Aims of Archaeology* (1904), laid out his technique of sequential dating, which uses analysis of potsherds to build a relative timeline for dating archaeological layers. Though controversial at first, Petrie's sequential dating method soon became a standard tool for archaeologists, who still use it today.

One of Petrie's protégés had come out to Egypt as an eager seventeen-year-old in 1891. Because of his artistic ability, he was eventually put to work sketching temples and inscriptions at the temple of Queen Hatshepsut in Thebes. Petrie liked him well enough, but after testing him at the dig site of Tell el-Amarna, he wasn't certain the boy had much of a future in archaeology. "Mr. Carter," he wrote, "is a good-natured lad whose interest is entirely in painting and natural history: he only takes on this digging as being on the spot and convenient . . . and it is of no use to me to work him up as an excavator."

Mr. Carter was Howard Carter, who in 1922 would elec-
trify the world with arguably the most famous archaeological discovery of all time: his dramatic, much-photographed
entry into the splendid and entirely intact tomb of Tutankhamun, pharaoh of Egypt in the fourteenth century
BC. Carter, who had been helped in opening the tomb by
the Metropolitan Museum of Art, toured America afterward, where King Tut fever took hold with special vehe-
mence. No Tutly detail was too fine to overlook; no Tutly
accoutrement too trivial for the public's adoring attention. "Some of the King's sandals are perfectly wonderful,"
judged *The New York Times*, "though difficult to describe."
Photos of the frayed, dilapidated objects bring to mind a
much-traveled flip-flop wrestled from the jaws of a starv-
ing Doberman. "I fully expect," continued the reporter,
"that in a few years' time we shall see our smartest ladies
wearing footgear more or less resembling and absolutely
inspired by these wonderful things." Popular history, Roar-
ing Twenties style.

Tutmania threatened to overshadow some other significant archaeological discoveries of the 1920s, most notably
the discovery of Sumerian civilization in Mesopotamia, an
area with brand-new borders that the British had recently
drawn up and labeled Iraq. Starting in 1922, the British
archaeologist Leonard Woolley, excavating at the royal city
of Ur and associated sites between the Tigris and Euphrates
rivers, put together the now-familiar picture of Mesopotamia as "the cradle of civilization." Sumer rivaled Egypt in its
antiquity, with the earliest urban settlements going back to
around 4000 BC.

In a mere half-century, history had staked a claim to clear working knowledge of human activities and early civilizations much further back in time than anyone had thought possible, and it could back that claim up with hard evidence. Almost as impressive, perhaps, was the dissemination of this knowledge through the newly emerging phenomena of mass media and global communication.* All this spectacular success came courtesy of archaeology, the modern scientific discipline that has done more for history than any other, and that made such rapid strides at the close of the nineteenth century and the dawn of the twentieth.

---

* Starting in the 1930s at Olduvai Gorge in Kenya, Louis and Mary Leakey found early human remains millions of years old. Exposed to avid readers through the pages of *National Geographic* magazine, the glamorous Leakeys would popularize the new disciplines of paleontology and paleoanthropology, which adapted archaeological techniques to further expand humanity's horizons backward in time. "Fossil man," it should be noted, had been the focus of scientific interest since 1856, when the first Neandertal fossils were found in Germany. Three years later, in 1859, Darwin published *The Origin of Species*; the phrase "deep time," which I've appropriated for this chapter, is usually applied to evolutionary or, as originally, geological timescales.

SIXTEEN

Vast Impersonal Forces

In the summer of 1870, Louisa Adams Kuhn, a wealthy forty-year-old American living in northern Italy, was thrown from a horse drawn cab in the spa town of Bagni di Lucca, injuring her foot. She was taken to the hospital, where a few days later, despite the less than serious nature of the wound, she developed tetanus. Her younger brother Henry, vacationing in London at the time, had already rushed to her bedside after receiving a telegram from Louisa's husband, Charles Kuhn. There Henry Adams stayed, while his sister, "as gay and brilliant in the terrors of lockjaw" as she had been in the glory of health, slowly succumbed to the illness. "Hour by hour the muscles grew rigid, while the mind remained bright, until after ten days of fiendish torture she died in convulsions," he later wrote in his autobiography, *The Education of Henry Adams*.

It was Henry Adams' first close experience of death, and it shattered him, stripping away forever the illusion of security that life, and privilege, had offered him in his first three decades. The chapter in which he tells the story is titled "Chaos," and the reader moves numbly with Adams from the deathbed of a vivacious, beloved sister straight into the horror of war, which convulsed Europe the day after Louisa died. The one merges inevitably into the other, death into death, as a young man's disillusionment is mirrored in a continent's: "man became chaotic, and before the illusions of Nature were wholly restored, the illusions of Europe suddenly vanished, leaving a new world to learn."

It's a very different story only a few pages earlier, as we take in the pleasures of Victorian London in the company of this accomplished descendant of two U.S. presidents, already himself a noted writer and soon to be a noted historian. The Industrial Revolution had transformed Britain and America and was transforming Europe as well; the first transatlantic telegraph cable had been laid a few years before; steamships and railways had dramatically shortened travel time between America and Europe, as between London and the continent. Progress was the watchword. A decade earlier, Charles Darwin had thrown the world into a tizzy with the publication of *The Origin of Species* (1859), in which he established the fact of evolution and offered his theory of natural selection to explain how it worked. Darwinism was denounced by alarmed church leaders, but it also seemed to give an intellectual blessing to the idea of progress, which the Victorians had inherited from their Enlightenment predecessors and worshipped like a shining deity. In London in June, Henry Adams had basked in the glow, though protected as ever by the dark, distancing lens of irony (he was skeptical that Darwinism could be proved): "Never had the sun of progress shone so fair. Evolution from lower to higher raged like an epidemic. Darwin was the greatest of prophets in the most evolutionary of worlds." And yet . . .

The war that broke out the day after Louisa Adams Kuhn died was the Franco-Prussian War, which Adams was looking back on from more than three decades' distance as he wrote in the early 1900s.* This war, which created the modern German state, is almost forgotten today, overshadowed in our consciousness by the cataclysmic horrors that followed it. But it turned Europe upside down, and the aftermath—Germany's ensuing drive to create not just a modern state but a first-class world empire to rival those of France and Britain—left a growing sense of looming disaster.

And it wasn't only politics. Culturally, Europe was at the pinnacle of glory, reveling in world empire, technological progress, and scientific achievements that promised yet greater marvels just around the corner. Everything should have been *wunderbar*. The problem was precisely the general perception of being on a pinnacle, since any paths leading from a pinnacle can go in only one direction, and it isn't up. Darwin, we should recall, had also introduced the idea of extinction. This was Darwinism's downside: the fear that progress might be replaced by its opposite. When the German-Jewish writer Max Nordau articulated such anxieties in the title of his widely read book *Degeneration* (1893), this word had already come into common use. The idea of degeneration braided together Europeans' most obsessive *fin-de-siècle* insecurities—racial purity, class conflict, cultural decay, imperial decline—in a nightmare vision of a potential Darwinian world.

Historians, like other writers in this age, looked for ways to grasp such anxieties and grapple with them. Science had

---

* The Prussian chancellor Otto von Bismarck provoked the way-overconfident French emperor Napoleon III into declaring war on July 14. The war resulted in the unification of Germany under Bismarck, the end of France as the big power on the continent, and decades of unresolved hostility and mutual suspicion between France and Germany, setting the stage for the stubborn trench warfare of World War I.

neat mechanical laws that dictated the workings of nature's forces, which, harnessed and domesticated, had clanked and chuffed their way with such success along the rails of progress. History, scientific historians reasoned, must have them, too. For disillusioned Henry Adams, the metaphor of choice was the dynamo, which impressed him with "its occult mechanism" when he saw it at the Chicago Exposition in 1900. He developed a whole "dynamic theory of history" around it, which he propounds at the end of his book, and which "defines Progress as the development and economy of Forces." Later, he would elaborate his theory to include the second law of thermodynamics, which says that entropy will always increase in a closed system.

Eventually, he predicted that civilization would collapse in 1921. He died in 1918, by which time events may well have led him to entertain the possibility of revising his estimate forward.

Of course, the idea that history is ruled by laws like those of science had been around for a long time before Henry Adams got a hold of it. Thucydides hints at the possibility, suggesting that his work will be valuable to future generations because, human nature being what it is, similar things will happen again. In most periods, we can find some historians confidently asserting history's usefulness as a tool for predicting the future, along with others who reject the prophet's role. This was the case even before the prediction of specific outcomes was enshrined as the supposed heart of the scientific method, but as scientists flaunted their predictive powers more and more, historians watched and fidgeted, and some yearned to set themselves up in the same role.

An early proponent of such views in the nineteenth century was Auguste Comte, one of the founders of sociology (his word), who was a close friend of Henri de Saint-Simon, one of the founders of socialism (not his word). Though he read little history and never wrote any, Comte put forward a scheme by which human consciousness progressed in historical stages, from theological to metaphysical to "positive" or scientific. He believed that, with his generous assistance, humanity was about to break through into the third, highest, stage.

Comte's thought was influenced by his friend Saint-Simon, the early socialist, but it was Karl Marx who, a few decades later, built a new edifice for socialism on the foundation of what he saw as immutable historical laws. Engaging with Hegel, who had seen history as governed by "world spirit," Marx (with Friedrich Engels) brought Hegel down to earth, proposing that history is determined solely by material considerations. And this, famously, came down to economics, and the conflict between economic classes. "The history of all hitherto existing societies," Marx and Engels wrote in *The Communist Manifesto* during the turbulent year of 1848, "is the history of class struggles." They predicted that historical materialism would lead to the abolition of private property and the withering away of the state.

The long awaited storm finally broke, and it left people more desperate than ever for fragments to shore against their ruin. Two young historians, Oswald Spengler and

Arnold Toynbee, stepped into the breach by proposing their own sweeping, and ultimately conflicting, visions of history's laws. An exhausted public attributed to each of these Saturnine figures—one German, the other British—an aura of magisterial omniscience that rivaled the star status accorded the great Ranke in the previous century. Both, too, suffered declines in their reputations later in their careers that continued after their deaths. They were men of the moment, though not perhaps in the way they would have liked.

Like the Franco-Prussian War, World War I is overshadowed for us by what came later. We need to be Vicos, imagining ourselves into the shock and despair that the hammer blows of artillery and machine-gun fire inflicted not just on shell-shocked troops but on an entire civilization. We are helped in the effort by a familiar body of literature, perhaps, at least if we read attentively. (Is there anyone who hasn't read *All Quiet on the Western Front* in school?) But historians, especially those who aspire to be scientists, habitually conceal feelings like shock and despair. Even Henry Adams did, when he wrote history.

In keeping with their portentous times, Spengler and Toynbee both focused on an old chestnut with new relevance: the rise and decline of civilizations.* Spengler, a German schoolteacher and polymath, wrote the first volume of the book that would make him famous, *The Decline of the West*, before World War I, but it didn't come out until 1918, when the war was almost over. "Decline" evokes a long

---

* We'll ignore the nasty question of what exactly makes a civilization.

Gibbonian sweep of time, but a more accurate translation of the title would be "The Downfall of the West," or even "The Collapse of the West," both of which are closer to the German word, *untergang*, that Spengler uses.

He gets right to the point: "In this book," he begins, "is attempted for the first time the venture of predetermining history. . .". Spengler's basic idea was not new: Civilizations have life cycles analogous to those of plants and animals. But other versions of the idea usually mixed in some leavening mechanism like Vico's *ricorso*, which would let the cycle start over again. For Spengler, a lifespan was just that, a lifespan, and when it was over, it was all over. *Kaput*. There was no regeneration, and no passing on the flame of civilization to the next one in line. Though Spengler makes it quite complicated (the two volumes together run to 900 pages in the English translation), the ultimate prediction, then, is always death: "Each Culture has its own new possibilities of self-expression which arise, ripen, decay, and never return." The book sold phenomenally well in Germany, and it's not hard to see why Germans bought it. If their civilization's lifespan was predetermined, win or lose, then they were no worse off in defeat than they would have been in victory. Spengler died in 1936, having expressed strong reservations about the Nazis but having still offered rather aloof endorsement.

Arnold Toynbee, who lived until 1975, also saw civilizations as undergoing a natural cycle of birth, growth, and decay, but unlike Spengler, he did not believe that their lifespans were predetermined. Instead, Toynbee suggested in his most famous formulation, civilizations rose and fell in a pattern of "challenge and response," which depended on whether individual leaders were able step up and effectively mobilize their followers in the face of new adversities. If so, then a civilization could go on indefinitely. Toynbee also differed from Spengler in his belief that new civilizations could arise from the pieces of older ones.

Toynbee laid all this out in his massive, twelve-volume *A Study of History* (1934–61), in which he examined no fewer than twenty-six global civilizations, pointing to examples that he claimed exemplified his theory of "challenge and response." Toynbee possessed wide learning and, unlike Spengler, he enjoyed a long and successful academic career. He taught at Oxford, the University of London, and other prestigious institutions, and was a highly sought-after guest lecturer at American universities after World War II. He wrote popular and much-discussed articles for *Time* magazine, and was interviewed for newspapers and television. For many mid-twentieth century Britons and Americans, Arnold Joseph Toynbee was History personified.

The problem was that his theory didn't hold up to scrutiny. As subsequent close analysis of his book has shown, Toynbee cherry-picked his examples to fit the theory. If a "challenge" was needed to pair up a "response," or vice-versa, there was always something around to fit the bill. Instances that fit the theory made it into the book, but numerous other ones that went against it didn't. Toynbee looked at history and he saw what he wanted to see.

So, perhaps, did his readers, and Spengler's, find what they needed in these massive and comforting works of rationalization. We can readily understand how Toynbee would go over well in an Anglo-American world that had just responded successfully to the challenge of two catastrophic world wars, just as Spengler would help demoralized German readers come to terms with their bitter defeat in the first one.

While European historians theorized about grand laws of history on a global scale, American historians for the most part stayed closer to home, entranced by what they came to see as the vigor of their young nation. The colonial period had produced histories of particular colonies, often written by prominent leaders: John Smith, William Bradford, Cotton Mather, Thomas Hutchinson; a spate of books about the Revolutionary War came out in the 1780s and 90s, including one by Mercy Otis Warren, a prominent anti-federalist during the debate over the Constitution.

In the early decades of the nineteenth century, the Americans fell swiftly under the spell of the Rankean school. Many studied in Berlin, from where they imported the nationalistic preoccupations and scientific self-presentation of the Germans. As the century progressed, American universities filled to overflowing with serious young Rankean scholars. The prototype, though not an academic, was George Bancroft, whose long life nearly spanned the nineteenth century: He was born in 1800 and died in 1881. Like many of his colleagues, he came from a patrician New England family. Bancroft studied history in Gottingen and Berlin, and later served as the U.S. ambassador to Germany, also in Berlin. His major work, a ten-volume *History of the United States*

(1834–82) took so long to complete, however, that he had to go back and prune the unrestrained boosterism of his early volumes after he finished the last one. Such gushing now seemed naive; the latest scientific historians no longer went in for that sort of thing.

The big exception to this trend was Francis Parkman, a lone storyteller in a hall full of scientists. Like most of the others, Parkman was raised in the East (and educated at Harvard), but unlike them he looked west, not east, for his training. His first book, *The Oregon Trail* (1846) narrates his event-filled journey across the Rockies, and may still be read with pleasure and interest. After this autobiographical travel book, he turned to history proper with a series of thrilling and thoroughly researched accounts of the run-up to the American Revolution. The first one, *History of the Conspiracy of Pontiac* (1851), tells the story of the Ottawa Indian leader who masterminded an effective guerilla campaign by various tribes against British control in the Great Lakes region after the end of the French and Indian War.

Parkman then embarked on his biggest work, *France and England in North America* (1865--92), which would ultimately fill eight volumes. Plagued by illness, depressed by the death of his wife, and hindered by poor eyesight, Parkman nevertheless retraced the routes of his subjects through the wilderness, visited the sites of the battles he wrote about, interviewed scores of settlers and pioneers, and spent time living with Indians, in addition to carrying out more traditional research. It is largely owing to Francis Parkman that we have clear pictures not only of Pontiac, but also of the explorer LaSalle, and the dueling generals, Montcalm and Wolfe.

The year after Parkman's last volume in his *France and England* series came out, a young professor at the University of Wisconsin named Frederick Jackson Turner published an essay entitled "The Significance of the Frontier in American History." Turner, a Wisconsin native, had received his PhD from Johns Hopkins with a dissertation on the Wisconsin fur trade. He now argued forcefully that the frontier had been a unifying and energizing force in American history, molding newly arrived immigrant groups into a homogenous whole, and stamping the resulting nation with a unique character and destiny. Turner's influential thesis was largely endorsed by other historians and by the public. But the frontier had just closed when Turner's essay was published, and in subsequent works Turner had less success fitting his ideas into the new directions the nation had taken, although he had earlier suggested (against the Rankeans) that each generation of historians must reinvent history for itself.

Such questions were addressed by the next generation of "progressive historians," though one of the most influential of them, Charles Beard, is best known for his revisionist take on the U.S. Constitution. In *An Economic Interpretation of the American Constitution* (1913), Beard argued rather ingeniously that the framers had produced a document that reflected not their self-proclaimed political ideals, but the narrow economic interests of the socioeconomic groups to which they belonged. Beard's contemporary, the intellectual historian Carl Becker, also revisited the framers, but from the more orthodox perspective of their roots in Enlightenment political theory. He was less orthodox, though, later on, and by the 1920s he was rejecting the prevalent Rankean assumptions; he and Beard were among the first academic historians in the United States to openly break with the model of historian as objective fact finder. They argued that the historian's job was not to turn in objective assessments for the ages, which they said was impossible anyway, but to examine the myths that societies use to comfort themselves.*

So far, we have described two main groups of historians: most recently, the scientists, clinging to the crumbling ruins of Rankean objectivity in America and Britain; but also those British historians outside of the scientific fold, the Whigs, as represented by George Macaulay Trevelyan, great-grandnephew (or something) of Thomas Babington Macaulay and a leading voice in British academic history into the 1950s.

Both were facing difficulties by the middle decades of the twentieth century. The scientific historians were bedeviled by the uncomfortable knowledge that science itself was advancing into areas in which full objective knowledge was recognized to be flatly impossible, as publicized by the well-known "Heisenberg uncertainty principle." Historians could try their best to ignore science, though, and many did

---

* At this point, it would probably be wise to point out that as history gets broader, so to speak, the process of simplifying it, already suspect on historiographical grounds, becomes even riskier. In other words, from here on in, more and more will be left out, for which distortion I hope a cheerful admission of my own profound limitations may serve as an excuse. At the same time, I trust the average reader's greater familiarity with recent historians and their work will at least partly make up the deficiency.

so quite successfully. It was harder to ignore the decades of mechanized mayhem that culminated in World War II, and especially in the Holocaust, and that was a problem for the Whigs, for whom human progress was an article of faith.

While the scientists and Whigs were fighting it out over Anglo-American history, an exciting new approach to history had arisen in France: the celebrated "Annales school," originated by Lucien Febvre and Marc Bloch, and named for the journal they founded in 1929, the *Annales d'histoire économique et sociale*. These cultural historians picked up on the model offered earlier by Jacob Burckhardt, whose *Civilization of the Renaissance in Italy* had few imitators, if many readers. But developments in the meantime in fields such as psychology and anthropology were almost begging to be applied to cultural history, and the brilliant scholar-writers of the Annales school would be among the first to do so.*

The aim of the Annales historians was the same ambitious one stated by Burckhardt, and indeed claimed by others as well: to give a portrait of a whole culture or society. Yet they also wished to be scientific, though in a very non-Rankean way. Instead of politics, war, and diplomacy, which they spurned as "event-fixated history" (*histoire événementielle*), and instead of chasing the abstract spirit or essence of an age, the Annales historians would use the latest techniques from psychology and anthropology to explore the inner life, the *mentalités* of past cultures, to give a picture from the inside out, as it were.

* Another was the great Dutch historian Johan Huizinga, whose *The Waning of the Middle Ages* (1919) was perhaps the most influential work of cultural history since Burckhardt. The Annales writers recognized their debt to Huizinga.

Perhaps the most impressive Annales historian was the great Fernand Braudel, a student of Lucien Febvre's, who was captured while serving in the French army during the fall of France in 1940. Held in Lubeck, Germany, as a prisoner of war for the duration, he wrote one of the most remarkable works of twentieth-century historiography, *The Mediterranean and the Mediterranean World in the Age of Philip II* (1949) entirely off the top of his head. Treating the Mediterranean basin as a cultural, economic, and geographical unity, Braudel extends his prodigious memory from the confines of Lubeck into what seems like every nook and cranny of the great inland sea that has played such a vital part in history. One gets the feeling, reading it, that here, perhaps, the inclusive and ever-inquisitive spirit of Herodotus has found new expression.

Indeed, if scientific history was under siege from various insurgents on both sides of the Atlantic by the middle of the twentieth century, we might be forgiven for thinking that it was the Father of History himself who had come back to pound on the gates. Many of these new approaches represent interests clearly displayed by Herodotus, but ones that Thucydides had long ago brusquely pushed to the margins. In the anthropological preoccupations of the Annales school, we see Herodotus's exuberant disquisitions on Scythians, Cimmerians, or Libyans; in the broad civilizational canvases of Spengler and Toynbee, we see Herodotus's large-scale ranging of Asia against Greece.

Finally, from the ranks of the amateurs as well as the academics, we also find greater numbers of popular histories—storytelling histories, that is—directed at a wide audience of general readers. The sometimes-painful divide between academic and popular history is sharpest in America, perhaps, where history established itself contemporaneously with its great Rankean migration into the universities. That left the academics to write for each other, inviting the Barbara Tuchmans, the Will and Ariel Durants, and latterly the David McCulloughs, Stephen Ambroses, and Doris Kearns Goodwins to fill the void. For readers have always loved history. And these writers, along with all of the academic historians who know that secret, are also the heirs of Herodotus.

SEVENTEEN

The Return of the Storyteller

In the spring of 1952, a young American historian named Natalie Zemon Davis arrived in France for six months of research toward her doctoral dissertation in the archives of Lyon. The beauty and freshness of the French countryside left her speechless, she later recalled, letting us in on the beginning of a lifelong love: "The rich fields, so carefully delineated, the borders of poplars along the horizon, ancient-roofed houses clustered in village patterns, flowers everywhere—in front of houses, in windows, in fireplaces." Other things struck her, too, as a progressive, socially engaged young woman coming from 1950s America. The food delighted her, naturally. But she also felt a sense of freedom after the oppressive stiffness of a nation tightly gripped by the Cold War and the McCarthy era.

Davis was interested in the social history of early modern France, and she had chosen to investigate the unrest—grain riots, strikes by workers in the printing industry, and a Protestant sectarian uprising in 1562—that had roiled Lyon in the sixteenth century. One of the first things she did on arriving was explore the city in search of a monument to her hero Marc Bloch, the social historian of French feudalism who, with Lucien Febvre, had helped found the Annales school. A Lyon native, Bloch had worked in the French Resistance during World War II and had been captured and shot by the Germans in 1944, in the aftermath of the Allied invasion at Normandy.* There was no monument to Bloch, though there was one to the Resistance fighters in general.

It's both ironic and fitting that Annales writers such as Bloch and Fernand Braudel fought Germans in the war, since one of the impulses behind the Annales school had originally been to resist the narrow focus on war, politics, and diplomacy that had originated with Ranke and other German scientific historians. As we've seen, the Annales historians also embraced a scientific approach, but a more expansive one incorporating methods from anthropology, psychology, and other emerging disciplines to explore society and culture as a whole. This perhaps was their most positive contribution: to break the legacy of Thucydides, the embalmed assumption that the only fit subject for a scientific approach to history was war and politics. Though that approach would continue to have its defenders (most notably the conservative British historian G. R. Elton in the 1960s), its credibility would not recover from the blow.

Yet at the same time the Annales revolution left room for an entrenched defense of that other pillar of the Rankeans, the assumption that scientific, objective history was possible in the first place. Other postwar historians outside the Annales group also increasingly looked to the so-called "social sciences" for models of how to do history, and as

---

* Bloch's influential book *The Historian's Craft* was posthumously published in an unfinished state in 1949. Together with R.G. Collingwood's *The Idea of History* (1946), Edward Hallett Carr's *What is History?* (1961) and G. R. Elton's *The Practice of History* (1967), these four make up a near-canonical "quartet" of classic works on historiography that appeared after the war. Only relatively recently have they found a worthy successor in Richard J. Evans' valuable contribution, *In Defense of History* (1997), to which I am indebted in this chapter.

a result the idea of scientific objectivity enjoyed a strong resurgence among European and American historians during the Cold War years.

It took a number of different forms. In Britain, the titanic figure of Lewis Namier reacted against the twentieth-century obsession with ideological fault-lines. Instead, he sought explanations in more down-and-dirty motivations such as ego and greed. His book *The Structure of Politics at the Accession of George III* (1929) attacked the traditional interpretation of eighteenth-century British politics as driven by the clash between liberal Whigs (representing the mercantile classes, Parliament, and limits on royal power) and conservative Tories (representing the landed gentry, the Crown, and absolute royal power). Not a bit of it, Namier sniffed: instead it was all about personal advancement through opportunistic networking. Namier's individualistic approach gained few adherents in the 1930s, but it caught on in the Cold War environment of the 1950s, especially among British academic historians. Half a century later, historian Richard J. Evans remembered being told as an undergraduate in the 1960s that Namier had hit upon "the ultimate way of doing history." That verdict would soon be overturned. As Evans recounts, neither Namier's assumptions nor his research have stood up to scrutiny. Ideology matters, although no one would dispute that greed and ego do, too.

Namier, a Polish immigrant to Britain (his original name was Ludwik Nemierowski), was a friend, admirer, and one-time patient of Sigmund Freud, the Viennese doctor who had struggled so mightily to create a science of the mind. Namier's psychological approach to history, though, was not specifically Freudian. But by the 1960s and 1970s, other historians were attempting to apply Freudian psychology to history; the less than stellar results have been widely enough observed as not to require much elaboration here. The curious reader may wish to test a roomful of history professors by saying the word "psychohistory," but the reader whose curiosity is matched by prudence will take care to stand near the door while doing so.

The debacle of the shrinks was paralleled by the debacle of the number-crunchers, as another cadre of giddy would-be technicians sought to squeeze history into a scientific box by "quantifying" it. This approach saddled itself with the preposterous name of Cliometrics; the speciousness of measuring a muse should elicit our skepticism all by itself. It, too, can be traced at least in part to the Annales historians, one of whom, the formidable Emmanuel Le Roy Ladurie, would declare (in 1979): "History that is not quantifiable cannot claim to be scientific." Most historians would agree with this statement, though the smartest might add: "History that is quantifiable cannot claim to be scientific, either." Nor should it need to.

But if some of their adherents' more ambitious claims were, in retrospect, ludicrously overblown, and if many of their early practitioners produced work that turned out to be distinctly cheesy, both of these approaches did have much of value to offer. The trick is knowing when and how to use them. The judicious application of Freudian and other psychological concepts has provided insights into many historical questions, just as the proper use of statistical analysis and other numerical techniques have opened valuable perspectives on many others. Neither one, however, can come close to solving all of history's problems—or even many of the most interesting ones—on its own.*

These currents took decades to play themselves out, but the heady sense of pioneering objectivity they fed into was already crackling in the air as Natalie Zemon Davis dug into the Lyon archives over the summer of 1952. Some of this energy was also generated by the "vast impersonal forces" we explored in the last chapter. Davis' research, for example, was geared toward testing "the ideas of Marx on religion as a superstructure reflecting material interest and of Max Weber on Protestantism as encouraging the capitalist spirit."** Another of her aims was shaped by the Annales school that she admired so: "to compile a quantitative social-history portrait of who the Protestants were in Lyon, their occupation, their quartier, their status." As she notes with justifiable pride, she was the first to do this, and indeed one of the first American historians to conduct archival research in France. "Why aren't you studying your own history?" she recalls being asked at the time by puzzled Lyonnaise. But the archives brought her alive partly because her immersion in them required such a deliberate

---

* See Peter Gay's balanced and enlightening book, *Freud for Historians* (1985) or (for Cliometrics) the discussion in Richard J. Evans, *In Defense of History*, pp. 31ff.
** Marxist historical theory has influenced many non-Marxist historians. Its most prominent practitioner was E. P. Thompson, whose book *The Making of the English Working Class* (1963) set out to rescue the late Victorian and Edwardian laborer from historical obscurity. Marxism's intellectual influence has extended well beyond the end of the Cold War. The late nineteenth-century German sociologist Max Weber proposed that Protestantism played a central role in the economic rise of Europe. His famous thesis of a "Protestant work ethic" has entered common usage (and has stealthily appeared already in this book).

act of imaginative will. Soon even the details of the room in which she worked savored of bygone time: "the smell of its old wood, the shape of its windows, the sounds from the cobblestone street or running stream. The room was a threshold in which I would meet papers that had once been written on and handled by people of the past." It was Alice's mirror, or the magical wardrobe of Narnia.

Of course, if Natalie Zemon Davis was one of the first Americans to do this kind of work in France, she was a pioneer in other ways, too. Her mother, apparently, was as shocked that a nice Jewish girl from an affluent Detroit suburb would want to become a historian as she was by Natalie Zemon's choice, at nineteen, to marry a goy mathematician named Chandler Davis. Yet this remarkable young woman possessed the capacity not only to make her choices and stick with them, but to continue growing within their bounds as well.

Her eye-opening stint (the first of many) in the archives completed, Natalie Zemon Davis returned to the University of Michigan at Ann Arbor to face two life-changing consequences of those choices. She became pregnant, with the first of three children she and her husband would raise in the 1950s. And her husband got into serious trouble with the government, largely over something she herself had done. She had researched and written most of a pamphlet protesting the unconstitutional activities of the House Un-American Activities Committee, which had been published by the University of Michigan Council for the Arts, Sciences, and Professions. Chandler Davis, as treasurer of the organization, wrote the check to have the pamphlet printed, and it was he upon whom the congressional inquisitors now set their sights. As she notes dryly, their sexism worked in her favor: they assumed that anything accomplished by a married couple was the responsibility of the man. The persecution lasted years. Fired from his job as assistant professor at Ann Arbor and blacklisted, Chandler Davis would ultimately serve a six-month prison term for contempt of Congress.

In the meantime, Natalie Zemon Davis continued her work as a scholar while raising a family, switching back and forth (as she puts it) between sixteenth-century Calvinist tracts and *Pat the Bunny*. "Having children helped me as a historian," she observes. "It humanized me; it taught me about psychology and personal relations and gave flesh to abstract words like 'material needs' and 'the body'; it revealed the power of family, rarely treated by historians in those days." By the 1960s, she had moved on from what she came to regard as the simplistic Marxist analysis of her youth, toward a sense of history that included multiple perspectives: economic, religious, social, psychological, and, increasingly, anthropological.

She also felt a growing need to make a place for women in her picture of the past, a realization that was reinforced in the 1970s by the emergence of feminism. As with other professions, women had to fight for a place in history departments, and even if they gained admittance they often faced a barrage of subtle slights. "At many a department meeting," she remembers, "I was the only woman present, and might have to suffer the indignity of some senior historian addressing everyone else as Professor So-and-so and me as

Mrs. Davis." She spent a good part of that exciting decade commuting between Toronto, where the family had moved in the 1960s, and Berkeley, where she taught for six years starting in 1971. In both places she took part in groundbreaking seminars, colloquia, and informal networks with other women historians and graduate students.

It was at Berkeley that she first came across a sixteenth-century book by a French judge, Jean de Coras, called *Memorable Decree*. The book "told the story of a celebrated case of peasant imposture in a Pyrenean village: a man who seemed to be accepted as husband by another man's wife for three years or more. My first reaction was: 'this has got to be a film!'" A few years later, it was: *The Return of Martin Guerre* (1982), with Davis as historical consultant to screenwriter Jean-Claude Carrière and director Daniel Vigne, who had already embarked on the project when Davis, casting about for someone to direct the film, met them and began the unusual partnership. The movie starred Gérard Depardieu as the imposter Arnaud du Tilh. It was widely distributed and did very well critically and commercially, winning numerous awards.

The story was a well-known one both in its own time and later. Juan de Coras, the author of *Memorable Decree*, had been one of the judges at the impostor's trial, and his book enjoyed a substantial readership. Michel de Montaigne commented on the tale, and Alexander Dumas *père* was among several writers who adapted it. Martin Guerre, a well-to-do peasant, disappears mysteriously one day from the small village of Artigat, in the Pyrenes. Years later, he suddenly returns and takes up his old life—but after several years of placid cohabitation, his wife Bertrande unaccountably claims that the man she has been living with is not in fact Martin Guerre at all. The man is tried, and just as he seems about to persuade the court of his innocence, the real Martin Guerre appears, and the impostor is exposed and executed.

While excited by the possibilities the film offered for conveying the reality of village life, Davis also chafed at the degree of simplification necessary to put the complex story into a two-hour screen format. She soon decided to write a historical account of the events themselves. "Influenced by thinking about cinematic narration," she tells us, "I decided to tell the prose story twice, first as it unfolded and was seen at each stage in the village, then as recounted by the storytellers: Judge de Coras, a young lawyer in the court, Montaigne and others. I hoped to suggest to readers some of the parallels between establishing what was true about identity and establishing what was true about history."

With her two versions of this tale—one cinematic, another historical—Davis made a distinctive contribution to a brand new genre of historical writing called microhistory. As the name suggests, microhistory takes a small scale slice of history—usually a village or small town over short period of time—and holds it up as a sort of case history to help address larger problems or issues. One pioneer of the genre was Emmanuel Le Roy Ladurie, the Annales-trained booster of quantification whom we met a few pages ago. Ladurie's brilliant book *Montaillou: The Promised Land of Error* (1975; English translation 1978) used the records of Inquisition interrogators to reconstruct details of life in the village of Montaillou, where heretical Cathar beliefs had taken hold in the fourteenth century. Another early micro-historian was the Italian scholar Carlo Ginzburg, whose book *The Cheese and the Worms* (1976; English translation 1980) explores popular culture in sixteenth-century Italy by examining the testimony of one man, a miller known as Menocchio, who was also tried by the Inquisition. As the reader will have gathered, microhistory tends to rely on records kept by often hostile or repressive authorities, which are preserved until historians find them in archives centuries later. What's particularly striking about microhistory is the way in which these historians turn the records against the interrogators, exploiting the official archives to "interrogate" the victims all over again, but with radically different aims. By allowing people who were often the victims of terrible abuses to tell their own stories, or rather by teasing those hidden stories out the documents left by the powerful, microhistorians give voice to the voiceless past.

Microhistory also reflects a renewed interest in narrative—that is, good old fashioned storytelling—that academic historians begin to demonstrate in the 1970s, and that has only gotten stronger since. Part of this new awareness, it is true, was forced on historians by the literary theorists who rose to prominence around the same time, and whose ideas go under the general heading of postmodernism. Some of these critics launched a full-on frontal attack on history, arguing (in terms that recall Aristotle) that historical texts were no different from fictional ones. Everything was a text, and one text was as good as another. Facts were out; modalities of discourse were in.

In response, history took a famous "linguistic turn" in the 1980s. Instead of desperately seeking objectivity, historians now pursued "self-reflexivity," which meant the ability to consider the limits of one's own understanding (never a bad thing, after all). Some of them used "postmodern" tricks to fine effect; Simon Schama comes to mind, particularly in his superb portrait of the Dutch Golden Age, *The Embarrassment of Riches* (1988). Other more conservative historians reacted angrily against such newfangled balderdash; sparring continued into the 1990s. A truce of sorts was declared after the historians pointed out that if one text was as good as another, then the theorists' own texts were no better than the historians'. Postmodernism, hoist by its own canard.

By the time *The Return of Martin Guerre* came out, Natalie Zemon Davis had been at Princeton for several years, where she taught for the remainder of her extraordinarily distinguished career (and where she still holds an emerita position). One of her colleagues there was a young British historian named Peter Brown, who arrived in 1983 from Berkeley, where he had taught for five years. Before that, he had been medievalist at Oxford, and before that he had been a Protestant boy from Ireland at a boarding school in England in the years after World War II.

At boarding school he had been steered into the study of Greek, which came with a certain amount of baggage in England in those days. For English boys of a certain class, the study of ancient Greek was a ticket back to a clean, crisp world ruled by virtuous reason, before the arrival of Christianity and dark superstition—a ticket to a world that had never existed, really, but that had been woven into airy semi-existence two centuries earlier by the likes of Edward Gibbon. To an Irish boy, however, the study of Greek meant something very different. In England, religious identity had long been a part-time occupation; the Irish were doing it 24/7. Peter Brown, as he later recalled, came from a world where religion soaked into every aspect of daily life and communal identity, whether Catholic or Protestant. At six, he had been very nearly swept up in the exotic world of cowboys, but one looming existential question held him back: "were cowboys Catholics, or were they Protestants?"

And so for him Greek was a gateway not to the chilly, white marble temples of Periclean Athens or Augustan Rome, but to the altogether moister, warmer world of the New Testament and the early fathers of the Church. The classical period, the age before Christianity, felt to him as if it lacked both substance and relevance. "Only the ancient world in its fateful last centuries could explain the world in which I myself lived—a Protestant in an Ireland dominated by a Roman Catholicism which claimed direct continuity with the post-Roman medieval past. . ."

This was the world that Peter Brown would devote himself to understanding and explaining. It is the same "Dark Age" that Gibbon had dismissed as featureless, vitiated, decaying. Ultimately, Brown would reinvent that world, reviving it and giving it a new name: the World of Late Antiquity. He would inspire—is still inspiring—several generations of historians to follow him in finding new meaning, new vitality, and above all new complexity in that world. As has been observed, Peter Brown is one of the few living scholars to have invented a whole new field of study virtually on his own.

Like Natalie Zemon Davis, Brown stresses the mysterious but definite role that the scholar's environment plays in shaping his or her learning. An important one for him was the Lower Reading Room of the Bodleian Library at Oxford. This large, expansive set of halls on the ground floor of the great old sandstone building contains the books and periodicals most commonly needed by students and scholars in classics, ancient history, early Christianity, and philosophy. It's a spacious universe bounded by walls of books, broken only by high windows, with carrels and long tables arranged in rows across the floor. Readers have accustomed seats and territorial interests; the place breathes and sighs with polite glances, deferential gestures, small incursions, hidden flirtations.

This was Peter Brown's space for a quarter century, from his undergraduate days in the 1950s through his postdoctoral research, for which he won a coveted junior fellowship at All Souls College in the 1970s. Looking back from 2003, he finds that this environment is "as distant to modern scholars and as much in need of patient reconstruction as are the quiet study circles of a late antique philosopher or the noisy, petulant world of a late Roman *grammaticus*." He particularly remembers a clergyman—not an Oxford scholar, but an expert on St. Augustine nevertheless—who came in every day from his vicarage in some quiet Oxfordshire village. The man wore bedroom slippers,

Brown recalls. "Frequently, the slippers appeared to win out over the books, and he would fall asleep. A prim young man at that time, I wondered if I could trust the views of so somnolent a person on the Donatist schism." But this old fellow "stood for a wider world of learning" than could be embraced by seminar rooms, colloquia, and scholarly conferences. It was for such people—"for persons of learning and general culture who were not necessarily academics"— as well as for his fellow scholars that Brown wrote his first book, he tells us. That book was *Augustine of Hippo* (1967), a reinterpretation of the saint's life which Brown went out of his way to see was published by a commercial publisher, not a university press.

Over the next decade, it was followed by others—*The World of Late Antiquity* (1971), *Religion and Society in the Age of Saint Augustine* (1972), and *The Making of Late Antiquity* (1978)—that together put forward a radical and compelling alternative to Gibbon's old picture of cultural decay in the late Roman world. Brown shows us instead a world seething with change, a world barely containing the religious and spiritual energy that is transforming it. (It helped, too, to give it a new name. Late Antiquity is a lot easier to respect than a Dark Age.)

It's hard to imagine a greater contrast with the dozing, slipper-wearing readers of the Lower Reading Room than Berkeley in 1978. The era of student activism was over, but Berkeley was still a magnet for the new and radical. This must, we feel, have something to do with Peter Brown's arrival there, for the self-described "prim" young man had carved out a place for himself on the academic cutting edge.

Now, though, he found himself pushed to reconsider the obvious by students asking questions that no sophisticated British undergraduate would be caught dead uttering, but that the relatively untutored and far more curious Americans had no problems blurting out. Why did Christianity replace paganism? How did the early church expand so rapidly? And, in this age of gender and sexual revolutions, what was it about sex that got the early Christians in such a lather?

The result was another flurry of books focusing on these new issues: *The Cult of the Saints* (1981), *Society and the Holy in Late Antiquity* (1982), and *The Body and Society: Men, Women, and Sexual Renunciation in Early Christianity* (1988). These books, as well as his scholarly articles published during this period, reflect the emphasis that Brown now put on the figure of the holy man as an important repository of popular, local spiritual yearning throughout the Mediterranean world. It's a measure of the awe in which Brown was held by this time that holy men started popping out of the woodwork in history departments across America. Suddenly, every graduate student in sight had a pet holy man.

Brown completed *The Body and Society* at Princeton, though he calls it very much a "Berkeley Book." At Princeton a new area of interest solidified around issues to do with rhetoric and power, which shows how this fluid scholar both shaped and was shaped by the intellectual trends of the day. Power was perhaps the hottest academic topic of the 1980s, and in Berkeley Brown had struck up a casual if energetic friendship with the power maestro himself, French theorist Michel Foucault. Brown's books of the early 1990s reflect this new concern, such as *Power and Persuasion in Late Antiq-uity* (1992) and *Authority and the Sacred* (1995).

By the middle to late 1990s, Brown's interests were shifting again, to the process of Christianization in the lands and former lands of the Roman Empire. In 1996 Brown published perhaps his most ambitious book, a volume that, with *Augustine* and *The Body and Society*, this reader would rate as one of three masterpieces. The title, *The Rise of Western Christendom*, perhaps gives a mistaken idea of its scope, since in covering Western Christendom Brown brings his vast learning to bear on Eastern Christendom as well, including Byzantine Christianity and other eastern traditions. This book, which is aimed at the general reader, amounts to Brown's most succinct rebuttal of Gibbon. He begins the preface by explaining: "This book hopes to tell in its own way a story that is already well known in its general outlines."

Less familiar, however, is the picture Brown paints of a bumptious and energetic Christianity jostling with demons and pagan gods from the Fertile Crescent to Iceland, over the space of seven centuries. In eighth-century England, Anglo-Saxon kings were held to be descended from the pagan gods, and this illustrious line of descent had to be reconciled with Christian faith:

> *As long as power based upon genealogies was taken seriously, the gods were taken seriously...Solemn figures even in their decline, they were like an ancient dynasty that had once ruled the earth until forced to abdicate in favor of the Christ of modern times. As Christian kings, their human descendants still bore*

traces of their distinctive, towering stature. Indeed, the more they did so, the more effective they would be as defenders of the Church.

How human that is! "To be noble was to live well," he continues, "to be seen to live well and to foster the memory of a past that lay always on the edge of the Christian present. . ."

And that, come to think of it, is a pretty good description of the historian's noble purpose—to foster the memory of a past that will always lie just beyond the edge of the present.

History Comes of Age

The peculiar genius of the English language, it is sometimes said, lies in its unusual capacity to absorb bits and pieces of other languages seemingly without limit, yet without itself ever being bent out of shape. Perhaps history is something like that. A hybrid from the start, it has proved remarkably resourceful not only in scavenging useful methods and approaches from other disciplines, but also in molding itself to the needs and interests of those who pursue it.

We may wonder at what point the process is finished, but the answer to that must be Frederick Jackson Turner's answer to the Rankeans: that each generation must reinvent history for itself. For each generation, something new. Yet, there it is, the same, somehow.

So it's probably merely the blinkered view of one moment's historical perspective that gives the impression of a maturation in historical practice over the course of the past half-century or so. The 1960s saw a confrontation of sorts, familiar to anyone with an interest in the subject, between two versions of history. In one corner was Edward Hallett Carr, British historian of the Soviet Union, who in his bracing little book *What Is History?* (1961) championed a seemingly newfangled relativist approach. Look at the historian before you look at the history, Carr advised, because all historians are products of their own time and culture. (We suspect that this was part of what Turner was getting at, and he probably wasn't the first one.) In the other corner glowered G. R. Elton, staunch defender of the scientific view, whose book *The Practice of History* (1967) insists that history ought to be based on factual narratives carefully constructed around a framework of political events.

Both still retain much of their original sharpness on rereading, yet where to an undergraduate in the 1980s they locked blades with a loud clamor of steel, now they seem to slide off each other without engaging. Yes, and your point is what exactly? Of course, historians are products of their cultures, but then so is everybody. Of course, history needs to be about politics—and anything else we're interested in. These are yesterday's battles, fought and won by those who went before, which is precisely why they feel so inconsequential now. What seems to have emerged since then, perhaps, is a consensus that history doesn't *have* to be about anything other than the human past, but it *can* be about any aspect of it. Our attitudes have migrated from the policing of history as a zero-sum game toward a summoning of the playful to Mary Poppins's bottomless portmanteau.

And it is bottomless, at least for all practical purposes. If historians downed pens right now, we could still never catch up on our reading.

Part of history's maturity, too, I'd venture, comes from the recent resolution of another old struggle: that between the Herders, who've insisted that the past is irreducibly alien and the people who live there can't possibly have anything in common with us, and the Voltaires, who've insisted that people in the past are just like people now, only with bad teeth.

The historians I am most entranced by handle this one with a grace so effortless that it seems instinctive. They simply hold both possibilities in their minds equally, ready to jiggle one or the other in a flash of emphasis as the evidence warrants. They don't make assumptions either way, in other words. They recognize—and surely this is progress— that an instance of one of these outcomes doesn't have to prevail in all circumstances: in some respects, people in the past may be shockingly different from us; in some other respects, however, they may be quite recognizable. If the evidence isn't clear, the good historians possess the discipline to entertain both possibilities as open, and proceed from there. That bespeaks an intellectual flexibility that earlier historians don't seem to have had. Pressed to pin this development, if such it is, on one historian, I'd blurt out the name of Arnaldo Momigliano, the great Italian historian and immigrant to Oxford who taught Peter Brown and many others, but that would be sheer intuition.

Here in the new millennium, history has conquered all comers, gaining strength from those who've proclaimed themselves its mortal foes. It was once a narrow Greek literary genre. Most recently, it has co-opted the ferocious postmodernists, who set themselves to drain it of meaning but only ended by presenting it with a new set of powerful tools.

History is everywhere; we live in it. We certainly fight over it. In Japan and Saudi Arabia, they rewrite the textbooks regularly; in South Carolina, they refuse to "rewrite history" by accurately labeling the statue of a racist ex-governor.

The past is now a precious commodity, and that makes historians precious, too. For anyone can steal the past, but it takes a historian to recover it. We can only hope that, more often than not, one will be there to do so.

Suggested Reading

On the assumption that readers of this book will have a higher than average interest in pursuing further reading, I have tried to suggest helpful books along the way, as it were, in footnotes. I have also used the footnotes to sketch my major debts in the same way, and for much the same reason.

Two historians, Ernst Breisach and Donald R. Kelley, have recently offered up-to-date and comprehensive scholarly accounts of the history of history. Their books are readily available and are excellent; I've relied heavily on them. Each has a full bibliography, which I why I'm not offering one here.

Ernst Breisach, *Historiography: Ancient, Medieval, and Modern.* Third Edition. Chicago, 2007.

Donald R. Kelley, *Faces of History: Historical Inquiry from Herodotus to Herder.* New Haven, 1998.

Donald R. Kelley, *Fortunes of History: Historical Inquiry from Herder to Huizinga.* New Haven, 2003.

Donald R. Kelley, *Frontiers of History: Historical Inquiry in the Twentieth Century.* New Haven, 2006.

One reason I wished to write this book was that general readers had no counterpart to such scholarly works, a situation that was remedied as my book was being completed by John Burrow's *A History of Histories: Epics, Chronicles, Romances and Inquiries from Herodotus and Thucydides to the Twentieth Century* (New York, 2008). I look forward to reading it, and regret that I was unable to lean on it for my own far less erudite effort. But perhaps the two books may be seen as complementing each other. Professor Burrow's much fuller account offers readers a luxurious and spacious ride, while I've tried to build mine for speed and agility. If his is a Rolls Royce, mine hopes to be an MG.

From the vast body of books on historiography, here are a few fairly accessible ones that I have found particularly informative, insightful, and stimulating:

Fernand Braudel, *On History* (Chicago, 1980). By the leading historian of the Annales school.

Frances FitzGerald, *America Revised* (Boston, 1979). A great American journalist examines the teaching of history in the United States and finds it sorely wanting. Dated now, but still compelling; read it with James Loewen's book, *Lies My Teacher Told Me.*

J. H. Hexter, *Doing History* (Bloomington, 1971), Witty and enjoyable.

H. Stuart Hughes, *History as Art and as Science* (Chicago, 1975).

James W. Loewen, *Lies My Teacher Told Me: Everything Your American History Textbook Got Wrong* (New York, 1995, rev. 2007). A professor at the University of Vermont sets the record straight in a delightfully entertaining way.

Arnaldo Momigliano, *The Classical Foundations of Modern Historiography* (Berkeley and Los Angeles, 1990) and *Essays in Ancient and Modern Historiography* (Middletown, CT, 1977). This great Italian historian (and immigrant to Britain) taught Peter Brown and an entire generation of excellent British historians.

Barbara Tuchman, *Practicing History: Selected Essays* (New York, 1982). Ruminations on writing history by a leading popular historian.

John Vincent, *An Intelligent Person's Guide to History* (London, 1995). Opinionated, cranky, and a lot of fun. This book was also the center of a lively controversy after being turned down by the publisher that initially contracted it.

Gordon S. Wood, *The Purpose of the Past: Reflections on the Use of History* (New York, 2008). By a leading historian of colonial and revolutionary-era America.

Curious readers may also benefit from Maria Lúcia Pallares-Burke, *The New History: Confessions and Conversations* (Cambridge, 2002), which offers profiles and interviews of nine leading historians (including Keith Thomas, Quentin Skinner, Asa Briggs, Jack Goody, and others whom I don't mention in this book but perhaps should have, as well as Natalie Zemon Davis and Carlo Ginzburg, whom I do mention). These and other historians belong to the "new history" generation profiled in a famous 1966 article in the *Times Literary Supplement*. In addition, an excellent book that didn't make its way into my text but that general readers may enjoy is David Hackett Fischer, *Historians' Fallacies: Toward a Logic of Historical Thought* (New York, 1970). Don't let the title throw you—it's very funny in addition to being accessible and lucid. A professor of American history, Fischer, of course, has gone on to write numerous bestselling works of popular history.

Finally, readers interested in the origins of history will have noted my references (in footnotes in Chapter 1) to the work of G. E. R. Lloyd on early Greek science. Professor Lloyd has recently expanded his research to include early Chinese thought. His recent book *The Ambitions of Curiosity: Understanding the World in Ancient Greece and China* (Cambridge, 2003) offers a penetrating and informative comparison of the enterprise of rational inquiry in these two cultures, with special reference to the contrasting social and political contexts that shaped Chinese and Greek knowledge traditions.

Acknowledgments

I'd like to thank my parents for their support during the writing of this book (and all the other times, too, for that matter). I'd also like to express my appreciation for the loving understanding shown to me by my brother Aaron Wells, his wife Elisabeth Bickford Wells, and especially their son, my nephew Theo (to whom this book is dedicated). Thank you for putting up with an uncle's unwilling absence from too many brunches.

My dear friend Catherine Conybeare gave me the benefit of her always astute and informed intelligence during the most difficult part of the book, selecting which historians to include and which to leave out. Thank you for that, Catherine, and for putting me on to Gregory of Tours, and for your friendship all these years. I'd also like to thank the amazing Kim Denton and her equally amazing daughter Brooke Stevens, who gave me James Loewen's *Lies My Teacher Told Me*, which immediately occupied a big place in my thinking. While I'm thanking Brooke, I should also thank all my other friends at the A.C.A.P. After School Program for generously giving me time to finish my homework.

Thanks also to the staffs of the following institutions: Feinberg Library at SUNY Plattsburgh; Starr Library at Middlebury College; the Wadhams Free Library and the Westport Library Association of Westport, NY; and Firestone Library at Princeton. Special thanks to Tim Hartnett and Patty Bentley at Feinberg and Liz Rapalee at Wadhams for all their expert help on so many occasions.

As always, my agent, Ed Knappman of New England Publishing Associates has offered me the highest level of professional representation, and has been a steady source of advice and support as well. I'm grateful also to the people at Lyons Press who contributed so much to the book's final form: Melissa Hayes (copyeditor), Kim Burdick (layout), Libby Kingsbury (interior design), and finally my very patient editor, Tom McCarthy. Thank you all.

Notes

Chapter One

15   *"Thucydides, the Son of Olorus..."* Thucydides IV: 104 and V: 26 (Rex Warner trans.)

Chapter Two

35   *But bitter comments of this sort...* Livy, *The Early History of Rome* (Harmondsworth, 1971) p. 34.

38   *After the conflict at Actium...* Tacitus, *The Complete Works of Tacitus* (New York, 1942), p. 419.

Chapter Three

42   *alone in the midst of a howling mob...* Josephus, *The Jewish War* (London, 1981) , p. 183.

47   *From that time on...* Eusebius, *The History of the Church* (London, 1989), p. 304.

48   *My book will start...Ibid,* pp. 2 and 3.

53   *It seems that the life...* Ammianus Marcellinus, *The Later Roman Empire* (London, 1986), p. 88.

54   *Scrupulous honesty...Ibid,* p. 420.

54   *The rest I leave...Ibid,* p. 443.

56   *his wounds began to fester...* Gregory of Tours, *History of the Franks* (London, 1974), p. 363.

57   *I have spent...*Bede, *A History of the English Church and People* (Harmondsworth, 1968), p. 336.

58   *the river ran dry...Ibid*, pp. 46–47.

59   *the first Roman...Ibid*, p. 40.

59   *in his own English tongue...Ibid*, p. 250.

Chapter Four

65   *And though she brought...*Procopius, *The Secret History* (Harmondsworth, 1966), p. 84.

65   *she murmured most ungratefully...*Edward Gibbon, *The Decline and Fall of the Roman Empire* (New York, undated, Modern Libarary, Vol. 2, p. 481 (italics original).

67   *It was one of the glories...*J. B. Bury, *History of the Later Roman Empire* (New York, 1958), Vol. 2, p. 419.

71   *the upper part of his head...*Einhard, *The Life of Charlemagne* (Coral Gables, FL, 1952), p. 50.

72   *concealed his knowledge of the rumors...Ibid*, p. 48.

76   *The man was as hard...*Michael Psellus, *Fourteen Byzantine Rulers* (Harmondsworth, 1966), p. 46 (slightly altered).

77   *The lady in question...Ibid*, pp. 180–81.

77   *The fact is, Zoe...Ibid*, p. 182.

82   *Now that I have returned...*Anna Comnena, *The Alexiad* (Harmondsworth, 1969), p. 460.

83   *The truth is that...Ibid*, p. 116.

Chapter Five

84   *If you had been there...*Fulcher of Chartres, *The History of the Expedition to Jerusalem* (Knoxville, TN, 1969), p. 122.

84   *It was a time...Ibid,* p. 123.

86   *How many Muslim women's...*Quoted in Carole Hillenbrand, *The Crusades: Islamic Perspectives* (New York, 2000), p. 298.

87   *The Rock has been cleansed...Ibid,* p. 299.

89   *No, probably not until the end of time...*Quoted in Amin Maalouf, *The Crusades Through Arab Eyes* (New York, 1984), p. 235.

90   *one of the most attractive Byzantine intellectuals...* Robert Browning, *The Byzantine Empire* (Washington, D.C., 1992), p. 213.

91   *There were lamentations and cries...*Nicetas Choniates, *O City of Byzantium* (Detroit, 1984), p. 315.

92   *The girl's father...Ibid,* p. 324.

94   *I can assure you...*Geoffroy de Villehardouin, *The Conquest of Constantinople* (Harmondswotth, 1963), pp. 58-9.

94   *No one could estimate...Ibid,* p. 92.

94   *And it was so rich...*Robert of Clari, *The Conquest of Constantinople* (New York, 1966), p. 101.

98   *They disregarded the changes...*Ibn Khaldun, *The Muqaddimah* (Princeton, 1967), Vol. 1, p. 9.

99   *For on the surface history...Ibid,* p. 6.

100   *undoubtedly the greatest work...*Quoted in *Encyclopedia Britannica*, 15th Edition, Volume 9, p. 148.

Chapter Six

107   *What do you think...*Quoted in Hollway-Calthrop, Henry, *Petrarch: His Life and Times* (New York, 1907), p. 73.

108   *every step brought some suggestion...Ibid,* p. 78.

108   *Well, I have found...Ibid*, p. 77.

121   *It was certainly good judgment...*Atkinson, James B. and David Sices (ed. & trans.), *Machiavelli and His Friends: Their Personal Correspondence* (DeKalb, IL, 1996), p. 335.

121   *I was sitting on the toilet...Ibid*, p. 336.

122   *so that they all stood around ...Ibid*, p. 337.

122   *let him gallop...Ibid.*

123   *My very dear Machiavelli...Ibid*, pp. 338–39.

127   *the first great work...*Gilbert, Felix. *Machiavelli and Guicciardini: Politics and History in Sixteenth-Century Florence*, p. 301; Hale, J. R., "Introduction," in Guicciardini, Francesco, *The History of Italy and the History of Florence* (trans. Cecil Grayson), p. vii.

Chapter Seven

131   *I agree ...*Tacitus, *Complete Works*, p. 710.

Chapter Eight

146   *left Seville with as much finery...*Bartolomé de Las Casas, *History of the Indies* (New York, 1971), Book I, Chapter 37.

148   *without speaking, acting, or moving...*Ibid., Book III, Chapter 29.

148   *to reflect on the misery...*Ibid., Book III, Chapter 79.

150   *When the cleric Las Casas...*Ibid., Book III, Chapter 102.

152   *he, to all appearances, slept...*Ibid., Book III, Chapter 160.

158   *he was not sure...*Ibid., Book III, Chapter 129.

159   *Greed increased every day...*Ibid., Book III, Chapter 79.

161   *principal and most able descendants...*Quoted in Hanke, Lewis, *The Spanish Struggle for Justice* (Philadelphia, 1949), p. 170.

Chapter Nine

165   *all the time turning...*Montaigne, *Essays* (Harmondsworth, 1958), pp. 347.

176   *Those who will find it...*Pierre Bayle, *Historical and Critical Dictionary* (Indianapolis, 1965), p. 101.

177   *This can humiliate...*Ibid., p. 102.

Chapter Ten

182   *those numerous Plays...*Boyle, Robert, *Occasional Reflections upon Several Subjects* (London, 1848), p. 31.

189   *the frightful Spectacle...*Behn, Aphra, *Oroonoko, or The Royal Slave: A True History* (New York, 1997), p. 65.

194   *the two foremost minds...*Giambattista Vico, *The New Science of Giambattista Vico* (Trans. Max Harold Fisch and Thomas Goddard Bergin: Ithaca, NY, 1948), p. 104.

195   *the best method of philosophizing...*Ibid., p. 74.

195   *But in the night of thick darkness...*Ibid., p. 96.

Chapter Eleven

206   *I would like to discover...*Quoted in Lanson, Gustave, *Voltaire* (New York, 1966), p. 108.

206   *Ideas have changed the world...*Quoted in Black, J. B., *The Art of History* (New York, 1965), p. 34.

211   *had rendered that polite nation...*Gibbon, Edward, *Memoirs of My Life* (New York, 1969), p. 87 (all three quotations in this paragraph).

211   *After a painful struggle...*Ibid., p. 85.

212   *Popish missionaries suffered under...*Ibid., pp. 60-61 (both paragraphs).

214   *My temper is not very susceptible...*Ibid., p. 134. Italics very much original. Tully is Cicero (Marcus Tullius Cicero in full).

214   *It was at Rome...*Gibbon, Edward, *Autobiography* (London, 1959), p. 160.

215   *for myself having supported...*Gibbon, Edward, *Letters of Edward Gibbon* (London, 1956). Vol. II, p. 63.

215   *final deliverance...*Gibbon, Edward, *Memoirs,* p. 180.

216   *At every step as we sink...*Gibbon, Edward, *Decline and Fall,* Chapter 48 (Vol. II, pp. 865–867) (both paragraphs).

218   *In the preceding volumes...*Ibid., Chapter 71 (Vol. III, p. 865).

218   *the attacks of barbarians...*Ibid., Chapter 71 (Vol. III, p. 863).

219   *long put the kiss of death...*Vryonis, Speros, Jr., "Hellas Resurgent," in L. White (ed.), *The Transformation of the Roman World* (Berkeley, 1966), p. 100.

Chapter Twelve

223   *Ossian has replaced Homer...*Both Herder and Goethe are quoted in Kelley, Donald R., *The Faces of History* (New Haven, 1998), p. 238, to which I'm indebted here.

228 *I read more than one*...Quoted in John Barker, *The Superhistorians*, pp. 150–51 (all three paragraphs).

230 *memoirs, diaries, letters*...Ibid., p. 151.

231 *Everything, both general and individual*...Quoted in Friedrich Meinecke, *Historism* (New York, 1972), p. 503.

234 *That was no lecture*...Quoted in Georg G. Iggers and Konrad von Moltke, "Introduction," in Leopold von Ranke, *The Theory and Practice of History* (Indianapolis, 1973), p. xxxi.

235 *When all the documents*...Quoted in Richard J. Evans, *In Defense of History* (New York, 1997), p. 18 (where Evans also mentions the warning that Planck's teacher gave him).

Chapter Thirteen

238 *At Lincoln Cathedral*...Quoted in John Clive, *Macaulay: The Shaping of a Historian* (New York, 1973), p. 122.

242 *he was, from temper*...Lord Macaulay, *The History of England* (Harmondsworth, 1979), p. 153.

243 *The perfect historian*...Quoted in Margaret Cruikshank, *Thomas Babington Macaulay* (Boston, 1978), p. 109.

244 *We do not consider ourselves authorized*...Quoted in Charles Firth, *A Commentary on Macaulay's History of England* (London, 1938), pp. 249–50.

244 *I went prepared to listen*...Ibid., pp. 254–55 (both paragraphs).

Chapter Fourteen

250 *The only way for us*...Quoted in Wolfgang Leppman, *Winckelmann* (New York, 1970), p. 113.

255   *In the powerful outline*...Ibid., p. 162.

256   *enabled him at all times*...Alexander Dru (ed.), *The Letters of Jacob Burckhardt* (New York, 1955) p. 5.

258   *My eyes were wide*...Ibid., pp. 49–50. Italics original.

258   *Ranke is on close terms*...Ibid., pp. 68 and 70.

259   *'ists' and 'isms' of every kind*...Ibid., p. 96.

259   *Part of the pleasure*...Ibid., pp. 98–99.

261   *To each eye, perhaps*...Jacob Burckhardt, *The Civilization of the Renaissance in Italy* (London, 1950), p. 1.

262   *We must insist upon*...Ibid., p. 104.

262   *I would not have gone*...Alexander Dru (ed.), *The Letters of Jacob Burckhardt* (New York, 1955) p. 152.

263   *In order to be reelected*...Ibid., p. 205.

Chapter Fifteen

265   *all of the best English*...Heinrich Schliemann, *Ilios* (New York, 1881), p. 25.

266   *we had nothing to keep*...Ibid., p. 26.

266   *struck upon a large*...Ibid., pp. 40–41.

267   *human bones, male and female*...Quoted in Peter Warren, *The Aegean Civilizations* (New York, 1989), p. 14.

272   *the prehistoric script of Crete*...Ibid., p. 21.

276   *Mr. Carter is a good-natured*...Quoted in Margaret S. Drower, *Flinders Petrie: A Life in Archaeology* (London, 1985), p. 194.

277   *Some of the King's sandals*...Howard Carter, *The Discovery of Tutankhamun's Tomb* (New York, 1976), p. 39.

Chapter Sixteen

279 *as gay and brilliant in the terrors...*Henry Adams, *The Education of Henry Adams* (Boston, 1918), p. 287.

280 *man became chaotic...*Ibid., p. 289.

280 *Never had the sun of progress...*Ibid., p. 284.

282 *defines Progress as the development...*Ibid., pp. 380-81 and 474.

283 *"The history of all hitherto..."* Karl Marx and Friedrich Engels, *The Communist Manifesto of Karl Marx and Friedrich Engels* (New York, 1963), p. 1.

285 *In this book...*Oswald Spengler, *The Decline of the West* Vol. I (New York, 1926), p. 3.

Chapter Seventeen

294 *The rich fields, so carefully...*Natalie Zemon Davis, *A Life of Learning*. American Council of Learned Societies Occasional Paper No. 39, 1997 (Charles Homer Haskins lectures), p. 12. Available online at www.acls.org/Publications/OP/Haskins/1997_NatalieZemonDavis.pdf. These autobiographical lectures, named for the medievalist Charles Homer Haskins (author of a classic revisionist work, *The Renaissance of the Twelfth Century*), are excellent sources on the formation of leading contemporary historians; I am indebted to this one for most of the biographical details about Natalie Zemon Davis in this chapter.

296 *the ultimate way of doing history...*Evans, *In Defense of History*, p. 29.

297   *History that is not quantifiable*...Ibid., p. 33.

298   *the ideas of Marx on religion*...Davis, *Life of Learning,* pp. 12 and 13.

300   *Having children helped me*...Ibid., pp. 15-16.

300   *At many a department meeting*...Ibid., p. 22.

301   *told the story of a celebrated*...Ibid., pp. 23-24.

302   *Influenced by thinking about*...Ibid., p. 26.

305   *were cowboys Catholics*...Peter Brown, *A Life of Learning*. American Council of Learned Societies Occasional Paper No. 55, 2003. (Charles Homer Haskins lectures), p. 9. Available online at www.acls.org/Publications/,OP/Haskins/2003_PeterBrown.pdf. I am indebted to this lecture for the biographical details on Peter Brown in this chapter.

305   *Only the ancient world*...Ibid., p. 7.

306   *as distant to modern scholars*...Ibid., p. 10.

309   *This book hopes to tell*...Peter Brown, *The Rise of Western Christendom* (Oxford, 1996), p. viii.

309   *As long as power*...Ibid., p. 306 & 307.

Index

A

Achilles, 11
Adams, Henry, 279–82
Aemilianus, Scipio, 25–26
Agamemnon, 11
Agricola, 37
aklea, 3
al-Athir, Ibn, 88–89
Alexander the Great, 21–22
Ambrose, Steven, 293
Annals, 37
Arcangeli, Francesco,
    248, 249
Aristotle, 22–23
Arouet, François-Marie, 203
Austen, Jane, 189

B

Baeda, 57–61
Bancroft, George, 287–88
Baronio, Cesare, 135–36
Baronius, Caesar, 135–36
Bayle, Pierre, 174–77
Beard, Charles, 289–90
Becker, Carl, 289–90
Behn, Aphra, 185–90

ben Matthias, Joseph,
    41–43
Berossus, 29
biography, 49, 51
Biondo, Flavio, 115–16,
    132–33
Bloch, Mark, 291, 294–95
Boccalini, Traiano, 134
Books from the Foundation
    of the City, 33–34
Boyle, Robert, 182–85
Bradford, William, 287
Brasidas, 15
Braudel, Fernand, 292, 295
Brown, Peter, 304–10
Bruni, Leonardo, 111–14
Burckhardt, Jacob,
    256–63, 291
Burns, Robert, 224

C

Caesar, Julius, 32–33
calendars, 60–61
Camden, William, 138–39
Carr, Edward Hallett,
    311–12

Carrière, Jean-Claude, 301
Carter, Howard, 276–77
Cato the Elder, 31–32
Champollion, Jean-Fran-
    çois, 274–75
Charlemagne, 69–70
Choniates, Michael,
    90–91, 95
Choniates, Nicetas, 89–95
Clarke, Deist Samuel, 204
Clio, 3
Columbus, Christopher,
    141–43
Comnena, Alexius, 77–80
Comnena, Anna, 78–83
Comte, Auguste, 283
Constantine, 46–47
Copernicus, Nicolaus, 143
Croesus, 9
Crusades, 84–87
Curchod, Suzanne,
    210–12
Curtius, Ernst, 264–65

D
Darwin, Charles, 280–82
Davis, Chandler, 299–300
Davis, Natalie Zemon,
    294–95, 298–304
de Coras, Jean, 301, 302

de Las Casas, Bartolomé,
    145–62
de Montaigne, Michel, 50,
    165, 301, 302
de Montfaucon,
    Bernard, 180
Defoe, Daniel, 189
Demetrius, 29
Descartes, Rene, 165–69
Dialogus de Oratoribus, 37
Diderot, Denis, 202
Diocletian, 46
divine retribution, 7
Droysen, Johann
    Gustav, 257
du Châtelet, Émilie, 200–
    201, 202, 205–6, 209
du Tilh, Arnaud, 301
Dumas, Alexander, 301
Durant, Ariel, 293
Durant, Will, 293

E
Einhard, 70–72
Einstein, Albert, 235–36
Eliot, George, 189
Elton, G. R., 295, 312
Engastromenos, Sophia,
    265–67
Eusebius, 45–52

Evans, Arthur, 270–73
Evans, Richard J., 296

F
Febvre, Lucien, 291, 294
Fielding, Henry, 189
Flacius, Matthias, 134–35
*Fragments of Greek History,
    The*, 18–19
Fulcher, 84–85
Fursey, 59

G
Gassendi, Pierre, 168, 193
Genealogies, 8
Germania, 37
Gibbon, Edward, 210–20
Ginzburg, Carlo, 303
Giovanni, Signor, 247–48
Goodwins, Doris
    Kearns, 293
Gregory of Tours, 55–56
Grimm, Jacob, 257
Grimm, Wilhelm, 257
Grote, George, 264, 265
Guerre, Martin, 301–2
Guicciardini, 125–28
Guicciardini,
    Francesco, 230
Guiscard, Robert, 78–79

H
Halicarnassus, 6
Hecataeus, 8
Herder, Johann Gottfried,
    198, 223–24
Herodotus, ix–xv, 1–2, 4–18,
    23–24, 27, 50
Histories, 1, 7–10, 37
history
    Alexander the Great and,
        21–22
    authors of, 29
    Christians and, 44–45
    church, 47–48
    cultural traditions and, 2
    cyclical view of, 26
    Jews and, 44–45
    as literary genre, 18,
        22–23
    parents of, 5
    patriotic, 133–34, 137
*History of the Christian
    Church*, 52
History of the Franks, 56
Hobbes, Thomas, 164
Holinshed, Raphael, 137
Homer, 2–3
Hume, David, 222
Hutcheson, Francis, 221
Hutchinson, Thomas, 287

I

Iliad, The, 2–3

Ionia, 4, 5

J

Jacoby, Felix, 18–19

Jewish Antiquities, 43

Jewish Wars, The, 42, 43

Johnson, Samuel, 223

Journey Around the World, 8

K

Khaldun, Ibn, 95–106,
    191–92

klea, 3

knowledge, search for, ix–xv

Kugler, Franz, 257

Kuhn, Louise Adams,
    279, 280

L

Ladurie, Emmanuel Le Roy,
    297, 302–3

Leibniz, Gottfried Wilhelm,
    169–74

Libri ab Urbe Condita, 33–34

Life of Constantine, 47, 50

Lives of the Caesars, 50–51

Livingstone, David, 273

Livy, 33–38

London, William, 163, 182

Lucretius, 193

Luther, Martin, 129

Lygdamis, 6

M

Mabillon, Jean, 177–80

Macaulay, Thomas Babing-
    ton, 237–46, 290

Machiavelli, Niccoló,
    117–25

Macpherson, James, 223

Manetho, 29

Marcellinus, Ammianus,
    52–55

Marlowe, Christopher,
    248–49

Martorelli, Jacopo, 253

Mather, Cotton, 287

McCullough, David, 293

Melanchton, Philip, 129–30

Menander, 29

microhistory, 302–3

Miletus, 3–4

Mill, John Stuart, 221

Momigliano, Arnaldo, 313

Moralia, The, 50

N

Namier, Lewis, 296–97

Neibuhr, Barthold Georg, 227–28
Newton, Isaac, 193–94
Nithard, 72–74
North, Sir Thomas, 50

O
Odyssey, The, 2–3
Ossian, 223, 224

P
Panyasis, 6
Parallel Lives, 49–50
Parkman, Francis, 288–89
Peloponnesian War, The, 12, 13, 14
Pericles, 13–14
Persian empire, 7–8
Petrarch, 107–11, 202–3
Petrie, William Matthew Flinders, 275–76
Photius, 75
Pickel, Conrad, 132
Pictor, Quintus Fabius, 29–31
Planck, Max, 235–36
Plutarch, 49–50
poetry, 2–3, 5
Polybius, 24–28
Polycrates, 7, 9

Pope, Alexander, 203
pride, 7
Procopius, 62–68
Psellus, Michael, 75–77

R
Ranke, Leopold, 226–36, 244–46, 257, 258
rational thought, 3–5, 12–13, 18
realpolitik, 14
Richardson, Samuel, 189
Robertson, William, 222
Rousseau, Jean-Jacques, 202, 209

S
Sallust, 33
Samos, 6–7
Schama, Simon, 304
Schliemann, Heinrich, 264, 265–70, 272, 273
Scott, Walter, 224–26
Simocatta, Theophylact, 74
Sleidanus, Johannes, 136
Smith, Adam, 222
Smith, John, 287
Solon, 9
Spengler, Oswald, 283–87
St. Alban, 58–59

Stanley, Henry Morton, 273
Suetonius, 50–51
suggested reading, 315–18
Swift, Jonathan, 203

T
Tacitus, 37–39, 130–32
Thales of Miletus, 4, 5
Thucydides, 11–18, 27–28
Timaeus of Taormina,
    23–24, 27
Toynbee, Arnold, 283–87
Trevelyan, George
    Macaulay, 239, 290
Trevelyan, Hannah, 240
Trojan War, 11
Tuchman, Barbara, 293
Turner, Frederick Jackson,
289, 311

V
Valla, Lorenzo, 114–15
Vergil, Polydore, 137–38
Vico, Giovanni Battista,
    190–99

Vigne, Daniel, 301
Virginal, 38
Vlacic, Matija, 134–35
Voltaire, 200, 201–10
von Schleiden, Johann
    Philip, 136

W
Warren, Mercy Otis, 287
Weber, Max, 298
William of Tyre, 87–88
Winckelmann, Johann
    Joachim, 247–56
Woolf, Virginia, 189
Woolley, Leonard, 277

X
Xenophon, 21
Xerxes, 10

Y
Young, Thomas, 274

Colin Wells is the author of *Sailing from Byzantium: How a Lost Empire Shaped the World* and *The Complete Idiot's Guide to Understanding Saudi Arabia*. He studied English, history, and classics at the University of California, Los Angeles and Oxford University before returning to the Adirondack region of northern New York State, where he grew up and where he now lives. He welcomes readers' comments at his Web site, www.colinwellsauthor.com.